WILDLAND RECREATION

WILDLAND RECREATION

ECOLOGY AND MANAGEMENT

William E. Hammitt
Professor of Forest Recreation
Department of Forestry, Wildlife, and Fisheries
University of Tennessee
Knoxville, Tennessee

David N. Cole
Research Ecologist
Systems for Environmental Management
Missoula, Montana

A WILEY-INTERSCIENCE PUBLICATION

JOHN WILEY & SONS
NEW YORK   CHICHESTER   BRISBANE   TORONTO   SINGAPORE

*To S. Ross Tocher, Professor of Outdoor Recreation
at the University of Michigan from 1965 to 1981,
who knew the field of wildland recreation management.*

Library of Congress Cataloging in Publication Data:

Hammitt, William E.
   Wildland recreation.

   "A Wiley-Interscience publication."
   Includes bibliographies.
     1. Wilderness areas—United States—Recreational use—
Management. 2. Wilderness areas–Environmental aspects—
United States. I. Cole, David N. II. Title.

GV191.4.H35 1987   333.78'0973   86-23403
ISBN 0-471-87291-1

Printed in the United States of America

10 9 8 7 6 5 4 3 2 1

Preface

Wildland Recreation: Ecology and Management is concerned with ecological resource problems that arise in wildland areas as a result of recreational use and how these problems can be managed. For our purposes wildland recreation areas are defined as natural areas that are used primarily for dispersed recreation. Everything from wilderness and wildland rivers to primitively developed campgrounds and off-road-vehicle areas are included in our definition of wildland recreation.

The book is intended as a textbook in such disciplines as forest and natural resources recreation, outdoor recreation, park management, geography, and environmental conservation. It should also serve as a useful reference for recreation resource managers already practicing in the field. In addition, it is intended that the ecological treatment of resource impacts will be of interest to ecologists, foresters, wildlife managers, and others who are trained in the biological sciences yet lack training in the area of recreation resources management.

Although the focus of the book is on recreation caused impacts to wildland resources, we have not ignored the social and economic factors involved in managing these impacts. Public policy has made these areas available for recreational use and managers must aim to provide public benefits as well as protect the resource base that provides these benefits. The material is presented in five parts. Part I defines wildland recreation and resource impacts, presents an overview of ecological/recreational impacts, and considers the sensitivity of wildland resources to recreational use. Part II deals with the ecology and impacts occurring to the soil, vegetation, wildlife, and water resources of wildland recreation areas. Spatial and temporal patterns of these impacts are also included in this section. Part III discusses the importance of environmental durability, visitor use, and user characteristics in determining the nature and magnitude of recreational impacts.

Part IV explores strategies and methods for monitoring and managing visitors and site conditions in wildland recreation areas. Finally, Part V summarizes the book and the importance and challenges of managing ecological impacts.

Portions of the book can be useful without reading the entire text. Parts I and V provide an overview on recreational impacts. Part IV can be useful for managers looking for available management alternatives. Part II is helpful for people wanting a basic understanding of the ecological impacts resulting from recreational use.

Several of our colleagues have contributed to the preparation of this book, for which we are greatly appreciative. We are particularly indebted to Joe Roggenbuck, Richard Strange, and Bruce Hastings for reading portions of the text. The U.S. Forest Service is acknowledged for contributing a significant portion of the photographs. Both the Department of Forestry, Wildlife, and Fisheries of the University of Tennessee, Knoxville, and the Forest Service Intermountain Research Station, Missoula, Montana, contributed space and services during the years of manuscript preparation. Final editing and typing of the manuscript were admirably performed by Sheila Ray. Most sincerely, Sally and Forest Park Hammitt are thanked for the many hours of loneliness they accepted during the writing of the book.

WILLIAM E. HAMMITT
DAVID N. COLE

Knoxville, Tennessee
Missoula, Montana
January 1987

Contents

of Problems. *Strategic Purpose. Types of Undesirable Visitor Actions. Direct vs. Indirect Approaches.* References.

I INTRODUCTION

1 Recreation Use and Resource Impacts

Recreational use of wildland areas has increased dramatically in recent decades. Along with this increase in recreational use have come human disturbance and degradation to the natural conditions of wildland areas. Examined in this book are the nature and degree of these disturbances and ways they can be managed. First, we need to define wildland recreation and recreation resource impacts. Then, we must consider the importance of recreational-ecological impacts and the role of the wildland recreation manager at balancing use and preservation of wildland areas.

WHAT IS WILDLAND RECREATION?

Although most types of recreation are fun and nonwork oriented, their goals and benefits are usually diverse. The notions of recreation as constructive, rewarding, and restorative are at least as important as the notion of recreation as fun (Brockman and Merriam 1973). For our purposes recreation is defined as activities that offer a contrast to work-related activities and that offer the possibility of constructive, restorative, and pleasurable benefits.

This broad definition provides room for a tremendous variety of activities. We are restricting ourselves here to recreational activities conducted outdoors in wildland areas that are dependent on the natural resources of these areas (Fig. 1). In *wildland* recreation the importance of the environment or setting for activities is greater than in *developed* recreation situations. Moreover, these wildland settings are largely natural,

National Park Service
U.S. Department of the Interior
NPS Photo by Richard Frear
365-180-75C

Although there are five campgrounds within the park, many campers prefer to tramp out on their own in the backcountry. Camping permits required for all backcountry camping are available from rangers at park headquarters or the visitor centers within the park.

Shenandoah
National Park
Virginia

Figure 1. Recreational activities in wildland areas are greatly dependent on the natural resources of these areas. (*Photo:* National Park Service.)

and management strives to maintain a natural appearance. Facility development is limited both in areal extent and function. Facilities in wildland areas are limited to small sites, if present at all, and are more likely to enhance visitor safety and resource protection than visitor comfort and convenience (Fig. 2). Accessibility is more difficult with wildland recreation. Distances from urban populations are greater. Roads tend to be low standard and less frequently maintained, if present at all. Where absent, trails may or may not be provided. Finally, use tends to be dispersed, creating a social environment with less emphasis on certain types of social interaction. Interaction takes place in smaller groups, with less interparty contact.

Most wildland recreation takes place on public lands such as those managed by the U.S. Forest Service, National Park Service, or state park departments. These lands may or may not be specifically designated for recreational use. For example, wilderness areas and campgrounds are designated on National Park Service lands while adjacent and interven-

Figure 2. Recreational facilities in wildland areas are limited in both areal extent and function, and are more likely to enhance visitor safety and resource protection than visitor convenience. (*Photo:* W. E. Hammitt.)

ing Forest Service land permits recreational use but emphasizes other uses, such as timber production. Similarly, wildland recreation use also occurs on private lands not specifically designated recreation areas. However, most wildland recreation occurs on public lands, and most of the management responsibility falls on public agencies.

This book, then, deals primarily with the recreational use of publicly owned and managed lands. Although many different activities are involved, they are generally dispersed over large areas, resulting in low user density. This dispersal makes management difficult because such a large area is used and disturbed. Moreover, because maintenance of natural or natural-appearing conditions is so important, considerable management of both users and resources is required to avoid excessive resource damage.

WHAT IS RECREATION RESOURCE IMPACT?

Disturbance to natural areas as a result of recreational use has typically been defined as *resource* or *ecological* impact. As pointed out by Lucas (1979), the term *impact* is a neutral term. When combined with *ecological* it refers to an objective description of the environmental effects of recreational use. Objectively, an impact can be a positive or negative change. In wildland recreation a value judgment has been placed on the term *impact*, denoting an undesirable change in environmental conditions. Of concern to the recreation manager are the type, amount, and rate of undesirable change occurring to the resource base as a result of recreational use. We define undesirable change to the resource base to mean degradation to the soil, vegetation, wildlife, and water resources of a wildland area.

Recreation resource managers are understandably concerned with ecological impacts because many of them have the responsibility of maintaining the quality of recreational resources. This is particularly true for wildland recreational areas, as many are national parks or designated wilderness areas where a major goal is to preserve natural conditions. To deal effectively with the problem of environmental disturbance in recreation and natural areas, resource managers need to understand recreational impacts in sufficient detail to determine how much and what kind of change is occurring and is acceptable (Cole and Schreiner 1981).

RECENT TRENDS IN WILDLAND RECREATION USE

The severity of ecological impact problems in wildland areas stems from an ever-increasing participation in wildland types of recreation. Studies conducted over long periods of time, documenting escalating trends in ecological impacts, are nonexistent; however, trend data on wildland recreation use is available for the last 35 years. Examination of these trends in recreational use provides an indication of the associated trend in impact.

The ecological impacts resulting from recreational use are particularly critical in wilderness and backcountry areas because management objectives for such areas stress maintaining high levels of natural integrity. (When using the term *wilderness*, we mean areas specifically designated as wilderness by Congress; backcountry is a more generic term for areas that are not roaded.) Use of wilderness areas has increased at a rate faster than most other wildlands. For example, recreational visits to U.S. Forest Service wilderness increased fourteenfold between 1946 and 1970 (Stankey 1973). Forest Service wilderness areas in California showed an average 16 percent annual increase in use for the 1970 to 1975 period (Hendee, Stankey, and Lucas 1978). Although rates of increase have slowed down over the last decade, use is still increasing. Moreover, the land base on which use occurs is decreasing. Designated wilderness acreage is growing, but nondesignated backcountry is shrinking drastically as areas are designated wilderness or becoming roaded.

Of wildland recreation activities on national forests, increases in winter sports have been most rapid in recent years (Table 1). Use nearly tripled between 1966 and 1979. While much of this represents increased use of developed downhill ski areas, participation in cross-country skiing and snowmobiling has also increased dramatically. Hiking and mountain climbing also increased nearly threefold over this period. Similar increases have occurred on lands outside the national forests. A public survey conducted in 1965 for the Bureau of Outdoor Recreation showed that 9.9 million Americans hiked or backpacked. This had increased to 28.1 million Americans when the survey was repeated in 1977.

Backcountry camping figures for the National Park Service have been kept on a nationwide basis only since 1972. However, individual parks have trend data over a longer period of time. For Great Smoky Mountains National Park, backcountry overnight use was about 105,000 user nights in 1975, a 53 percent increase over 1972 use levels and a 250 percent increase over 1963 use (Bratton, Hickler, and Graves 1978). Between 1967 and 1972, backcountry camping in Yosemite National Park increased 184 percent, from 78,000 to 221,000 user nights. Overnight use in the Shenandoah National Park backcountry quadrupled between 1967 and 1974; total backcountry use of Rocky Mountain National Park increased more than seven times between 1966 and 1976 (Hendee et al. 1978).

River recreation has also been rapidly expanding. The history of whitewater floating on the Colorado River through the Grand Canyon is a classic example. Prior to 1960 fewer than 650 people had *ever* floated the river; 10 years later 10,000 people were floating the river *every* year. Between 1966 and 1972 the number of people floating the river increased

TABLE 1. National Forest Recreation Use by Activity
(Thousands of Visitor-Days)

Activity	1966		1979	
	Use	Percent of Total	Use	Percent of Total
Camping	39,564.5	26.2	54,780.3	24.9
Recreational travel (mechanical)	31,301.1	20.7	49,536.5	22.5
Fishing	14,709.1	9.7	16,776.0	7.6
Hunting	13,118.6	8.7	15,327.9	6.7
Recreational residence use	7,960.5	5.3	6,651.6	3.0
Picnicking	7,887.5	5.2	8,874.2	4.0
Winter sports	5,219.6	3.5	14,485.0	6.6
Hiking and mountain climbing	4,277.8	2.8	11,176.9	5.1
Organizational camp use	4,287.2	2.8	4,086.8	1.8
Boating	4,006.5	2.6	7,072.1	3.2
Viewing scenes and sports entertainment	3,926.8	2.6	8.321.1	3.8
Resort use	4,003.5	2.6	4,308.9	1.9
Swimming and scuba diving	3,076.9	2.0	4,632.3	2.1
Horseback riding	2,065.9	1.4	3,166.4	1.4
Visitors information services	2,058.8	1.4	4,121.8	1.9
Gather forest products	1,241.7	.8	3,916.1	1.8
Nature study	796.4	.5	1,210.9	.5
Waterskiing and other water sports	641.0	.4	888.0	.4
Games and team sports	585.5	.4	832.8	.4
Total	150,728.9	99.6	220,165.6	99.6

Source: U.S. Forest Service.

sixteenfold, from 1,067 to 16,432 (Table 2). Leatherberry, Lime, and
Thompson (1980) report that ownership of kayaks and canoes has increased much faster than ownership of other types of water craft. Between 1973 and 1976 there was a 68 percent increase in number of
canoes and a 107 percent increase in number of kayaks. This accelerating
trend in river use has led public resource agencies to restrict use on

TABLE 2. Travel on the Colorado River through the Grand Canyon of Arizona

Year	Number of People
1867	1[a]
1869–1940	41
1941	4
1942	8
1943	0
1944	0
1945	0
1946	0
1947	4
1948	6
1949	12
1950	7
1951	29
1952	19
1953	31
1954	21
1955	70
1956	55
1957	135
1958	80
1959	120
1960	205
1961	255
1962	372
1963–1964	44[b]
1965	547
1966	1,067
1967	2,099
1968	3,609
1969	6,019
1970	9,935
1971	10,385
1972	16,432
1973	15,219
1974	14,253[c]

Source: U.S. Forest Service.

[a] Some contend that James White, a trapper fleeing Indians, floated through the Grand Canyon on a makeshift log raft two years before the famous expedition of John Wesley Powell.

[b] Travel on the Colorado River in those years was curtailed by the completion of Glen Canyon Dam upstream and the resultant disruption of flow.

[c] The downturn in visitation was the result of the institution by management of a quota system. The numbers applying for the available permits continued to rise sharply.

many rivers. The number of rivers with use restrictions increased from eight in 1972 to 38 in 1977 (McCool, Lime, and Anderson 1977). On some rivers the number of persons applying for a limited number of permits has been as much as 20 times the number of permits handed out. The waiting list to float through the Grand Canyon is so long that new applicants may have to wait over 10 years for a chance to float the river. Ecological impacts on river resources can be particularly severe because use is concentrated along a narrow linear corridor.

The most common activity causing ecological impact in wildland recreation areas is camping, whether by people in cars and recreational vehicles or by backcountry users. According to a 1979 survey, camping now ranks third, behind swimming and bicycling, among outdoor recreation activities. Cole and LaPage (1980) report that a national survey conducted in 1960 showed 3 to 4 million active camping households in the United States. This figure had grown to 12.4 million households by 1971 and to 17.5 million households by 1978. Camping grew at an average annual rate of 20 percent in the 1960s, 8 percent in the early 1970s, and less than 5 percent in the late 1970s. Much of the early interest in recreational impacts in the United States grew out of this rapid increase in camping during the 1960's.

Off-road vehicle use has also increased dramatically in recent decades. In the 1960 nationwide survey on outdoor recreation, so few people used off-road vehicles that they were not included in the survey; by 1982, 11 percent of people 12 years old and older used wheeled off-road vehicles, and 3 percent used snowmobiles (USDI National Park Service 1984). On national forest lands off-road vehicle use doubled during the 1970s to a 1979 use level of 5.3 million visitor days for wheel vehicles and 3.3 million visitor days for snowmobiles (Feuchter, 1980). Most vehicular recreation takes place on roads; almost 50 million visitor days of recreational driving took place on national forest roads in 1979. This is fortunate because the impacts of recreational vehicles, when used off roads, are unusually severe.

ECOLOGICAL IMPACTS OF WILDLAND RECREATION

All of these activities disturb the natural environment. Although the specific impacts associated with each activity differ to some extent, they all potentially can affect soil, vegetation, wildlife, and water. These effects and their interrelationships are laid out in Fig. 3. Some activities

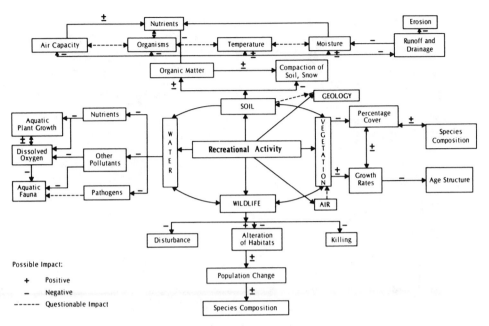

Figure 3. Recreational impact interrelationships in wildland areas. (*Source:* "Recreational Impact Interrelationships," by G. Wall and C. Wright in *The Environmental Impact of Outdoor Recreation,* 1977. Reprinted with permission.)

can also affect basic geology and air as the Fig. 3 shows; however, these impacts are less direct and often originate on areas adjacent to wildlands. Presented in this section is an overview of the major resource impacts that will be discussed in more detail in subsequent chapters. In particular, we want to stress the interrelated nature of these different types of impact. One theme that should come out in this book, particularly when we get to management, is that impacts do not occur in isolation; single activities cause multiple impacts, and each impact tends to exacerbate or compensate for other changes. Management solutions to impact problems must recognize this, or the solution to one problem is likely to be the cause of another.

Impact to soils starts with the destruction of surface organic matter and the compaction of soil or snow. Each of these changes alters basic soil characteristics related to aeration, temperature, moisture, nutrition, and the organisms that live in the soil. These changes, which adversely affect the ability of the soil to support plant life, are most visibly obvious in the barren, compacted soils of campsites (Fig. 4). Compaction, by

Figure 4. Campsites in wildland areas are typically characterized by a heavily impacted zone of compacted soil and absent of vegetation. (*Photo:* W. E. Hammitt.)

reducing water infiltration rates, increases runoff and, therefore, erosion. Erosional impacts are most severe on trails and in off-road vehicle areas (Fig. 5).

Most of these changes in soil condition inhibit the establishment of new plants and adversely affect the growth of existing vegetation. Moreover, trampling by feet and horse hooves and abrasion by skis and off-road vehicles directly injure and kill existing plants. Plant cover, growth rates, and reproductive capacities are all diminished. For trees, in particular, this alters the age structure of the population. On many campsites, for example, tree populations consist entirely of middle-aged and older trees; reproduction is totally lacking. Even these older trees are often scarred by ax marks, lantern burns, and nails (Fig. 6). Understory vegetation varies greatly in its ability to tolerate recreational impact. Since more tolerant species are more likely to survive on recreation sites, changes in species composition shift toward these more tolerant species. An ability to grow close to the ground is one important survival mechanism that partially explains the reduced height of most vegetation on recreation sites.

Figure 5. Hiking trails on steep slopes and at higher elevations where greater rainfall occurs are easily eroded. (*Photo:* W. E. Hammitt.)

Although the indirect effects of soil impacts on vegetation are particularly obvious, the relationship is also reversible. Loss of vegetation cover exacerbates such impacts as loss of organic matter and increased erosion. It also is related to wildlife impacts, particularly through alteration of habitats. For large animals the most serious impacts of recreation are direct, either outright killing or unintentional disturbance (harassment). Disturbance can reduce reproduction, as when a disturbed bird leaves her nest, lead to migration to more remote areas, or result in adaptation, as when a bear learns to rely on garbage as a food source. Smaller animals are more affected by habitat alterations. For example, soil impacts, such as loss of organic matter, remove a home and food source for many insects; vegetation impacts, such as a chopped-down tree snag, eliminate homes for cavity-nesting birds. Many of these animals have important effects on soils and vegetation, from their roles as decomposers and grazers and their place in ecosystem nutrient and energy cycles. Altered population structures, spatial distribution and abundance, and even behavior will, consequently, have an influence on soil, vegetation, and water as well.

Figure 6. Trees on older campsites are often scarred by the burns of gasoline lanterns. This tree has 13 lantern scars. (*Photo:* W. E. Hammitt.)

Water quality is reduced by inputs of nutrients, other pollutants, including increased sedimentation resulting from erosion, and contamination with pathogens. Pathogenic contamination may result from improper disposal of human waste; more commonly, contamination is caused by wild animals that carry disease organisms. Nutrients and pollutants may enter waters as a direct result of recreational use, as when surface films of oil and gasoline pollute lakes with heavy motorboat use. More insidious are the indirect sources such as the reduction in water quality caused by erosion triggered by recreational use. Again, this erosion is promoted by soil and vegetation impact. Water pollution, from many sources, depletes dissolved oxygen and alters aquatic plant and animal growth and survival.

THE IMPORTANCE OF ECOLOGICAL IMPACTS

All of these impacts occur, but so what? We can go out and measure most of the impacts, determining the *magnitude* of environmental change. It is a very different matter, however, to assess the *importance* or *significance* of these impacts. We might all agree that 95 percent of the spiders on the forest floor of a campsite have been eliminated by recreation use; we are unlikely to agree about how important a change this is. We might not even be able to agree on whether this is a positive or a negative change. In a recreational context, impacts only become good or bad, important or insignificant, when humans make value judgments about them. Those judgments are determined primarily by the type(s) of recreation an area is managed to offer, the objectives of various user groups, and the objectives of resource management.

Different areas offer different types of recreation. This fact has been formalized in the recreational opportunity spectrum, a classification of land based on the types of recreational opportunities they offer. More will be said about it in Chapter 10. The spectrum distinguishes, for example, between the opportunities for primitive recreation of a wilderness area and the ball-playing opportunities of an urban park. Both areas may have experienced, in some places, a conversion from native vegetation to a turf of Kentucky bluegrass. In the wilderness this presents a problem because loss of natural conditions is undesirable in wilderness. The importance of this change is probably related to how large an area is affected and the uniqueness of the vegetation that was lost. In the urban park the conversion is both important and beneficial because it greatly improves the quality of ball-playing. As we move along the recreational opportunity spectrum from developed and urban areas to remote and primitive areas, the same impact is likely to become increasingly negative and significant.

Even within the same area people vary in their opinions about impacts. Different recreationists have different ideas. A hiker, confronted with erosion of a hill used by motorcyclists, is more likely to react negatively than the motorcyclists themselves. Conflict, resulting from different perspectives on ecological impact, commonly occurs between motorized and nonmotorized recreationists whether recreation occurs on land, water, or snow. Similar conflicts and differing perspectives separate many hikers and users of horses and pack animals.

It is also interesting to compare the perspectives of the ecologist, recreationist, and manager. The ecologist is most likely to be concerned about impacts that impair the function of ecosystems or destroy unique features. Examples include removal of dead woody debris to burn in fires or elimination of an inconspicuous endangered plant, neither of which is likely to be noticed by many recreationists. Ecologists are also likely to evaluate the importance of a change in terms of how long it takes for recovery to occur. Using this criterion, erosion is extremely serious because it will take centuries to regenerate soils to replace eroded ones.

Recreationists, as a whole, seem to be more concerned with impacts that decrease the functionality of a site or with "unnatural" objects left by other parties. In Yosemite National Park, facilities (toilets, tables, etc.) and litter detracted more from enjoyment of backcountry campsites than other impacts (Lee 1975). To an ecologist such impacts are likely to be of little importance because they are easily reversible and do not greatly harm the function of natural ecosystems. Most recreationists do not even recognize ecological impacts. Knudson and Curry (1981) asked campers in three Indiana state park campgrounds for their opinions about ground cover conditions. Then, they compared these judgments to actual conditions (Table 3). More campers felt conditions were satisfactory or good on the less devegetated sites; however, even at Turkey

TABLE 3. Campsite Ground Cover Conditions and Visitor Opinions

	Versailles		Turkey
Cover Conditions	New	Old	Run
As rated by campers	---Percent of Campers ---		
Very poor	2	3	14
Poor	11	20	29
Satisfactory	53	39	47
Good	30	37	8
Excellent	4	1	2
Actual	-----Percent of Sites -----		
≥ 75 percent bare and disturbed	6	23	99

Source: Knudson and Curry, 1981. Reproduced with permission of the Society of American Foresters.

Run where 99 percent of the sites were over 75 percent denuded, most campers found conditions satisfactory. Over two-thirds of campers saw no tree or shrub damage, despite the fact that virtually every tree was damaged. Finally, a majority of those that did notice tree, shrub, and ground cover damage said it did not adversely affect their enjoyment.

While this lack of recognition and concern for impact characterizes most recreationists, there are exceptions. In wilderness areas there are undoubtedly visitors who are bothered by impacts. However, little research has been done of visitor perceptions of resource impacts in wildland areas.

The manager is usually caught somewhere in between. Maintenance of natural or natural-appearing conditions is important in most wildland areas; so is providing recreational opportunities—and recreation *always* disturbs natural conditions. Impacts that affect visitor enjoyment, particularly those that impair the functionality or desirability of sites, are a particular concern. Legislative mandates and agency guidelines provide additional constraints. Wilderness designation, for example, places some bounds on the types and levels of impact that can be tolerated. Different agencies also have differing perspectives. Even in designated wilderness, presumably subject to the same mandates, each managing agency has a different style. For example, the Fish and Wildlife Service has a particular concern with wildlife. The National Park Service is much more likely to restrict recreational activities to avoid resource impact than the Forest Service (Washburne and Cole 1983). In dealing with recreational impacts, managers must balance the concerns of ecologists, recreationists, other user groups, and the constraints of legislation and agency policies, and tailor all these to the peculiar situation of the area they manage.

THE MANAGER'S ROLE

While considering the importance of recreational impacts in wildland areas, it is easy for one to develop an antiuser bias toward these areas. Would these wildland recreation areas not be better off if recreational use did not occur on them? This is an unrealistic position to adopt and is certainly not the intent of this book.

Society and public policy have made these areas available for recreational use, and we must accept the propriety of use of wildland resources for recreational purposes. Humans, as recreationists, are to be a part of these wildland ecosystems. Because man is a part of all ecosystems, wildland management is an effort to maintain a natural site environment in which human impact and influence are minimized as much as possible, while still allowing for recreational use. We should *accept* the principle that recreational use can occur in wildlands, and that no matter how small, will produce an impact of some type. Management's role, in general, is not to *halt* change within wildland areas, but to manage for acceptable levels of environmental change. The challenge of the recreation resource manager is to find the proper balance between satisfying public desires for recreational experiences without creating substantial irreversible losses of wildland resources.

One of the primary tools for meeting this challenge is the development of management objectives related to visitor use and acceptable levels of resource impact. This important topic will be introduced in the next section and developed in more detail in Chapter 9.

RECREATIONAL CARRYING CAPACITY

In an attempt to plan for the increases in resource disturbance associated with increasing recreational use, managers and recreation researchers have repeatedly looked to the concept of carrying capacity for solutions. The concept of carrying capacity was borrowed from the disciplines of range and wildlife management. In these fields, carrying capacity refers to the maximum number of animals a given unit of land can support on a sustained basis without destruction of the resource base. In managing recreation areas it was hoped that a maximum number of users could be specified, above which recreation quality could not be sustained. Recent agency directives, from both the National Park Service and the Forest Service, have actually mandated determination of appropriate use levels or carrying capacities for parks and wilderness areas.

For a number of reasons, determining carrying capacities is neither simple nor particularly useful. First, managing recreation use and associated impacts differs considerably from managing cattle or other animals. In addition to concern with the physical ability of the resource to sustain use, there is an equally important concern with the effect of use on the recreational experience of the user (Wagar 1974). Social carrying capacity refers to these visitor experience aspects while ecological carrying capacity refers to resource aspects. Both are inextricably intertwined. As Frissell and Stankey (1972) note:

> The soil compaction and dying vegetation that accompanies excessive use of a site is of significance not only to the ecologist, but also to the social scientist, for the perception of declining esthetic quality might well be a more important constraint than reduced soil pore space.

More important than the greater complexity of recreational carrying capacity was a misunderstanding of how carrying capacity was used in a field such as range management. Setting carrying capacities for range animals only became common practice when private users were allowed to graze public lands and land managers did not have the time to oversee the operation and monitor changes in conditions. Capacities were conservative, set low so that private users would not damage public lands even in years when forage production was low. Actually ranges suffered from overgrazing in unproductive years while in productive years the limits were wasteful because many more animals could have grazed. On private lands experienced ranchers do not set carrying capacities; they monitor conditions—rainfall or forage condition, for example—and adjust numbers of animals to achieve their objectives.

In recreation it is possible to select a carrying capacity, but by itself it too will be wasteful. As we will see in subsequent chapters, the relationship between amount of use and amount of impact is not direct. Amount of impact is also affected by the timing, type, and distribution of use, the setting where use occurs, and mitigative actions taken by management. As Washburne (1982) notes:

> There is a separate carrying capacity for horses in meadows in the spring and another in the summer, one for campers who use previously established sites, one for campers who bring stoves rather than build fires, one for noisy and inconsiderate campers who walk through the camps of others . . . .

We will explore the importance of many of these variables that affect amount of impact. The point we want to make here is that while carrying capacities *can* be set, they must either be wasteful of legitimate recreational opportunities—set very low to allow for variations in all of the other factors affecting amount of impact—or they must be only a small part of a management program. They are not the key to management for which some have been looking. The key to management, in recreation as in range and wildlife management, is specifying management objectives and monitoring conditions.

These key elements of management will be discussed more fully in Chapters 9 and 10. In the following five chapters the ecological effects of recreation are described. The first task for management, once these impacts are understood, is to set objectives for how much impact is too much. In the terminology of Frissell and Stankey (1972), managers must set "limits of acceptable change" (Fig. 7). Change in nature is the norm; the natural variation in the rate and character of change is acceptable, except where it poses a safety hazard or, in nonwilderness areas, where it detracts substantially from desired recreational opportunities (i.e., insect infestations). Changes beyond this constitute man-caused change or impact. A certain amount of impact must be considered acceptable even in wilderness. The limit of acceptable change, a management judgment, divides acceptable impact from unacceptable. Management must decide where to draw the line and then hold that line through prescription of management programs (Stankey, McCool, and Stokes 1984).

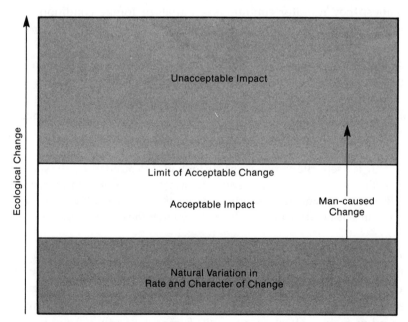

Figure 7. Model of acceptable ecological change in wildlands. (*Source:* Adapted from Frissell and Stankey 1972.)

However, it must be recognized that the decision of where to draw the line is one which can not be determined *entirely* by ecological criteria. The manager must be prepared to weigh policy, economic, and public use considerations as well when setting limits of acceptable resource change. This is particularly true in wildlands that are not congressionally established wilderness, for they are managed under a broader range of social and economic considerations. Management prescriptions can be based on ecological criteria, but only under the broad umbrella of these other factors.

THEMES OF THIS BOOK

This chapter has introduced the topics of wildland recreation and resource impacts. It has defined each topic and its importance to the management of wildland areas. Following this introductory chapter are three major parts to the book: the first dealing with ecological impacts to the four major resource components of wildland areas and the spatial-temporal distribution of these impacts; the second describing some key factors that affect resource impacts; and last, a section on the management of recreation resource impacts. Throughout the chapters comprising these topic sections will be a number of reoccurring themes. These themes form the basis for organizing the material of the book and are summarized below to serve as a guide to the reader.

1. The impacts caused by recreation use can be direct or indirect, are interrelated, and are often either synergistic or compensatory. Some are immediately obvious even to untrained eyes. Initials in trees and trampled vegetation are good examples. Others are only visible with microscopes, and some effects have never been identified or studied. Many of these more obscure impacts may be among the more significant. For example, the impact of recreation on soil organisms is very poorly understood, yet it is undoubtedly considerable. Moreover, soil organisms are particularly important to the energy and nutrient cycles of ecosystems so their disruption is serious. Some impacts such as disturbance of large wildlife species are almost impossible to identify because there is no way to know what their distribution and behavior were like prior to disturbance.

Many of the more obvious impacts are *direct*; that is, the observed change is a direct result of recreation use. Vegetation loss as a direct result of trampling is an example. Vegetation loss can also reflect poor growth and reproduction in soils that have been compacted by recreation use. This is an *indirect* impact, the result of soil compaction. Indirect impacts illustrate the interrelated nature of many impacts. Many synergistic relationships exist. Loss of organic matter makes a soil more susceptible to erosion and in turn tends to carry away organic matter. However, sometimes impacts are compensatory. For example, loss of native vegetation cover reduces competition for weedy species, which increases the vegetation cover. Soil moisture levels tend to be reduced because water infiltration rates are reduced, but the soil's capacity to hold water increases at the same time; the result is often little change in available moisture.

2. In addition to understanding what impacts occur—their severity and their interrelationships—it is also important to understand the spatial distribution of impacts and how they change over time. Most impact is highly concentrated. McEwen and Tocher (1976) note, for example, that probably no scenic site in North America is more heavily impacted than that at Athabasca Falls in Jasper National Park, Canada, yet the forest a few yards on either side of the falls is essentially undisturbed. In this book we will be concerned both with areas of concentrated use, primarily camp and picnic sites, but also water-recreation sites, off-road vehicle areas, and scenic sites, and with linear routes, trails and roads. In all cases undisturbed land is likely to exist a short distance from these places.

There is usually a tendency for these areas and routes to increase in number and size over time. In contrast to these changing spatial patterns, the severity of most impacts tends to increase rapidly with initial use, stabilize, and then remain relatively constant for long periods of time.

3. Both the nature and severity of impacts vary with type of recreational activity. We will be primarily concerned with impacts associated with picnicking, camping, skiing, or riding on trails and recreational boating. Each of these activities is unique in the impacts that result, their spatial distribution, and how they change over time. For example, water pollution is most serious with boating while erosion is most serious on trails, and vegetation damage is most serious with camping and picknicking.

4. Although more use tends to cause more impact, the use-impact relationship is seldom direct or linear. Usually, a little use causes most of the impact, and additional use causes less and less additional impact. The nature of this relationship varies widely between different types of impact. Since limits on amount of use are a frequently considered management response to impact, it is very important to understand how each type of impact responds to different levels of use.

5. Even within an activity such as camping, parties vary greatly in their potential to cause impact. This variation between parties is part of the reason that the use-impact relationship is not direct. The method of travel a party uses—foot, horse, or motorized vehicle—has a great effect on amount, type, and spatial distribution of impact. Other important user characteristics are the type of party, its size, and the behavior of individuals within the party. Knowledge and use of low-impact techniques are extremely variable between parties and have much to do with the impact they cause.

6. Another factor affecting impact is the ability of different environments to resist change. For example, different plant species and soil types vary in their ability to resist damage when used for recreation. Both *resistance* and *resilience* are important. Resistance is the ability to absorb use without being disturbed (impacted); resilience is the ability to return to an undisturbed state after being disturbed. Resistant sites may or may not be resilient and *vice versa*. Let's compare a bare rock site with a site of lush vegetation. The rock is highly resistant; it would take a stick of dynamite to disturb it, but once dynamited, the scar would be there for a long time. The lush vegetation is not at all resistant, being easily disturbed by a few footprints. However, it would recover in time even if it were greatly disturbed. Resistance varies with the activity. The bare rock would never show much evidence of trampling impact, but one campfire would leave a lasting scar. Obviously, it is best to locate recreation sites on resistant and resilient sites and to avoid use of sites that are neither. Appropriate management of sites that are resistant but not resilient is very different from those that are resilient but not resistant. Resistance and resilience vary seasonally with climatic conditions and the growth stage of plants.

7. When managing impacts it is important to understand their nature and their spatial and temporal patterns and then decide on limits of acceptable change. Then, armed with knowledge of how impacts relate

to amount and type of use and environmental conditions, the manager can manipulate these variables in such a way that impacts are minimized.

8. The final factor to consider in managing recreational impacts is the need to accept wildland recreation as an appropriate use of wildlands. However, recreational use of these areas, because they are easily impacted, is only appropriate if managed. The challenge of the recreation resource manager is to balance the public's desire for wildland recreation and at the same time, to maintain the natural conditions of wildland areas. We must manage for an acceptable level of recreational use and resource protection.

REFERENCES

Brockman, C. F., and L. C. Merriam. 1973. *Recreational Use of Wildlands.* 3rd ed. New York: McGraw-Hill.

Bratton, S. P., M. G. Hickler, and J. H. Graves. 1978. Visitor Impact on Backcountry Campsites in the Great Smoky Mountains. *Environmental Management* 2:431–442.

Cole, G. L., and W. F. LaPage. 1980. Camping and RV Travel Trends. In LaPage, W. F., ed. *Proceedings 1980 National Outdoor Recreation Trends Symposium.* USDA Forest Service General Technical Report NE-57.

Cole, D. N., and E. G. S. Schreiner. 1981. Impacts of Backcountry Recreation: Site Management and Rehabilitation—An Annotated Bibliography. USDA Forest Service General Technical Report INT-122.

Feuchter, R. 1980. Off-road Vehicle Use: The U.S. Forest Service Perspective. In Andrews, R. N. L., and P. F. Nowak, eds. *Off-road Vehicle Use: A Management Challenge.* (pp. 148–155). Office of Environmental Quality, Washington, DC.

Frissell, S. S., and G. H. Stankey. 1972. Wilderness Environmental Quality: Search for Social and Ecological Harmony. In *Proceedings, Society of American Foresters Annual Meeting.* (pp. 170–183). Hot Springs, Arkansas.

Hendee, J. C., G. H. Stankey, and R. C. Lucas. 1978. Wilderness Management. USDA Forest Service Miscellaneous Publication 1365. 381 pp.

Knudson, D. M., and E. B. Curry. 1981. Campers' Perceptions of Site Deterioration and Crowding. *Journal of Forestry* 79:92–94.

Leatherberry, E. C., D. W. Lime, and J. L. Thompson. 1980. Trends in River Recreation. In LaPage, W. F., ed. *Proceedings 1980 Outdoor Recreation Trends Symposium.* USDA Forest Service General Technical Report NE-57.

Lee, R. G. 1975. The Management of Human Components in the Yosemite National Park Ecosystem. Yosemite National Park, CA: Yosemite Institute, 134 pp.

Lucas, R. C. 1979. Perceptions of Non-Motorized Recreational Impacts: A Review of Research Findings. In R. Ittner, D. R. Potter, J. Agee, and S. Anschell, eds. *Recreational Impacts on Wildlands.* USDA Forest Service Conference Proceedings, No. R-6-001-1979.

McCool, S. F., D. W. Lime, and D. H. Anderson. 1977. Simulation Modeling as a Tool for Managing River Recreation. In *Proceedings: River Recreation Management and Research.* USDA Forest Service General Technical Report NC-28. pp. 304–311.

McEwen, D., and S. R. Tocher. 1976. Zone Management: Key to Controlling Recreational Impact in Developed Campsites. *Journal of Forestry* 74:90–93.

Stankey, G. H. 1973. Visitor Perception of Wilderness Recreation Carrying Capacity. USDA Forest Service Research Paper INT-142. 61 pp.

Stankey, G. H., S. F. McCool, and.G. L. Stokes. 1984. Limits of Acceptable Change: A New Framework for Managing the Bob Marshall Wilderness Complex. *Western Wildlands* (Fall). 5 pp.

USDI National Park Service. 1984. The 1982–1983 Nationwide Survey: Summary of Selected Findings. National Park Service, Washington, DC.

Wagar, J. A. 1974. Recreational Carrying Capacity Reconsidered. *Journal of Forestry* 72:274–278.

Wall, G., and C. Wright. 1977. The Environmental Impact of Outdoor Recreation. Department of Geology Publication Series 11, University of Waterloo, Waterloo, Ontario. 69 pp.

Washburne, R. F. 1982. Wilderness Recreational Carrying Capacity: Are Numbers Necessary? *Journal of Forestry* 80:726–728.

Washburne, R. F., and D. N. Cole. 1983. Problems and Practices in Wilderness Management: A Survey of Managers. USDA Forest Service Research Paper INT-304. 56 pp.

II IMPACTS TO RESOURCE COMPONENTS

2 Soil

Along with changes in the characteristics of ground vegetation, soil impacts are the most frequently mentioned of all the effects of outdoor recreational activities. An understanding of ecological impacts presupposes that the reader has had exposure to soil science concepts and terminology. A brief overview of soil characteristics and properties is given and must be understood to appreciate the major impacts of outdoor recreation on soils. Foremost among these characteristics are soil texture, structure, pore space, bulk density, and profile development. For additional information on soils, the following references are suggested: Wilde (1958), Brady (1974), and Foth (1978).

BASIC SOIL ECOLOGY

What Is Soil?

Soil, the basis of all terrestrial life, is commonly misunderstood. Much more than just inert dirt, soil is alive—produced and maintained by interactions between living organisms, rock, air, water, and sunlight (Dasmann 1972). Soils consist of four major components. Minerals and organic matter, both dead and alive, make up the solid portion; the soil solution, water and dissolved substances, and air occupy the pore spaces between solids. While all of these components are present in all soils, usually so intimately mixed that separation is rather difficult, their relative abundance and distribution vary greatly. These differences affect both the soil's capacity as a medium for supporting life and its response to recreational use.

Soil Texture and Structure

The mineral fraction of soils has been divided into classes based on the size of particles. *Sand* particles are 2.0 to 0.02 mm in diameter, *silt* particles are between 0.02 and 0.002 mm, and *clay* particles are less than 0.002 mm. Particles larger than sand are called coarse fragments. *Texture* describes the proportion of these various particle sizes in a soil. A sand soil contains a large proportion (at least 70 percent) of the relatively large sand particles; a clay soil contains at least 35 to 40 percent submicroscopic clay particles. Soils with about equal proportions of sand, clay, and silt particles are called loams. Many intermediate classes have also been defined (e.g. silty clay loam).

Sandy soils are *coarse* textured. The relatively large particles do not pack together tightly; consequently, pore spaces are large. Except when soils have recently been wetted, water only occupies small (*capillary*) pores, where it is held by absorption to the soil particles; air occupies the larger pores. Consequently, sandy soils hold more air and less water than soils with smaller pores (Fig. 1). Such soils drain readily and are apt to be excessively dry.

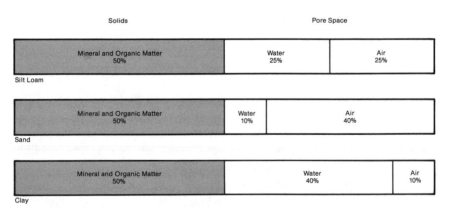

Figure 1. Difference in the relative proportion of solid particles, water, and air in representative silt loam, sand, and clay soils. (*Source:* W. E. Hammitt.)

Clay and silt soils are *fine* textured. They hold more water but less air than sand soils. They can remain waterlogged for long periods of time, providing poor aeration for plant growth. Moreover, despite large quantities of water, much water is held so tightly by the soil particles that it may be unavailable for use by plants. Soils containing equal amounts of sand, silt, and clay such as loam and silt loam soils generally have the best balance of water availability, drainage, and aeration.

Structure refers to how the individual soil particles of different sizes combine into aggregates. Clay particles and organic matter, in particular, promote the aggregation of many individual soil particles into clumps of various shapes and sizes. Thus, a fine-textured soil may appear coarse and may function in many ways as a coarse soil, because the fine particles coalesce into large granules with large pores between them (Spurr and Barnes 1980). Soil structure is particularly important in fine-textured soils where aeration can be a problem. Large pores around aggregates provide good water movement and aeration despite relatively small pores around individual particles. Organic matter can improve the structure in soils of various textures. In coarse-textured soils, organic matter can improve the water-holding capacity of the soil because of its capacity to absorb and hold water.

Favorable soil structure developed under forest conditions may be destroyed by removing the forest vegetation and exposing the soil surface directly to rainfall. The direct impact of rainfall can detach soil particles from aggregates. The detached particles clog spaces between aggregates, forming a crust that is relatively impervious to water. Less water entering the soil means that more is running across the surface, and this increases erosion. The effects of recreational trampling on soil structure can be even more profound. Destruction of leaf litter by trampling eliminates the possiblity of its incorporation into the surface soil horizon, decreasing the amount of organic matter that is so important to promoting good soil structure. More will be said about this and the serious effects of soil compaction later.

Pore Space

As was previously mentioned, the pore space is determined largely by the texture and structure of soils. Soils with a large proportion of large particles such as sands or with a compacted structure in which particles lie close together have a low *total porosity*. Soils that are medium-textured, high in organic matter, and uncompacted have a high total porosity. Soil pores have been divided into two size classes—*macro* and *micro*. The larger macropores allow the ready movement of air and percolating water, but they retain little water. In contrast, water is retained in micropores, but air and water movement is impeded. Sandy soils have low total porosity, but a large proportion of that porosity consists of macropores. Consequently, the movement of air and water is rapid (Brady 1974).

Despite a large total pore space, movement of air and water in fine-textured soils is relatively slow. Porosity is dominated by micropores, which are often full of water, leaving little pore space for air. Also the water occupying the capillary micropores is held tightly to clay particles by tension forces, contributing to the slow movement of water. The significant point here is that the size of individual pore spaces (macro or micro) is more important to the movement of air and water than total pore space.

Bulk Density

Bulk density is a soil weight measurement, defined as the mass (weight) of a unit volume of soil. It is determined primarily by the quantity of pore space within a given volume of soil. Thus, it is closely related to porosity. It is affected by the compactness of the soil and by the soil's composition, particularly its texture, structure, and organic matter content. Soils that are loose and porous will have low weights per unit volume (bulk densities), and those that are compact will have high values. Soils high in fine-textured material and organic matter will have lower bulk densities than soils high in sand and low in organic matter. The bulk densities of clay, clay loam, and silt loam surface soils normally range from 1.00 to as high as 1.60 g/cm^3, while sands and sandy loams vary from 1.20 to 1.80 g/cm^3 (Brady 1974). These differences, present under undisturbed conditions, should be kept in mind when using bulk density as a measure of compaction.

Variation in the relationships between soil texture, compaction, and bulk density is illustrated in Fig. 2. The increase in bulk density with compaction is more pronounced in fine-textured soils. Uncompacted, fine-textured soils have low bulk densities because the soil particles can be packed together more tightly than large particles. Consequently, fine-textured soils can be compacted to a greater density than coarse-textured soils.

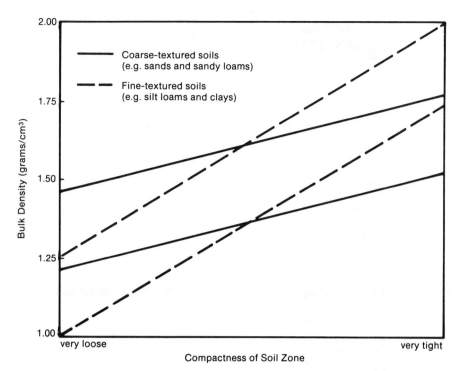

Figure 2. Generalized relationship between compactness and the range of bulk densities common in sandy soils and in those of finer texture. (*Source:* Brady 1974.)

Also, bulk density tends to increase with profile depth. This apparently results from a lower content of organic matter, less aggregation and root penetration, and compaction caused by pressure from the weight of overlying horizons. Compact subsoils may have bulk densities greater than 2.0 g/cm^3 (Brady 1974).

The Soil Profile

Soils are not uniform in texture and structure for a given depth. Examination of a vertical section of soil shows the presence of more or less distinct horizontal layers, differing in color, composition, and other properties. Such a section is called a *soil profile*. A typical soil profile will consist of four primary horizontal layers or *horizons* (Fig. 3). These primary horizons, the O, A, B, and C horizons, are subdivided further and may or may not be present in any given soil.

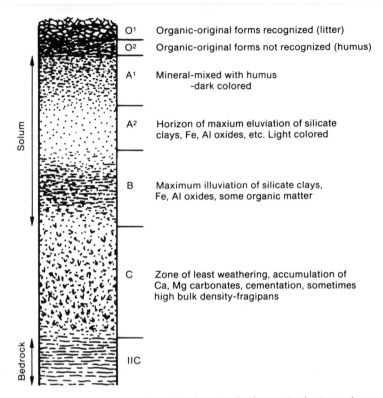

Figure 3. A conceptual mineral soil profile showing the four major horizons that may be present. (*Source:* Adapted from Buckman and Brady, 1969. Reprinted with permission of MacMillan Publishing Co., Inc. From *The Nature and Properties of Soils,* 7th Edition, by H. O. Buckman and N. C. Brady. Copyright(c) 1960, 1969 by MacMillan Publishing Co., Inc.)

The O, or organic horizon is formed above the mineral soil and often consists of both an O_1 and an O_2 horizon. The O_1 horizon consists of litter—recognizable leaves, twigs, fruits, and dead plants and animals. When this litter decomposes to an unrecognizable state, it is called humus, the primary component of the O_2 horizon. Surface organic horizons are extremely important to healthy soils. They cushion the impact of rainfall and other erosional agents, including recreational use, on underlying mineral horizons. They are important zones of biotic activity and help in the absorption of water. As a source of humus that can move downward into the soil, the organic horizons contribute to the maintenance of healthy soil structure, water relations, and aeration. They also are an important source of nutrients, critical to the maintenance of soil fertility. Unfortunately, the 0 horizon is often pulverized and removed by recreational use of sites receiving concentrated use.

The A horizon is the uppermost layer of mineral soil. It is characterized in moist climates by the leaching of nutrients by downward moving water and acid solutions. It is subdivided into an upper A_1 horizon, in which organic matter is constantly being added to mineral soil through litter decomposition and mixing by soil organisms and a lower A_2 horizon, a zone of leaching. Biotic activity is most concentrated in the A_1 horizon.

Below the A is the B horizon, characterized in moist temperate climates by the accumulation of iron and aluminum oxides and minute clay and organic particles, all derived from leaching of the A horizon above. In more arid regions, it is characterized by accumulation of soluble salts such as calcium carbonate. As a result, the B horizon is usually finer-textured and darker-colored than either the A horizon or the original parent material, except in arid regions where accumulated salts are light-colored.

The C horizon is below the zone of accumulation. It has been little affected by biotic activity and consists primarily of disintegrated parent material, similar to that from which the A and B horizons were derived.

IMPACTS ON SOILS

Manning (1979) provides a useful conceptualization of recreational impact on soils as a seven-step cycle (Fig. 4). Where present, the first step in the cycle is a reduction or removal of the leaf litter and humus layers—the 0 horizon. Trampling, surface runoff, and in some places raking of the site for aesthetic or fire safety reasons contribute to loss of this litter cover. The second step, a reduction in organic matter incorporated into the mineral soil, occurs in some places but not in others. Removal of surface litter cuts off much of the source of organic matter so that in time, as existing soil organic matter decomposes, soil organic matter should decline. Indeed this does occur in some places. In others, however, some of the pulverized surface organic matter is transported down into the soil by percolating waters where it accumulates in dark bands (Monti and Mackintosh 1979). In these cases soil organic matter actually increases in response to recreational use.

Regardless of what happens in the first two steps, the third step—

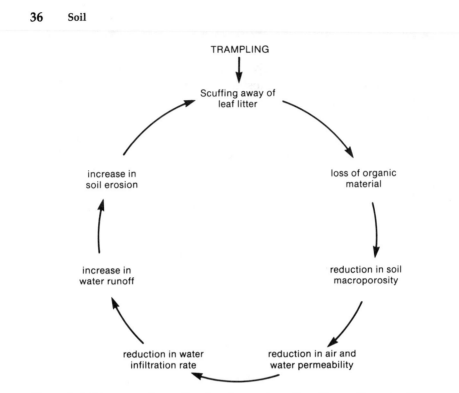

Figure 4. Soil impact cycle resulting from human trampling. (*Source:* "Impacts of Recreation on Riparian Soils and Vegetation," by R. E. Manning in *Water Resources Bulletin* 15(1):30–43. Reprinted with permission of the American Water Resources Association.)

compaction—always occurs. Susceptibility to compaction of soil by the pressures of trampling or vehicular travel is increased by loss of organic matter, both at the surface and in the soil, but it will occur anyway. Through compaction, soil particles are forced to pack together more tightly, eliminating much of the interstitial pore space. Soil structure is also disrupted as aggregates are broken up and forced together. The result is a reduction in total porosity and macroporosity; the volume of micropores is not greatly affected.

This reduction in macroporosity initiates a chain of events that carries through the sixth step of the cycle, with profound implications for the "health" of soils. Since macropores are the primary conduits for the free movement of air and water, their reduction seriously impedes soil aeration and the percolation of water into the soil. Because less water can move through the soil, less can enter the soil, and water infiltration rates are reduced. This can lead to reductions in soil moisture and resulting water stress on plants, although this impact is only pronounced in certain places at certain times. A more universal impact is increased surface runoff, the inevitable result of rainfall on soils with low infiltration rates. This greatly increases the potential for erosion, step seven, particularly if slopes are steep and soils are erosive. Severe erosion truncates soil profiles, and it exacerbates soil impacts by washing away even more surface organic matter, hence the view of the impact process as a never-ending cycle. Let's now take a look at how serious these impacts are in various recreational situations.

Organic Matter

The magnitude of organic matter loss varies with amount of use, the recreational activity involved, and environmental conditions. In desert areas, for example, where organic horizons are very thin and patchy, if present at all, any use of any kind rapidly eliminates organic matter. As it is so sparse to start out with, such losses represent a severe impact. In forested environments, effects vary between deciduous and evergreen forests. Deciduous forests accumulate much more leafy litter in the fall after the main use season. This can promote more rapid overwinter recovery. Litter loss is particularly pronounced and rapid on paths and trails. Trampling is highly concentrated, and the frequency of steep slopes and water channelization contribute to surface erosion of litter from much of the trail surface. On a newly opened nature trail in England, the passage of 8000 people reduced the volume of forest leaf litter by 50 percent in just one week (Burden and Randerson 1972).

Legg and Schneider (1977) found that after two seasons of camping, litter on forested campsites in Michigan was limited to one year's leaf fall, and the humic layer (the O_2 horizon) had been eliminated. The annual leaf fall is rapidly removed within several months after the beginning of each camping season even on light use sites (Fig. 5). In most cases hardwood litter is more rapidly eliminated during the main use season, but it recovers more rapidly over winter. Differences in litter cover, between light and heavy use sites, were much less pronounced after the fourth year of use (1972) than after the third. In a park in northwest Ontario, Monti and Mackintosh (1979) also reported that most organic litter is lost even with light use.

Loss of litter is less pronounced on campsites in wilderness areas

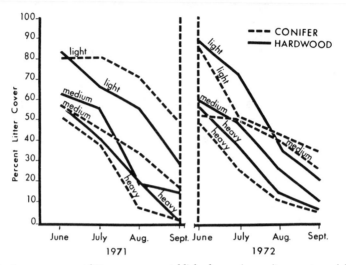

Figure 5. Average percent litter cover on established camping units over two visitor use seasons. Note the percent recovery during the off-season, Sept. 1971 to June 1972. (*Source:* Legg and Schneider 1977. Reproduced from *Soil Science Society of America Journal,* Volume 41, pp. 437–441, 1977 by permission of the publisher.)

where use is not so great. In what is now the Boundary Waters Canoe Area, Minnesota, litter and humus layers on campsites were reduced in thickness an average of 65 percent below undisturbed control areas (Frissell and Duncan 1965). In the Eagle Cap Wilderness, Oregon, about one-half of the organic horizon has been removed on campsites (Cole and Fichtler 1983). In some places, however, all organic matter has been removed. The mineral soil (A horizon) beneath was exposed over about 30 percent of the Eagle Cap campsites. On the most infrequently used sites little litter was lost. The thickness of organic horizons was reduced only 3 percent on soils used no more than a few times per year. This compares with reductions of 21 percent and 68 percent on sites used about 10 to 20 nights per year and over 25 nights per year, respectively.

Little litter is likely to remain on trails or campsites that are frequently used, particularly those with roaded access, after they have been used for several years. On lightly used campsites in more remote areas, however, little litter loss may occur if organic horizons are thick. This is very different from the situation with regard to soil compaction where substantial compaction occurs even on very lightly used sites. In places where litter cover is sparse, such as desert areas, even light recreational use can eliminate all litter.

As mentioned previously, there is some debate about what happens to surface organic matter once it is pulverized. Certainly, most of it is eroded away. However, several researchers report that some of the pulverized organic matter accumulates in the uppermost zone of the A horizon. On Eagle Cap campsites, for example, the organic matter content of the upper 5 cm of mineral soil was 20 percent higher on campsites than controls. Other researchers report the opposite. Settergren and Cole (1970) found organic matter to be mixed through the surface layers of control sites but absent in campsite soils.

Loss of soil organic matter is serious because it makes the soil more prone to many soil impacts that follow. Susceptibility to reduced rainwater infiltration and nutrient cycling and increased surface erosion, profile truncation, and soil compaction are all increased when organic matter is removed. Elimination of the surface litter and humus layers greatly reduces the soil's ability to capture rainwater, accumulate and replenish soil organisms and nutrients, and cushion the mineral soil against the impact forces that cause compaction.

Profile Truncation

Destruction of the protective organic horizon leads to an accelerated rate of wind and water erosion, which removes a large proportion of the fine-sized particles on the exposed soil surface. In addition, unprotected mineral soil is readily compacted by human trampling. As a result of the combination of organic matter destruction, wind and sheet erosion, and compaction, the soil profile is reduced in depth or truncated. Tree roots are commonly exposed and suffer mechanical damage as a result of soil profile truncation (Fig. 6).

The profile of heavily used campsites average 3 in. shallower than that on nearby control sites in the Missouri Ozarks (Settergren and Cole 1970). The profile of one badly abused campsite indicated that as much as 9 in. of surface soil had disappeared following extensive recreational use. In a study of Michigan backcountry campsites, the A_1 horizon was completely eroded from moderately and heavily used sites by the end of four seasons of use. In contrast, the A_1 horizons on control sites were over 5 cm deep, on average (Legg and Schneider 1977). Therefore, 5 cm had been lost in just four years.

Figure 6. Tree roots exposed by soil erosion and compaction. (*Photo:* D. N. Cole).

Soil Compaction

Compaction, whether by trampling, vehicular use, or some other source of pressure, is a commonly documented effect of recreational use. The major techniques used to document soil compaction are (Speight 1973):

Penetrometry.   Records the force necessary to drive a rod a known length into the ground

Bulk Density.   A direct measure of soil density (weight to volume ratio)

Permeability.   A measure of how rapidly water permeates the soil

Conductivity.   A measure of soil density based on conductivity to electricity or gamma rays

Although these methods measure different characteristics, they all document increased compaction, the forcing of individual soil particles into closer proximity, thereby reducing the area occupied by interstices (Manning 1979). Compaction of soils by recreational use is reflected in increased values for bulk density, penetration resistance, conductivity, and decreased permeability values.

Comparing the degree of compaction found in different areas is difficult because of differences in site conditions and measurement techniques. Bulk density values vary greatly between soil types; certain inherently dense, uncompacted soils (e.g., sands) have even higher bulk densities than soils on highly compacted recreation sites. Studies of campsites, picnic sites, paths, and trails report increases in bulk density of up to 0.5 g/cm^3. Examples of reported increases include 0.1 g/cm^3 on Eagle Cap Wilderness campsites (Cole and Fichtler 1983), 0.4 g/cm^3 on developed camp and picnic sites in Rhode Island (Brown, Kalisz, and Wright 1977), and 0.2 to 0.4 g/cm^3 on paths and trails (Liddle 1975). Dotzenko, Papamichos, and Romine (1967) recorded a bulk density of 1.60 g/cm^3 in a heavily used campground in Rocky Mountain National Park. In off-road vehicle areas, surface bulk densities over 2.00 g/cm^3 have been reported (Wilshire, Nakata, Shipley, and Prestegaard 1978). Weaver and Dale (1978) measured bulk density after experimentally trampling a grassland 1000 times by a hiker, a horse, and a motorcycle. Bulk density increased 0.2 g/cm^3 with hiker use and 0.3 g/cm^3 with horse and motorcycle use.

Soil penetrometer readings also show wide variation in amount of increase. Penetration resistance typically increased 71 percent on campsites in the Bob Marshall Wilderness, 89 percent in the Rattlesnake, 139 percent in the Mission Mountains, and 220 percent in the Boundary Waters Canoe Area (Cole 1983). In the Bob Marshall the median penetration resistance on sites used by parties with horses was 4.0 kg/cm^2 compared with only 2.6 kg/cm^2 on backpacker-only sites. Higher values and greater increases indicate increasing force needed to penetrate the soil, a reflection of increased compaction. While soil penetrometer readings are much easier to record than bulk density and more replicate readings can be taken, they vary with differences in water content and other soil characteristics. Consequently, comparisons between sites and even over time on the same site should be treated with caution.

In all soils the top layers of the mineral soil are the most compacted; organic horizons are not very susceptible to compaction. Except in areas used by off-road vehicles, compaction on recreation sites is seldom evident more than 5 to 6 in. below the surface (LaPage 1962). Compaction of ORV areas is evident at depths exceeding 3 ft (Wilshire et al. 1978). Unfortunately, it is compaction of the surface soils that is more critical to the alteration of water and air movement, vegetation rooting zones, and the habitat of soil organisms.

The degree of soil compaction is influenced by many soil factors, including organic matter, soil moisture, and soil texture and structure.

In general, the soils most prone to compaction are those with a wide range of particle sizes (e.g., loams), those with a low organic content, and those that are frequently wet when trampled. On dry, extremely sandy soils, compaction can even be beneficial. Total porosity remains high because the sand particles simply cannot be pushed together closely; however, some of the macropores are reduced to micropore size, allowing the soil to retain more water, thereby benefiting plant growth.

Degree of compaction varies seasonally. Recovery occurs over the winter season as compaction is lessened by frost action, lack of use, and possibly wind rocking of trees. If all use is curtailed, compaction of recreation sites can be expected to return to normal within about a decade. With continued use any overwinter recovery is short-lived. With the beginning of the next use season, recovery stops and renewed compaction eliminates any overwinter loosening by early summer (Legg and Schneider 1977). Figure 7 illustrates this well.

Evaluation of the significance of compaction *per se* is difficult. Certainly the effect of compaction on water and air movement can create serious problems. As the example of the dry, sandy soil illustrates, however, there are cases where a more dense soil can actually be beneficial. Two direct, plant-related, negative consequences of compaction are the hindrance of plant root elongation and the lack of suitable regeneration sites on compacted soils. Figure 8 illustrates the effects of compaction on the ability of seedling roots to penetrate soil. Serious root impedence occurs at much lower densities on the more fine-textured silt loam soil. On coarser soils, it is difficult to compact soils to a level where pores are too small to penetrate. A poorly developed root system decreases establishment of plants and, for established plants, reduces vigor and growth. Compaction reduces germination through its effect on the smoothness of germination sites. Seeds of different species require a diversity of microhabitats in which to germinate. Germination is usually greater on rough surfaces that offer heterogeneous habitats. Compaction typically creates a homogeneous, smooth surface on which germination is inhibited.

Macroporosity and Infiltration Rate

Compaction reduces the macropore space among soil particles, thus reducing soil aeration and the rate at which water enters and moves through the soil. A reduced infiltration rate, in turn, causes increased

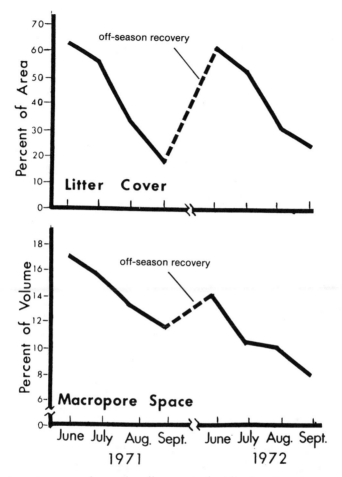

Figure 7. Impact recovery during the off-season is short-lived, as impacts resume at the beginning of the new camping season. (*Source:* Legg and Schneider 1977. Reproduced from *Soil Science Society of America Journal*, Volume 41, pp. 437–441, 1977 by permission of the publisher.)

surface water runoff. The increased runoff may change drainage patterns, accelerate erosion, and reduce available soil moisture.

On the central core of developed campsites, Monti and Mackintosh (1979) found that the area of macropore space declined from about 25 percent of soil volume to 2 or 3 percent. These changes are particularly pronounced on fine-textured soils where macropore space is low initially, and susceptibility to compaction is high on account of the smaller soil particles. However, even in sand dune soils, loss of macroporosity

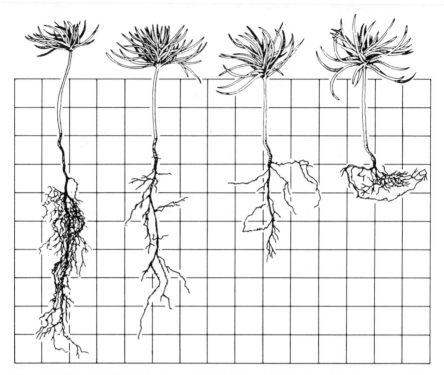

Figure 8. Effect of soil bulk density at 1.2, 1.4, 1.6, and 1.8 g/cm³ on Austrian pine seedling growth on sandy loam soil (2 cm grid). (*Source:* Zisa et al. 1980.)

can be severe enough to cause anaerobic (low oxygen) conditions (Liddle and Greig-Smith 1975). Smaller soil pore size reduces the mass flow and diffusion of air within the soil and curtails movement of nutrients (Liddle 1975). The movement of O_2 and CO_2 is retarded in the soil, which can lead to respiration and growth problems for vegetation (Legg and Schneider 1977). Root activity decreases as does the ability to absorb water and nutrients. The soil microbiota is adversely affected, and the decomposition of organic matter is slowed.

Legg and Schneider (1977) observed decreases in macropore space on newly opened campsites over a four-year period. In conifer stands macropore space declined from 31.6 percent (control measures) to 17.1 percent after two years to 8.6 percent after four years. The rate at which macroporosity is reduced diminishes with time; macroporosity probably stabilizes at some low level after about five years. Loss of macropores, after both two and four years of use, was greater on heavy sites than on moderate or light use sites. Even on light use sites, however, four years of use eliminated two-thirds of the macropores.

Reductions in water infiltration rates are probably the most important environmental consequence of compaction. On picnic areas in Connecticut, Lutz (1945) found reductions of 80 percent in sand soils and 95 percent in sandy loam soils. On the sandy loam sites the average length of time for the infiltration of one liter of water was 86 minutes in the picnic area and 4 minutes in the undisturbed area—a twentyfold difference. On the coarser textured sandy soil, loss of macropores was less severe, and infiltration on the picnic site was four times as fast as on the sandy loam picnic site; one liter infiltrated in 20 minutes.

James, Smith, Mackintosh, Hoffman, and Monti (1979) report a similar twentyfold reduction in infiltration on developed campsites in Ontario. Less severe reductions are characteristic of the less heavily used campsites in wilderness areas. In the Bob Marshall Wilderness, for example, Cole (1983) measured both instantaneous infiltration rates (the time it takes for the first centimeter of water to enter the soil) and saturated rates (the time for the first 5 cm of water). Instantaneous rates for campsites were less than one-third of controls, and saturated rates were one-sixth of controls.

More severe reductions in infiltration have been found in off-road vehicle areas. In one California area, infiltration rates were almost 40 times slower on motorcycle tracks than in adjacent undisturbed areas (Wilshire et al. 1978). Organic matter content and soil texture and structure greatly influence both infiltration rates and the severity of reductions in infiltration rates.

Compaction appears to occur rapidly with light use. Even in wilderness areas low use sites are usually nearly as compacted as high use sites. In the Boundary Waters Canoe Area, increases in bulk density were two-thirds as high on sites used fewer than 12 nights per year as on sites used over 60 nights per year (Marion and Merriam 1985). In the Eagle Cap, Missions Mountains, and Rattlesnake Wildernessses increases in penetration resistance and infiltration rates were significantly greater on sites used fewer than five nights per year than on sites used many times more (Cole and Fichtler 1983). Macroporosity is also greatly reduced even at low use levels. The relation between compaction-related impacts and amount of use is highly curvilinear—a little use causes most of the impact. This is different from the case of litter loss, where it often takes at least a moderate amount of use before a substantial amount of litter is lost.

Soil Moisture

Soil moisture usually decreases as compaction increases since compaction reduces infiltration and the amount of water available to the soil. However, compaction can also increase the amount of capillary pore space and consequently the moisture-holding capacity of soils. This situation is explained by the fact that when the soil is compacted, noncapillary pores too large to hold water against the force of gravity may be reduced to capillary sizes where they can hold water. Lutz (1945) found the field capacity of trampled sites on sandy loam soils to be 8.9 percent higher than on control sites. Field capacity is the amount of water held in the soil after any water added to the soil has had a chance to drain downward. This increase in field capacity comes at the expense of reduced air capacity and, ironically, a reduced rate of water infiltration.

Settergren and Cole (1970) conducted one of the more detailed studies of soil moisture on a campground in the Missouri Ozarks. Both the field capacity and the permanent wilting point—the moisture left after plants have removed all the water they can—were reduced on campsites. The most significant measure of moisture—that available to plants—was about the same on campsites and controls. At no time was moisture at the 12 in. depth unavailable to plants, although recharge after precipitation and the rate of moisture depletion were both much slower on campsites (Fig. 9). Note the more rapid loss of moisture in dry June and the more rapid increase after late August rains on controls. Although adequate moisture was available at the 12 in. depth, available moisture dropped to zero at the surface in late August. This must be fairly common, given the severe wilting and stag-heading of tree crowns. These seasonal moisture limitations in surface soils are responsible, along with compaction, for creating a poor rooting environment for trees near the surface. A scarcity of shallow roots limits the ability of trees to utilize any surface moisture recharge that occurs in late summer.

The inability of the compacted soil surface to take up water restricts soil moisture recharge, which is particularly important to the survival of herbaceous vegetation during dry months. Many of the annual grasses, sedges, and herbs forming the recreation area ground cover vegetation during the early part of the summer succumb later to severe surface moisture limitations.

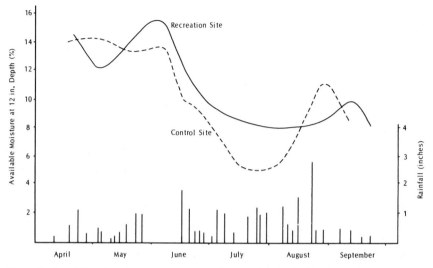

Figure 9. Rainfall and moisture availability, Missouri Ozarks, 1973. (*Source:* Settergren and Cole 1970.)

The effects of recreational use on soil moisture are complex and variable, being related to factors such as soil compaction, texture, organic content, density of forest cover, and exposure to sun and wind. Generally, effects on soil moisture content are probably of less importance than many of the other impacts that have been discussed. They are probably most significant where available moisture declines in soils that were inherently droughty under undisturbed conditions.

Soil Erosion

Erosion is the most permanent, and therefore serious, of soil impacts. While soil compaction, loss of organic matter, and some other impacts will recover to some degree during periods of nonuse, erosion usually continues, once initiated, whether use continues or not. Gully erosion of trails, in particular, is likely to continue even without use. Most erosion is not caused by trampling or camping. Soil is eroded mostly by wind and water; recreational activities provide the circumstances for erosion and increase its rate of occurrence but are seldom the actual agents of erosion.

Although the most important agent of soil erosion is water, wind is an important erosional force in peat or sandy soils. Wind erosion of sand dunes is the best example of large-scale erosion triggered by recreational activity (Speight 1973). Where recreation destroys the vegetation that stabilizes dunes, the sand is freely moved by wind. Tens of hectares may be eroded at a single site, causing dune erosion to be the most obvious and often quoted impact of recreation in Great Britain. In the United States, wind erosion of dune ecosystems is primarily a problem in the national seashores of the Park Service, lakeshore parks on the Great Lakes, and desert dune areas used by off-road vehicles. Boardwalks to channel visitor use and prohibitions on camping and vehicular traffic are common means of limiting vegetation disturbance and resulting wind erosion.

Water erosion in recreation areas occurs primarily in two forms: sheet and gully. Sheet erosion of campsites, picnic areas, and other fairly level recreation sites occurs when water flows in a sheet across broad expanses of ground, picking up material as it moves. This impact was discussed earlier in this chapter under the heading of "Profile Truncation." Gully erosion, an even more serious problem to recreation management, occurs where water is concentrated in channels. This increases its erosive power. Gully erosion is a common problem on roads, trails, and sometimes on stream banks. Ketchledge and Leonard (1970) have measured trail erosion in the Adirondack Mountains that amounts to an increase in both trail width and depth of 1 in. per year. Surface erosion of up to 2 ft was reported on footpaths near campsites along the Colorado River in Grand Canyon; 1 ft reductions were common (Dolan, Howard, and Gallenson 1974).

Paths created by horses and trail bikes create conditions that invite accelerated gully erosion. Shod horses tend to loosen and move soil rather than compact it. Consequently, equestrian trails in steep areas develop as narrow trenches, which deepen and widen over time. Four-wheel drive vehicles and trail bikes in the steep and moist southern Appalachian Mountains make trails that erode in places to depths of 6 to 8 ft. (Fig. 10). In an off-road vehicle area in California, the annual erosion rate was estimated to be 11,500 tons per km^2. This is 30 times higher than the rate at which the U.S. Bureau of Reclamation considers erosion to be a serious problem (Wilshire et al. 1978). In a study of riverways, Hansen (1975) could not attribute much of the streambank erosion that was occurring to canoe use. Much was natural; some was linked to vehicular access by people fishing, picnicking, or simply watching the floaters.

Figure 10. Off-road vehicles have caused excessive erosion on this trail in the Cherokee National Forest, Tennessee. (*Photo:* W. E. Hammitt.)

The extent of erosion on a recreation site is determined by many factors. Slope, drainage, and climate are important. Erosion is likely to be more serious on steep slopes where water tends to be channelized and in climates with infrequent but intense rainfall. A sparse ground-cover vegetation and lack of an organic horizon also make a site prone to erosion. The most erosive soils are homogeneous-textured soils, particularly those high in silt or fine sands and low in organic matter. Shallow soils may quickly erode down to bedrock.

Other Soil Impacts

Additional impacts, which have been investigated in less detail, include effects on temperature, organisms, and chemistry. Loss of vegetation and surface organic horizons removes an insulating layer, which leads to a greater range of soil temperatures. Temperatures are higher in summer and during the day; they are lower during winter and at night. During winter, soil in trampled areas was observed to be frozen to a depth of 3 to 4 cm whereas under taller vegetation in minimally used areas, the soil temperature remained above freezing (Chappell, Ainsworth, Cameron, and Redfern 1971).

The effect of snowmobiles on soil temperature regimes can be particularly pronounced. Compaction of snow reduces its insulating ability. Wanek (1971) found the duff layer (0 horizon) under snowmobile trails to be 11°C cooler than under the undisturbed snow. The A_1 soil horizon under the compacted snow froze approximately one month earlier and thawed an average of 2 to 3 weeks later in the spring. This shortened growing season can be detrimental to the life cycle of flowering plants, particularly those in alpine ecosystems. As Wanek (1974) states:

> The colder temperatures retard the growth and flowering of early spring flowers and reduce their seed productivity and viability. In addition, perennial herbs having large underground storage organs often perish due to intracellular ice crystals producing cytolysis, dehydration, or extracellular ice masses which disrupt tissues. (p. 50)

Changes in soil temperature regimes and decreases in organic matter and air pore space also affect soil organisms. Colder temperatures under snowmobile trails were the presumed cause of a hundredfold reduction in soil bacteria and a two to tenfold reduction in soil fungi (Wanek 1971). Speight (1973) summarized the influence of trampling on bacteria in woodland soils, where bacteria decreased by about one-half. Nitrifying bacteria, which need an abundance of oxygen, were unable to survive in the trampled soils, while anaerobic bacteria were twice as abundant as other forms. Both the abundance and diversity of soil arthropods and earthworms decrease with the increasing intensity of recreational activity (Speight 1973). Although *very* poorly understood, impacts on soil organisms may be among the most significant of all recreational impacts, as soil organisms play a crucial role in the cycling of energy and nutrients in the ecosystem.

Several changes in soil chemistry have also been recorded on recreation sites. Several studies have found increases in soil pH on campsites; recreation use somewhat reduces acidity. Results of changes in the concentration of various nutrients have been notably inconsistent. Cole and Fichtler (1983) found that Mg and Ca concentrations doubled and that Na increased significantly on campsites in the Eagle Cap Wilderness. The authors suggest that the pH and nutrient increases "probably resulted from the scattering of materials, such as campfire ashes, excess food, and soap, as well as from reduced leaching as a result of slower infiltration rates." Chappell et al. (1971) found decreases in nitrate and phosphate, compounds that were unaffected by use in the Eagle Cap. Probably a number of soil impacts, particularly reductions in organic matter, reduced aeration, and impoverishment of soil organism populations act to reduce concentrations of certain soil nutrients; however, this tendency can be compensated for by pollution of the site and reduced leaching. Most of these changes are small, and perhaps they are generally of little importance.

Impacts Associated with Campfires

Soil impacts resulting from collecting and burning wood in campfires are quite different from those associated with other activities on campsites and trails. Therefore, they will be discussed separately here. The removal of firewood need not cause the serious problems suggested by some proponents of banning campfires. Nutrient supplies should not be severely depleted in areas where wood is gathered. The majority of soil nutrients supplied by trees are contained in the leaves, needles, and small trees, not the larger branches and small boles of trees that are usually used for firewood (Weetman and Webber 1972). Neither will soil organic matter be substantially reduced. Again, the majority of organic matter added to the system comes from leaves and twigs, tree components seldom collected for firewood. The trampling of leaf and small twig litter is likely to have more of an effect on carbon cycling than the gathering of firewood (Bratton, Strombert, and Harmon 1982).

The most serious effects of firewood gathering result from the collection of large pieces of downed wood, those larger than several inches in diameter. Decaying wood of this size plays an important role in the environment that has only recently been appreciated. Moreover, its role cannot be replaced by any other component of the ecosystem. Decaying wood has an unusually high water-holding capacity, making it important to the water relations of droughty sites in particular. It also accumulates nitrogen, phosphorus, and sometimes calcium and magnesium. Therefore, use of this wood could result in nutrient impoverishment. Decaying wood is the preferred germination site for certain plant species and is a preferred growing medium for microorganisms. Ectomycorrhizal fungi, which develop a symbiotic association with the roots of many plants, improving their ability to extract water and nutrients from infertile soils, are frequently concentrated in decaying wood. Thus, removal of large pieces of wood can be detrimental to soil productivity.

Generally, the area affected by firewood removal is small and locally concentrated. However, this activity can greatly increase the area of disturbance around campsites. In Great Smoky Mountains National Park the area disturbed by firewood gathering was more than nine times the size of the devegetated zone around campsites (Bratton, Hickler, and Graves, 1978).

The area disturbed by burning of firewood in campfires is even smaller; however, the effects are considerably more serious. Fenn, Gogue, and Burge (1976) examined the effects on soil of burning 140 lbs of wood, a much larger amount than would be burned at one time in most campfires. Their fires altered organic matter to a depth of 4 in. and destroyed 90 percent of the organic matter in the surface inch of soil. Unfortunately, the only other information on campfire effects must be extrapolated from studies of forest and slash fires. In such fires it is common to lose most organic matter, nitrogen, sulfur, and phosphorus and to reduce the soil's moisture-holding capacity and infiltration rate (Tarrant 1956). Since the effects of campfires are so dramatic, many managers try to concentrate them in one place to avoid excessive damage.

SUMMARY

1. Recreational use causes reductions in surface organic horizons and compaction of mineral soil. Compaction leads to loss of macroporosity and reductions in water infiltration rates. This reduces aeration and water movement in the soil, altering the character of soil organism populations and adversely affecting plant vigor and growth. Increased surface runoff often results in accelerated erosion, causing both profile truncation and gully erosion.

2. Where it occurs, erosion is the most serious of these impacts because it is essentially irreversible. Recovery rates vary greatly, particularly with factors like amount of biotic activity, length of the growing season, and the nature of temperature and moisture fluctuations. Erosional losses are likely to require centuries to recover. Most other impacts should usually recover in a decade and many can be speeded up through human intervention.

3. Compaction-related impacts, particularly reduction in macroporosity and infiltration, occur rapidly with low use. Initial low use causes most of the change, with further use causing less and less additional impact. If surface horizons are thick, loss of litter is less rapid and is only pronounced when use levels are moderate to high. Amount of erosion is related more to site factors than amount of use because the main agents of erosion are water and wind, not trampling.

4. Activities engaged in and type of use affect what impacts occur as well as their severity. Camping and picnicking cause most of these impacts to be severe because use is highly concentrated; however, erosion is less pronounced because use areas are generally flat. On trails, erosion is the most serious problem because of steep slopes and channelization of water. Erosion problems are aggravated when use is by horses or motorized vehicles, because they often loosen the soil rather than compact it. This makes it more easily moved by water, the main agent of erosion.

5. Susceptibility to impact varies between soils and with site factors. Compaction is most pronounced on fine-textured soils, soils with a wide variety of particle sizes, and soils low in organic matter. Erosion is most pronounced in soils with homogenous textures, particularly those high in silt and fine sand and low in organic matter. Erosion is more likely on steep slopes, shallow soils, places with sparse vegetation cover, and places where runoff is concentrated.

REFERENCES

Brady, N. C. 1974. *The Nature and Properties of Soils.* 8th ed. New York: Macmillan, 639 pp.

Bratton, S. P., M. G. Hickler, and J. H. Graves. 1978. Visitor Impact on Backcountry Campsites in the Great Smoky Mountains. *Environmental Management* 2(5):431–442.

Bratton, S. P., L. L. Strombert, and M. E. Harmon. 1982. Firewood Gathering Impacts in Backcountry Campsites in Great Smoky Mountains National Park. *Environmental Management* 6(1):63–71.

Brown, Jr., J. H., S. P. Kalisz, and W. R. Wright. 1977. Effects of Recreational Use on Forested Sites. *Environmental Geology* 1:425–431.

Burden, R. F., and P. F. Randerson. 1972. Quantitative Studies of the Effects of Human Trampling on Vegetation as an Aid to the Management of Semi-natural Areas. *Journal of Applied Ecology* 9:439–457.

Chappell, H. G., J. F. Ainsworth, R. A. D. Cameron, and M. Redfern. 1971. The

Effect of Trampling on a Chalk Grassland Ecosystem. *Journal of Applied Ecology* 8(3):869–882.

Cole, D. N. 1983. Campsite Conditions in the Bob Marshall Wilderness, Montana. USDA Forest Service Research Paper INT-312.

Cole, D. N., and R. K. Fichtler. 1983. Campsite Impact on Three Western Wilderness Areas. *Environmental Management* 7(3):275–288.

Dasmann, R. F. 1972. *Environmental Conservation.* 3rd ed. New York: Wiley, 473 pp.

Dolan, R., A. Howard, and A. Gallenson. 1974. Man's Impact on the Colorado River in the Grand Canyon. *American Scientist* 62:392–401.

Dotzenko, A. D., N. T. Papamichos, and D. S. Romine. 1967. Effects of Recreational Use on Soil and Moisture Conditions in Rocky Mountain National Park. *Journal of Soil and Water Conservation* 22:196–197.

Fenn, D. B., G. J. Gogue, and R. E. Burge. 1976. Effects of Campfires on Soil Properties. USDI National Park Service, Ecological Service Bull. No. 5.

Foth, H. D. 1978. *Fundamentals of Soil Science.* 6th ed. New York: Wiley, 436 pp.

Frissell, Jr., S. S., and D. P. Duncan. 1965. Campsite Preference and Deterioration in the Quetico-Superior Canoe Country. *Journal of Forestry* 63:256–260.

Hansen, E. A. 1975. Does Canoeing Increase Streambank Erosion? USDA Forest Service Research Note NC-186.

James, T. D., D. W. Smith, E. E. Mackintosh, M. K. Hoffman, and P. Monti. 1979. Effects of Camping Recreation on Soil, Jack Pine (*Pinus banksiana*), and Understory Vegetation in a Northwestern Ontario Park. *Forest Science* 25:233–249.

Ketchledge, E. H., and R. E. Leonard. 1970. The Impact of Man on the Adirondack High Country. *The Conservationist* 25(2):14–18.

Legg, M. H., and G. Schneider. 1977. Soil Deterioration on Campsites: Northern Forest Types. *Soil Science Society American Journal* 41:437–441.

Liddle, M. J. 1975. A Selective Review of the Ecological Effects of Human Trampling on Natural Ecosystems. *Biological Conservation* 7:17–34.

Liddle, M. J., and P. Greig-Smith. 1975. A Survey of Tracks and Paths in a Sand Dune Ecosystem. I. Soils. II. Vegetation. *Journal of Applied Ecology* 12:893–930.

Lutz, H. J. 1945. Soil Conditions of Picnic Grounds in Public Forest Parks. *Journal of Forestry* 43:121–127.

Manning, R. E. 1979. Impacts of Recreation on Riparian Soils and Vegetation. *Water Resources Bulletin* 15(1):30–43.

Marion, J. L., and L. C. Merriam. 1985. Recreational Impacts on Well-established Campsites in the Boundary Water Canoe Area Wilderness. University of Minnesota Agricultural Experiment Station Bulletin, AD-SB-2502, St. Paul, MN. 16 pp.

Monti, P., and E. E. Mackintosh. 1979. Effects of Camping on Surface Soil Properties in the Boreal Forest Region of Northwestern Ontario, Canada. *Soil Science Society of American Journal* 43:1024–1029.

Settergren, C. D., and D. M. Cole. 1970. Recreation Effects on Soil and Vegetation in the Missouri Ozarks. *Journal of Forestry* 68:231–233.

Speight, M. C. D. 1973. Outdoor Recreation and Its Ecological Effects: A Bibliography and Review. Discussion Paper in Conservation 4, University College, London. 35 pp.

Spurr, S. H., and B. V. Barnes. 1980. *Forest Ecology.* 3rd ed. New York: Wiley, 687 pp.

Tarrant, R. E. 1956. Effects of Slash Burning on Some Soils of the Douglas-Fir Region. *Soil Science Society American Proceedings* 20:408–411.

Wanek, W. J. 1971. Snowmobile Impacts on Vegetation, Temperatures, and Soil Microbes. In M. Chubb, ed. Proceedings of the 1971 Snowmobile and Off the Road Vehicle Research Symposium. Department of Park and Recreation Resources, Technical Report No. 8, Michigan State University, East Lansing. pp. 116–129.

Wanek, W. J. 1974. A Continuing Study of the Ecological Impact of Snowmobiling in Northern Minnesota. Final Research Report for 1973–1974, Center for Environmental Studies, Bemidji State College, Bemidji, MN. 54 pp.

Weaver, T., and D. Dale. 1978. Trampling Effects of Hikers, Motorcycles, and Horses in Meadows and Forests. *Journal of Applied Ecology* 15:451–457.

Weetman, G. F., and B. Webber. 1972. The Influence of Wood Harvesting on the Nutrient Status of Two Spruce Stands. *Canadian Journal of Forest Research* 2:351–369.

Wilde, S. A. 1958. *Forest Soils: Their Properties and Relation to Silviculture.* New York: Ronald Press, 537 pp.

Wilshire, H. G., J. K. Nakata, S. Shipley, and K. Prestegaard. 1978. Impacts of Vehicles on Natural Terrain at Steven Sites in the San Francisco Bay Area. *Environmental Geology* 2:295–319.

Zisa, R. P., H. G. Halverson, and B. B. Stout. 1980. Establishment and Early Growth of Conifers on Compact Soils in Urban Areas. USDA Forest Service Research Paper NE-451. 8 pp.

3 Vegetation

Along with water, vegetation is probably the most important resource component affecting visitor selection of recreation sites. Vegetation adds to site desirability by providing shade, screening for campsite privacy, and attractiveness or botanical interest. At the same time, vegetation can be susceptible to damage, particularly from recreational trampling. Consequently, it is often highly altered on recreation sites. Of all changes that occur as a result of recreation, impacts on vegetation are the most readily evident to users (Fig. 1).

VEGETATION IMPACT PARAMETERS

In contrast to soils, researchers have studied only a few vegetational parameters in their attempt to describe the impacts of recreational use. Moreover, understanding these parameters requires less specialized knowledge about vegetation ecology than is required for soil ecology. Consequently, we will not need to devote as much space to describing vegetational parameters as we did with soils.

Amount of Vegetation

The most common impact parameter studied is vegetation cover, usually defined as the percentage of the ground area covered by the vertical projection of aboveground plant parts. Usually the researcher will lay

Figure 1. Impacts to vegetation in zones above treeline are often severe, long lasting, and readily visible to users for some distance. (*Photo:* W. E. Hammitt.)

down some sample unit, such as a quadrat 1 meter on each side and estimate the percent of the quadrat area covered by vegetation. For example, Cole (1982) estimated vegetation cover on campsites, using the mean cover of vegetation in fifteen 1 m^2 quadrats systematically dispersed around each site. Other standard techniques for measuring or estimating cover include line intercepts and point intercepts (Mueller-Dombois and Ellenberg 1974).

Regardless of the technique, the intent is to provide a measure of the amount of vegetation present in the area under study. By comparing such a measure on a recreation site before and after recreational use, the effects of recreation on vegetation can be identified. Where recreational use has already occurred, vegetation impacts can also be identified by comparing vegetation cover on recreation sites with cover on adjacent undisturbed sites. The assumption, in this case, is that the undisturbed site (the control) is similar to what the recreation site was like before it was used. Thus, this means of evaluating impact will only be accurate if researchers carefully select controls that are environmentally similar to recreation sites. This requires considerable experience.

Although uncommon in the impact literature, other measures of amount of vegetation that have been used are density and biomass. Density is simply a count of the number of individual plants in some unit area (e.g., 10 trees/100 m^2). Density can be useful for large, discrete individuals such as trees; it is less useful when working with grasses and plants that grow in clumps where it is difficult to distinguish between individuals. Thus, it has become standard to measure density of trees and sometimes shrubs and cover of the ground level of vegetation. Biomass is a measure of the weight of vegetation in a unit area. It is determined by clipping the vegetation, drying it to remove water, and then weighing it. While this provides a more objective measure of amount of vegetation than cover does, this method is destructive and quite time-consuming. Therefore, it is seldom used.

Vegetation Composition

In addition to recording amount of all vegetation, it is common also to record cover for individual species. This information is used to characterize species composition, particularly of the ground level vegetation. The term *species composition* is used to refer to the mix of species that occupies any site. As with total vegetation, recreational impacts on the cover of individual species can be identified. Some researchers have grouped species into classes of particular interest. This allows them to study the effect of recreation on such classes of plants as exotic species and species exhibiting different growth forms. Exotic species are those that are not native to any given area. Such species commonly increase in importance on recreation areas, thriving on disturbed areas where native species have difficulty growing. Growth forms are classes of species grouped on the basis of similarities in their structure, form, and function. Studying how different growth forms respond to recreation use has been helpful in understanding how and why different plants vary in their susceptibility to impact.

Tree Condition

A third common parameter of interest is tree condition. In most cases, researchers have documented the percent, number, or density of trees that have been inflicted with certain types of damage such as root exposure or severe scarring. A few studies have also tried to relate tree growth to recreational use to determine what effect recreation has on growth.

IMPACTS ON VEGETATION

Most vegetation types have a vertical structure that consists of a number of horizontal strata. Although not common to all vegetation types, three important and distinct strata are the ground cover layer, shrubs and saplings, and mature trees. In the following discussion we will explore recreational impacts on each of these three layers.

Ground Cover

Ground cover vegetation is profoundly impacted by visitor use, particularly as a result of trampling. Trampling affects ground cover vegetation both directly and indirectly. Ground cover is directly affected where trampling breaks, bruises, and crushes plants. It is indirectly affected where trampling causes soil compaction and other soil changes which, in turn, lead to changes in vegetation.

The direct effects of trampling are usually detrimental to plants. Although growth of a few species is stimulated by low levels of trampling, most species exhibit reduced abundance, height, vigor, and reproductive capacity on recreation sites. Where trampling is heavy and/or vegetation is fragile, plants are killed outright. Death occurs when plants are ripped out of the ground, have their regenerative tissues destroyed, or, in the case of annuals (plants that only live for one season), lose their ability to reproduce. Less severe trampling damage causes breakage without death; plant stems are knocked back and leaves are torn off. This reduces the area available for photosynthesis. Loss of photosynthesis, then, leads to reductions in plant vigor and can affect the ability to reproduce. For perennials (plants that live a number of years), repeated loss of photosynthetic area can ultimately cause death of the plant.

Problems resulting from direct impact to aerial plant parts are compounded by the problems of growing and reproducing in compacted soils. Compaction increases the mechanical resistance of the soil to root penetration. As was illustrated in Fig. 8 in Chapter 2, plants growing in soils with high bulk densities have fewer roots that only extend a short distance away from the plant. An important function of these roots is to grow into areas where water and nutrients can be extracted. When water and nutrients are depleted close to the plant, roots must be able to extend further away from the plant. Compaction makes this more difficult; as a result, plants cannot extract sufficient quantities of water and nutrients from the soil. This problem is compounded by two other consequences of compaction. Loss of macropores in the soil reduces soil aeration because most oxygen resides in the larger pores in the soil. Oxygen shortages also inhibit root growth, which in turn makes extraction of water and nutrients more difficult. Compaction also reduces water infiltration rates. With less water entering the soil, plant roots will more rapidly exhaust soil moisture adjacent to the plant. This accentuates the need for a large and healthy root system under conditions in which the size and health of root systems are deteriorating. Such indirect effects should cause more serious problems in environments where moisture and/or nutrients are scarce.

Compaction also inhibits the germination, emergence, and establishment of new plants. Seeds lying on a compacted surface crust are prone to dessication and less likely to receive proper incubation and moisture. Studies have shown that germination success is usually greatest on heterogeneous surfaces with a diversity of microsites (Harper, Williams, and Sagar 1965); a smooth, compacted surface does not provide such a diversity of microsites so germination is reduced. Should germination occur, a strong surface crust will make it difficult for the radicle (the incipient primary root) to penetrate the soil to provide stability, water, and nutrition. Even if the seedling successfully germinates and emerges from the soil, a number of indirect impacts make premature death likely.

The microclimate of trampled sites is more severe than in untrampled areas. Both vegetation and organic matter serve to moderate temperatures, keeping them from getting too high during the day or too low at night. Trampling, by removing vegetation and organic matter, indirectly subjects seedlings to a greater likelihood of both heat injury and freezing. Another common cause of death is frost heaving, a process in which freezing and thawing of the soil physically lift seedlings out of the soil. Although frost heaving does occur on undisturbed sites, it is most common in bare mineral soil, particularly soils that have been compacted.

The ultimate result of most of these effects of trampling is a reduction in amount of vegetation, usually expressed as a loss of vegetation cover. This type of impact is particularly pronounced on campsites. Even in wilderness areas campsites commonly lose most of their vegetation cover. For example, cover loss on campsites in the Eagle Cap Wilderness, Oregon, averaged 87 percent (Cole 1982); the average loss on sites in the Boundary Waters Canoe Area Wilderness, Minnesota, was 85 percent (Frissell and Duncan 1965). Cover loss on developed campsites is sometimes less pronounced because of more active maintenance programs and more durable vegetation. On developed campsites in Rhode Island, for example, Brown, Kalisz, and Wright (1977) found cover loss to be only about 50 percent. Loss of vegetation cover usually exposes underlying organic matter unless this layer has also been worn away and mineral soil or rock is exposed.

Ground cover vegetation can also be destroyed when it is disturbed by off-road vehicles. In the Algodones Dunes area of southern California, areas used by dune buggy and other off-road vehicle enthusiasts had only about 5 percent as many herbaceous plants as undisturbed areas (Luckenbach and Bury 1983).

Many studies have found that the loss of vegetation cover on lightly used sites is nearly as substantial as the loss on heavily used sites. This has been illustrated most frequently on wilderness campsites. For example, in studies in three western wilderness areas, cover loss on sites used only a few nights per year averaged between 55 and 71 percent (Fig. 2).

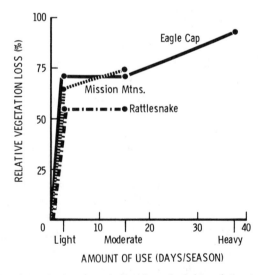

Figure 2. Median values of relative vegetation loss plotted in relation to amount of use in the Eagle Cap, Mission Mountain, and Rattlesnake Wilderness. For the Eagle Cap campsites, the numerical use frequencies are estimates. (*Source:* D. N. Cole.)

The curve that describes the relationship between vegetation loss and amount of use is not a straight line; it is curvilinear or hyperbolic, to be more precise. Some trampling studies (e.g., Cole 1985) have found a linear relationship between vegetation cover and the logarithm of amount of use. Cover loss increases rapidly with initial increases in use. Beyond some use threshold the rate of loss decreases as loss approaches 100 percent.

The finding that vegetation loss is so severe even on lightly used sites illustrates the susceptibility of ground cover to impact. Although susceptibility varies greatly between vegetation types, a topic that will be discussed in more detail in Chapter 7, the curvilinear relationship between amount of use and vegetation cover appears to always apply. This has important implications for management, implications that will be discussed more fully in Chapters 8 and 11.

Loss of vegetation usually occurs very rapidly once use of campsites begins. LaPage (1967) followed changes on developed campsites in old field grasslands in Pennsylvania over the course of the first three years they were used. After the first year of use, an average of 45 percent cover was lost on the campsites (Fig. 3). Plant cover increased over the

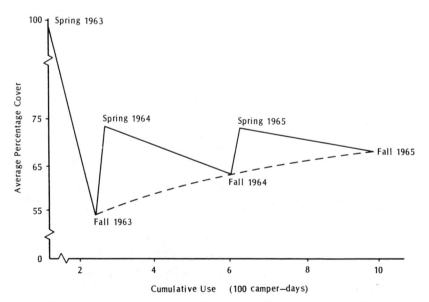

Figure 3. Changes in vegetation cover following the initial development and use of a car campground in Pennsylvania. (*Source:* LaPage 1967.)

winter when no recreational use occurred and then declined over the next use season. However, total cover at the end of the second and third use seasons was actually greater than it had been after the first season of use.

What was happening on these campsites was that the original native occupants of the sites were being replaced by new species that were more resistant to trampling. While vegetation cover increased from the end of the use season in 1963 to the end of the use season in 1965, the total number of species declined from 29 in 1963 to 23 in 1964 and 17 in 1965. This compares with 37 species found on the sites before use began. Most species were being eliminated by camping, but a few species were increasing in importance. As camping disturbance increased and competition with native species decreased, these trampling-resistant species were able to spread and increase total vegetation cover on the sites. A number of new species actually invaded the site. Four species that were not present before camping began appeared and spread on the sites in subsequent years. However, even with this increase cover remained reduced by about one-third.

Beyond loss of cover, this study illustrates several other common vegetation impacts. One is the decline in number of species—a characteristic of plant communities known as species richness. Species richness is one of the components, along with the relative abundance of individual species, of the concept of species diversity. A reduction in species richness almost always occurs where recreational use levels are high. At high use levels only trampling-resistant species can survive if any species can. The number of trampling-resistant species is always less than the number of original occupants of the site. However, the highest species richness usually occurs in areas that receive low to moderate levels of use. In such places the original occupants will be reduced in abundance but not eliminated. Less competition with these natives encourages the invasion and spread of trampling-resistant species. Richness is high because both the original occupants and the trampling-resistant invaders occupy the site simultaneously.

Another type of impact reflects the fact that species differ greatly in their resistance to impact. As seen in the Pennsylvania campsite example, some of the original species that occupied the campsites were eliminated much more rapidly than others; indeed, some species actually increased in cover, and other species invaded the site. The most common species before use, cinquefoil, was eliminated entirely after three seasons of use while bluegrass, originally found in only a few places, became the most common species on the campsite. Over time such changes led to development of a plant community with a different species composition than was originally there.

Change in species composition is usually evaluated by reporting differences in the cover of all individual species, either over time or between recreation sites and undisturbed controls. Such lengthy lists of species make it difficult to compare the severity of shifts in species composition in different places. To provide an index of change in species composition, Cole (1978) proposed an index that measured the dissimilarity in composition between two sites. This index, the floristic dissimilarity index, can vary between 0 and 100 percent. A value of 0 means that both sites are identical in terms of both the species there and their relative abundance. Realistically, this value is not possible in nature; even under undisturbed conditions there is considerable variation in species composition, often on the order of 25 percent or so. A value of 100 percent means that the two sites have no species in common.

This index has been used to quantify change in species composition on campsites in a number of recreation areas. On campsites in the Boundary Waters Canoe Area, the original forest-floor occupants tend to be fragile, and there are a number of trampling-resistant species to invade campsites. Consequently, compositional shifts are pronounced, and the floristic dissimilarity index averaged 88 percent (Marion 1984). On campsites high in the mountains of the Rattlesnake Wilderness, Montana, most of the native dominants are resistant to trampling, and few invader species can grow successfully at such high elevations. The floristic dissimilarity there averaged only 27 percent, little more than one would expect when comparing undisturbed plant communities (Cole and Fichtler 1983).

Whether any individual species will be resistant to trampling or not is largely dependent on its structure or form and characteristics of its life cycle. Plant characteristics that tend to make a plant resistant to trampling (as modified from Speight 1973) include:

1. A low-growing rather than erect stature and growth form

2. A tufted growth form

3. Arming with thorns or prickles

4. Leaves in a basal cluster (rosette)

5. Stems that are flexible rather than brittle or rigid

6. Small, thick leaves

7. Flexible leaves that can fold under pressure

8. The ability to initiate growth from tissues at the base of plant parts (e.g., intercalary meristems at the base of grass leaves) in addition to growth from tissues at the tip of parts (apical meristems)

9. The ability for perennials (plants that live for a number of years) to initiate seasonal regrowth from buds concealed below the soil surface where they are not subject to the direct effects of trampling

10. The ability to reproduce vegetatively from suckers, stolons, rhizomes, or corms as well as sexually through seeding

11. A rapid rate of growth

12. The ability to reproduce when trampling pressure is low

While no species will possess all of these characteristics, many highly resistant species will possess a number of them. For example, bluegrass, the species that increased so dramatically on the Pennsylvania campsites, is capable of growing low to the ground (it is capable of erect growth when undisturbed and prostrate growth when disturbed) and has flexible folded leaves, intercalary meristems, buds protected below the ground surface, and the ability to reproduce from rhizomes and initiate rapid growth when injured. For these reasons it is a common lawn grass as well as a common invader of recreation sites.

Many of the most resistant species are exotics, many of which are native to Eurasia. At high elevations in the mountains, exotic species are uncommon. At lower elevations, however, exotics often dominate the vegetation along trails and on campsites. In the Boundary Waters Canoe Area Wilderness, for example, Marion (1984) found at least one exotic species on 62 percent of the campsites he surveyed. One campsite had 12 different exotic species. Three exotic species were among the 10 species found on the largest number of campsites. On campsites in the Bob Marshall Wilderness, Montana, three of the four most common species on campsites were exotics (Cole 1983).

Generally, researchers have found that graminoids (grasses and grasslike plants such as sedges and rushes) possess more adaptations that allow them to resist impact than other growth forms. Forbs, herbaceous plants other than graminoids, vary greatly in their resistance. Low-growing, tufted forbs with a basal rosette of small, tough leaves are common survivors on recreation sites. Two common examples, both exotic in the United States, are white clover and common plantain. Forbs that grow in the shade of deep forests are at the other extreme. In trying to gather in as much light as they can, they tend to be tall with large, thin leaves. Leaves generally lack tough outer layers so that absorption of light is maximized. They invest more of their energy in producing photosynthetic tissue than in producing tough support systems such as stout stems and branches. These adaptations make them highly susceptible to trampling damage. Low-growing shrubs are intermediate in their resistance to damage. They can usually survive low levels of trampling because of a tendency to have small, tough leaves and woody stems. Their stems are often brittle, however, and so they are usually eliminated at moderate use levels. The loss of shrubs on recreation sites is accentuated by slow rates of regrowth once stems are broken.

Tree seedlings are particularly sensitive and readily killed when trampled. Even in wilderness areas tree seedlings are almost completely eliminated on all but the most lightly used campsites. In the Eagle Cap Wilderness the average number of tree seedlings on a campsite of average size (200 m^2) was only six. The number on a comparably sized, undisturbed site was over 50. This represents an average loss of over 90 percent of all seedlings. Even on the most lightly used sites, those used no more than about five nights per year, about three-fourths of all seedlings had been eliminated (Cole 1982). Similar near-complete losses of tree reproduction have been reported wherever campsite impacts have been studied. They are likely to be even more pronounced on more heavily used, developed sites. For example, in a survey of 137 developed Forest Service camping and picnic sites in California, Magill and Nord (1963) found no seedlings at all on more than one-half of the sites. They also state that, where present, the continued survival of tree seedlings is doubtful.

Loss of ground cover vegetation occurs in campsites wherever trampling occurs. Along trails, ground cover is eliminated on the tread, either during construction or shortly after the start of use. Adjacent to the tread is a trailside zone that receives some trampling pressure and is also affected by habitat changes such as increased light levels caused by brush and tree removal during trail construction. This zone certainly experiences a change in species composition. Usually, vegetation cover will also be reduced, but sometimes the habitat changes will result in an increase in cover there. Cole (1978) studied loss of cover and change in species composition in this trailside zone in eight different vegetation types in the Eagle Cap Wilderness. Cover loss adjacent to trails was as high as 73 percent in some of the forested types and as low as 12 percent in subalpine meadows. Floristic dissimilarity varied from 37 to 82 percent; the most pronounced shifts occurred in the forested vegetation types.

Where trampling pressure is low, the height of the vegetation can be reduced without incurring a loss of vegetation cover. Vegetation with reduced stature is commonly found at the periphery of campsites and along the edge of trails. This vegetation forms a pronounced zone intermediate between the barren center of the campsite or trail and the undisturbed vegetation beyond. Lightly used trails, particularly those that were user-created, are also characterized by a short but complete vegetation cover. Other changes in plant morphology and physiology where plants are disturbed but not destroyed include a reduction in leaf area, carbohydrate reserves in roots, flower density, and number of seeds per flower (Liddle 1975; Hartley 1976). Liddle (1975) found that 400 passes by a light vehicle reduced the leaflet area of a relatively resistant clover species by 57 percent. When "trampled" by a tractor six times, the average number of flower heads on a species in the pea family decreased from 29 to one; no seed pods were found on trampled plants. With light foot traffic the number of branches can sometimes increase as a response to frequent damage of terminal buds.

An additional source of impact on ground vegetation, in many Western areas particularly, is grazing and trampling by stock. The trampling effects of stock are generally similar to those caused by humans, except that the potential for causing impact is much more pronounced. Horses weigh much more than humans, and their weight is concentrated on a small bearing surface. This greatly increases the pressure stock exert on both vegetation and soil. Moreover, shod hooves can cause substantial gouging and ripping of the ground. Grazing effects also lead to cover losses and changes in species composition. Changes in composition are accentuated by the fact that stock prefer to eat certain species if they are available. These preferred species, because they are defoliated more frequently, will often decrease and be eliminated more rapidly than other species.

Few data on stock impacts on meadows exist. Cole (1981) compared the cover and composition of some lightly and heavily grazed mid-elevation meadows in the Eagle Cap Wilderness. The more heavily used meadows had about 30 percent less cover than the lightly used meadow. Graminoids, which are generally more palatable than forbs, comprised only about 35 percent of the cover on the heavily used sites, compared with 80 percent on lightly used sites. The heavily grazed meadows also had more exotic species and more annuals.

Shrubs and Saplings

Although low-lying shrubs suffer from trampling as part of the ground cover vegetation, larger shrubs and saplings are usually large enough to avoid most of the direct effects of trampling. Most impact to this vegetation layer is the result of either damage caused by off-road vehicles or by the conscious removal of shrub and tree stems.

Both terrestrial off-road vehicles and snowmobiles can affect shrubs and saplings. Shrub cover was reduced 90 percent in an off-road vehicle area in southern California. Cacti and thorny plants that are usually spared from trampling damage can be run over and killed by vehicles.

Snowmobiles can be particularly damaging to shrubs and saplings. Ground cover plants are likely to be protected by the snow cover, although this is not the case if snow cover is shallow. Mature trees are likely to only incur trunk scars. Shrubs and small saplings, however, are often stiff and brittle during the winter and are readily snapped off when run over by snowmobiles. In some cases, damage to shrub stems causes them to put out sucker shoots. Wanek (1974) found that "most shrubs increase (number of stems and cover) where snowmobiles travel, primarily because of vegetative propagation." He points out that this may not continue indefinitely, because of disease or eventual failure to maintain the large root system of individual plants.

Removal of shrub and tree stems occurs along trails to make it easier for hikers and stock to use the trail. For example, standards on Forest Service trails in wilderness specify removing brush along a corridor 8 ft wide and 10 ft high. In more developed settings, removal of shrubs and saplings is even more pronounced. In terms of biomass removed, trail construction and maintenance are the activities that cause the most impact to shrubs and saplings in wildland recreation areas. The major exception would be in roaded areas where road construction and maintenance remove even more vegetation.

Although not as much biomass is involved, concern with removal of shrubs and saplings usually centers on campsites. Here, loss of stems occurs as a result of the development and expansion of sites as well as the felling of stems for tent poles and firewood. In the intersite zones of a developed campground in Michigan (intersite zones are the lightly used portions of the campground between high impact centers of activity—refer to Chapter 6), McEwen and Tocher (1976) found only 76 saplings per acre compared with 338 per acre in adjacent unused portions. Around long-established shelters along the Appalachian Trail in Great Smoky Mountains National Park, saplings less than 3 in. in diameter simply cannot be found within 200 ft of shelters; they have all been cut down and used for firewood. On campsites in Eagle Cap Wilderness, one-third of the trees had been felled; most of these felled trees were sapling size (Cole 1982).

Perhaps the most serious consequence of this type of impact is its long-term effect on maintenance of forested campsites. In short, removal of saplings from the immediate vicinity of campsites is cutting off the source of new trees to replace the current overstory when it eventually succumbs to old age. Tree reproduction is almost nil as a result of trampling. Removal of the few stems that do make it into the sapling size class forecasts the eventual conversion of forested sites into open vegetation types. Since campers have been shown to prefer the shading and privacy provided by both shrubs and trees (Cordell and James 1972), this is a highly undesirable change.

Mature Trees

The major impacts to mature trees on recreation sites result from mechanical damage. Much is caused consciously, if thoughtlessly, by visitors through a diverse set of acts that include removing limbs, driving nails into trunks, hacking trees with axes, peeling bark to use as kindling, and felling trees for tent poles or firewood. Other impacts are caused unconsciously; for example, trees are scarred by lanterns, and roots are exposed when stock are tied to trees. Finally, considerable impact to trees is caused by management. Examples include clearing trees along trails and in campsites and removing hazard trees in danger of falling on people.

In an intensive survey of tree damage on campsites in the Eagle Cap Wilderness, Cole (1982) found that over 90 percent of the mature trees had been scarred, felled, or had cut or broken branches (Fig. 4). Damage

Figure 4. Tree damage on a campsite in the Eagle Cap Wilderness, Oregon. (*Photo:* D. N. Cole.)

to many of the trees was relatively minor—lower branches had been broken or nails had been driven into trunks. Twenty-seven percent of these trees, however, bore trunk scars from chopping. Of these scars 22 percent were larger than 1 ft^2, and 67 percent were located below breast height, conditions under which the probability of decay is particularly high for these spruce and fir species. Another 33 percent of the trees on the campsites had been cut down.

Despite this level of damage to overstory trees, there was little evidence of recreation-related tree mortality or even loss of vigor, except where trees had been felled outright. The fact that more than six decades of recreational use have had little noticeable effect suggests that premature mortality of the overstory may not be a serious problem. Most other studies have also found little evidence of recreation-caused tree mortality. Recreation-caused loss of vigor and death occur most commonly where soils are thin and/or droughty or where trees are thin-barked and particularly susceptible to decay. Mortality of trembling aspen, a widespread thin-barked tree, was studied on 17 developed campgrounds in the Rocky Mountains. They were dying at a rate of about 4 percent per year, mostly as a result of canker diseases following mechanical injuries caused by campers (Hinds 1976).

Another place where tree mortality has been a serious problem is the Boundary Waters Canoe Area Wilderness. Merriam and Peterson have followed change over time on a handful of campsites established by the Forest Service in 1967. Just five years after use began, the average percent of original trees that had died was 15 percent; after 14 years 40 percent of the trees had died (Merriam and Peterson 1983). Aspen and birch dominate a number of these sites; their thin bark and the tendency for campers to peel off bark for kindling make them particularly susceptible to damage. Thin soils and pronounced erosion are also characteristic of these canoe-camping sites. It is not uncommon for almost all of the soil to be removed from surface tree roots. Once this occurs, death will follow before long.

Exposure of trees roots is a common occurrence on trails, river and lake banks, and campsites. Of 19 campsites with trees in Cole's Eagle Cap survey, 17 had trees with exposed roots. On a typical campsite about one-third of the trees had exposed roots. In the Boundary Waters, 84 percent of the trees on campsites surveyed by Marion (1984) had exposed roots. Once exposed, roots can suffer mechanical damage. Root exposure also makes trees more prone to wind throw.

In areas that receive large amounts of overnight stock use, tree damage can be especially pronounced. Most of this additional damage reflects the common practice of tying stock to trees. When tied in this way, most animals will paw up the ground, causing erosion and exposure of tree roots. Rope burns on the tree trunks leave scars and on small trees can girdle and kill the tree. Parties that travel with stock are also more likely to carry heavy canvas tents that require felled trees for tent poles. They are also more likely to carry axes and saws capable of felling trees for firewood. Not every stock party causes these avoidable types of impact, but enough do for tree damage in horse camps to be particularly pronounced.

To illustrate this difference, Cole (1983) compared the number of damaged trees on backpacker, horse, and outfitter campsites in the Bob Marshall Wilderness, Montana (Table 1). Backpacker sites were only used by backpackers; horse sites were used primarily by private horse parties, usually for only a few nights at a time; outfitter camps were sites occupied by outfitted parties for long periods of time, particularly during the fall hunting season. Seedling loss is the same—100 percent—on

TABLE 1. Tree Damage on Campsites Used Primarily by Backpackers, Private Horse Parties, or Outfitted Parties.[a]

Type of Use	Seedling Loss		Damaged Trees		Felled Trees		Trees with Exposed Roots	
	Median	Range	Median	Range	Median	Range	Median	Range
	Percent		Number of trees in disturbed area					
Backpacker	100	100 a	5	3–29 a	0	0–8 a	1	0–4 a
Horse	100	92–100 a	56	21–180 b	8	0–33 b	25	10–38 b
Outfitter	100	100 a	100	23–500 b	15	3–250 b	37	13–100 b

[a] Any two sets of median and range values followed by the same letter are not significantly different at the 95 percent confidence level, using the randomization test for two independent samples. Seedling loss is relative change.

all three classes of site; this damage is the inevitable result of trampling and does not vary with type of use. In contrast, there are large differences in damage to mature trees between the three types of sites. This damage is avoidable and related to the type of use occurring on the site.

Likewise, mechanical damage on developed sites can be much more common and serious than that on backcountry sites. Common types of damage on such sites include lantern scars and nails driven into trees to hang objects. In most older national forest and national park campgrounds, mature trees close to tables have numerous scars from gas lanterns. These scars, caused by heating, can weaken trees, particularly if the trees are thin-barked. Once weakening occurs, trees are more prone to breakage and, as hazard trees, must be removed by management. In recent years metal lantern holders have been erected on many sites to avoid this problem. The fact that people tend to stay much longer at developed sites accessible by road and can carry much more equipment provides more opportunity for damage; mature trees bear much of the brunt of this damage.

SUMMARY

1. Trampling affects vegetation both directly and indirectly. These interrelationships are diagrammatically presented in Fig. 5. Breakage and bruising reduce plant vigor and reproductive capacity; severe trampling kills plants directly. Plant vigor and reproductive capacity are also reduced as a result of the soil changes described in Chapter 2. Shrubs and

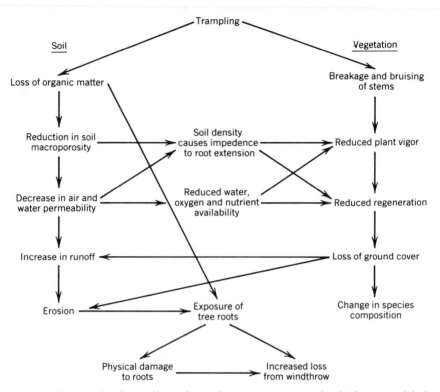

Figure 5. Direct and indirect effects of trampling on vegetation and soil. (*Source:* modified from "Impacts of Recreation on Riparian Soils and Vegetation," by R. E. Manning in *Water Resources Bulletin* 15(1):30–43. Reprinted with permission of the American Water Resources Association.)

saplings are removed to expand the campsite, clear the trail, or collect firewood. Mature trees are mechanically damaged by a variety of actions, conscious and unconscious, taken by both visitors and managers.

2. Of these impacts, the most serious is probably lack of tree regeneration. Even in the many situations where premature mortality is not a problem, the existing overstory will eventually die. On most campsites, however, there is no regeneration to replace these trees when they die. Most seedlings are killed by being trampled, and the ones that do survive are cut down in the sapling stage for firewood or tent poles. Finding a way to allow trees to grow into the larger sized classes is one of the major challenges to management of campsites.

3. Vegetation impacts occur rapidly during the initial development and use of recreation sites. Most impacts also reach near-maximum levels of impact even on relatively lightly used sites. This reflects the ground cover vegetation's low level of resistance to trampling damage. Damage to mature trees also occurs rapidly with only light use. However, amount of tree damage is strongly influenced by the type of use that occurs on the site. Stock use, for example, tends to cause more damage than use by parties without stock.

4. Susceptibility to damage also varies greatly between different environments. In this chapter we discussed vegetative characteristics that make a plant resistant to trampling impact. We also discussed how damage to mature trees is more pronounced for thin-barked trees and, where soils are thin, prone to erosion and/or drought. A more complete discussion of environmental durability will be provided in Chapter 7.

REFERENCES

Brown, Jr., J. H., S. P. Kalisz, and W. R. Wright. 1977. Effects of Recreational Use on Forested Sites. *Environmental Geology* 1:425–431.

Cole, D. N. 1978. Estimating the Susceptibility of Wildland Vegetation to Trailside Alteration. *Journal of Applied Ecology* 15:281–286.

Cole, D. N. 1981. Vegetational Changes Associated with Recreational Use and Fire Suppression in the Eagle Cap Wilderness, Oregon: Some Management Implications. *Biological Conservation* 20:247–270.

Cole, D. N. 1982. Wilderness Campsite Impacts: Effect of Amount of Use. USDA Forest Service Research Paper INT-288.

Cole, D. N. 1983. Campsite Conditions in the Bob Marshall Wilderness, Montana. USDA Forest Service Research Paper INT-312.

Cole, D. N. 1985. Recreational Trampling Effects on Six Habitat Types in Western Montana. USDA Forest Service Research Paper INT-350. 43 pp.

Cole, D. N., and R. K. Fichtler. 1983. Campsite Impact in Three Western Wilderness Areas. *Environmental Management* 7:275–286.

Cordell, H. K., and G. A. James. 1972. Visitor's Preferences for Certain Physical Characteristics of Developed Campsites. USDA Forest Service Research Paper SE-100.

Frissell, Jr., S. S., and D. P. Duncan. 1965. Campsite Preference and Deterioration in the Quetico-Superior Canoe Country. *Journal of Forestry* 65:256–260.

Harper, J. L., J. T. Williams, and G. R. Sagar. 1965. The Behavior of Seeds in Soil. I. The Heterogeneity of Soil Surfaces and Its Role in Determining the Establishment of Plants from Seed. *Journal of Ecology* 53:273–286.

Hartley, E. A. 1976. Man's Effects on the Stability of Alpine and Subalpine Vegetation in Glacier National Park, Montana. Ph.D. dissertation, Duke University, Durham, NC.

Hinds, T. E. 1976. Aspen Mortality in Rocky Mountain Campgrounds. USDA Forest Service Research Paper RM-164.

LaPage, W. F. 1967. Some Observations on Campground Trampling and Groundcover Response. USDA Forest Service Research Paper NE-68.

Liddle, M. J. 1975. A Selective Review of the Ecological Effects of Human Trampling on Natural Ecosystems. *Biological Conservation* 7:17–36.

Luckenbach, R. A., and R. B. Bury. 1983. Effects of Off-road Vehicles on the Biota of the Algodones Dunes, Imperial County, California. *Journal of Applied Ecology* 20:265–286.

McEwen, D., and S. R. Tocher. 1976. Zone Management: Key to Controlling Recreational Impact in Developed Campsites. *Journal of Forestry* 74:90–93.

Magill, A. W., and E. C. Nord. 1963. An Evaluation of Campground Conditions and Needs for Research. USDA Forest Service Research Note PSW-4.

Manning, R. E. 1979. Impacts of Recreation on Riparian Soils and Vegetation. *Water Resources Bulletin* 15:30–43.

Marion, J. L. 1984. Ecological Changes Resulting from Recreational Use: A Study of Backcountry Campsites in the Boundary Waters Canoe Area, Minnesota. Ph.D. dissertation, University of Minnesota, St. Paul.

Merriam, L. C., and R. F. Peterson. 1983. Impact of 15 Years of Use on Some Campsites in the Boundary Waters Canoe Area. Minnesota Forest Research Note 282, University of Minnesota, St. Paul.

Mueller—Dombois, D., and H. Ellenberg. 1974. *Aims and Methods of Vegetation Ecology*. New York: Wiley.

Speight, M. C. D. 1973. Outdoor Recreation and Its Ecological Effects: A Bibliography and Review. Discussion Paper in Conservation 4, University College, London. 35 pp.

Wanek, W. J. 1974. A Continuing Study of the Ecological Impact of Snowmobiling in Northern Minnesota. Final Research Report for 1973–1974. Center for Environmental Studies, Bemidji State College, Bemidji, MN. 54 pp.

4 Wildlife

The effects of wildland recreation on wildlife have received little attention, except those of hunting and fishing. This is because wildlife species are not stationary, as are plants, and the effects of impacts are not immediately obvious or easily measured. Nevertheless, numerous impacts to wildlife as a result of recreation have been documented, and in a few cases fairly well researched (Ream 1980). These studies show that human disturbances result in changes in wildlife physiology, behavior, reproduction, population levels, and species composition and diversity. The major source of the impact problem is the recreationist who innocently produces stressful situations for wildlife, primarily through unintentional harassment of wild animals. However, some wildlife are attracted to recreationists and alter their behavior in response to the presence of humans. Panhandler bears and campgrounds chipmunks that seek out human foods are typical examples.

While specific studies of impacts of recreation on wildlife are limited, this chapter reviews the major types of ecological disturbances caused by recreationists-wildlife interactions and the major impacts on some species of animals where management problems are most evident.

HUMAN-WILDLIFE INTERACTIONS

The response of wildlife to recreational disturbance is complex, being neither uniform nor consistent. Different species of wildlife have different tolerances for interactions with humans. While some species may be completely displaced from an area of concentrated recreational use, other species have actually increased in abundance. In general, species less tolerant of recreational disturbance will be replaced by those better adapted to the new environmental conditions (Kuss, Graefe, and Vaske 1984).

Even within a species, tolerance levels for interactions will vary by time of year, breeding season, animal age, habitat type, and individual animal experience with recreationists. Recreationists may produce critical situations at certain times and places and have no effect on the same species under other conditions. Seasonal and spatial effects appear to be strongly tied to habitat requirements and utilization. For example, if a species is already under physiological stress from limited food and other environmental factors, interactions with humans may be especially serious.

The relationship between amount of recreational use and wildlife impacts is not well understood. Very few studies have systematically examined the effects of varying numbers of visitors on wildlife. Even fewer wildlife studies have determined an accurate population count of organisms prior to the introduction of recreation. Thus, it has been difficult to document a uniform relationship between amount of recreational use and wildlife impacts. In fact, there may be no *uniform* relationship. Previous research indicates the complexity of the relationship by stating that the number of visitors cannot be considered in isolation from species requirements and habits, setting attributes, and type of recreational use. Various aspects of use intensity are also involved, including frequency and regularity of use and number of people at one time (Speight 1973). There is evidence that the effects of human-wildlife interactions depend more on the frequency of human presence than on the amount of total recreational use or on the number of people present at any one time.

While human-wildlife interactions are too complex to classify, an attempt to generalize about the form of impacts may be useful. The influence of wildland recreation on wildlife occurs in the forms of *direct* and *indirect* impacts. Direct impacts include the effects on animals caused by primary disturbances and interactions with humans. Indirect impacts are the secondary result of disturbances to habitat and other environmental parameters as a result of recreational use of natural environments. Although indirect impacts are secondary in nature of human-wildlife interactions, they are far more prevalent at affecting most wildlife (Speight 1973). According to Kuss et al. (1984), "Larger game species tend to be affected more by direct contact with people while smaller forms of wildlife appear to be more susceptible to indirect impact on habitat."

Recreational impacts on wildlife may also be classified as *selective* versus *nonselective*. Selective impacts are associated with recreational activities that focus on certain wildlife species. For example, nature study and collecting as well as hunting and fishing are often restricted to a limited number of species, and in some cases, unique or rare species. Nonselective impacts result from coincidental interactions by visitors of whatever wildlife they confront. Hiking, camping, and picnicking are activities that typically lead to nonselective impacts.

As with any attempt to generalize or classify complex phenomena, obvious overlap and interrelatedness exist among parameters. Hunting has been studied more than any other human-wildlife interaction and demonstrates well the difficulty of classifying impacts. While hunting would at first appear to be a form of direct, selective impact, it also results in indirect and nonselective forms of disturbance. Habitat manipulation for certain game species can have detrimental effects on non-game species. Introduction of exotic species for hunting purposes also has indirect impacts on native species. Regulated hunting of animals is considered to be very selective, resulting in the management of specific wildlife populations on a sustained basis. However, even here the impacts are not as selective as one might wish. Speight (1973) reports a study in which 30 percent of wildfowlers could not distinguish game species from rare, protected species. Salo (In Wall and Wright 1977) found that wounding rates in hunting appear to range between 24 and 30 percent. The point is best summarized, although exaggerated, by a chief naturalist at Yellowstone National Park who stated, "In order to get 5000 elk shot by hunters, it would be necessary to accept that in addition 196 moose, 17 men, and an undetermined number of bears, coyotes, bighorn sheep, antelope, bison, mule deer, and horses would be shot by mistake" (Fraser and Eichhorn 1969).

Obviously, the many parameters related to human-wildlife interactions are complex. Nevertheless, understanding these parameters is essential if recreational impacts on wildlife are to be managed.

RECREATION-WILDLIFE IMPACTS

The intrusion of humans into wildlife habitats during recreational activities can cause various types and levels of change in both animals and their habitat. These changes are not entirely detrimental to animals; while many animals are repelled by the presence of humans, others are attracted. Neither are all the changes a direct result of contact with humans; some are indirect. Figure 1 presents a conceptual framework of the major impacts associated with recreational activity in wildlife areas.

When recreational activity occurs in wildlife habitats, two forms of interaction can occur. The recreationists may interact with the animals directly or indirectly through altering the habitat. Direct interaction with wildlife results in two major types of impact: various levels of disturbance and harassment and the actual killing of animals. These two impacts, along with habitat modification, can lead to three responses by wildlife. First, the normal behavior of animals may be altered to various degrees, all the way from habituation to slight modifications to migration from impacted sites. Second, animals may be displaced completely to a new habitat or, in the case of sport hunting, displaced from the population. Third, all three impacts can cause a reduction in the reproductive level of many species. Ultimately, these impacts result in a

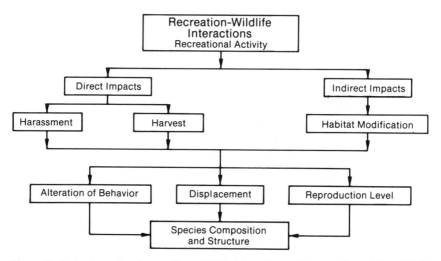

Figure 1. Major impacts of recreation-wildlife interactions. (*Source:* Adapted from Wall and Wright 1977.)

change in the species composition and structure of wildlife populations. The major impacts in Fig. 1 will now be briefly discussed.

Animal Disturbance and Harassment

Harassment, in its broadest sense, refers to "events which cause excitement and/or stress, disturbance of essential activities, severe exertion, displacement, and sometimes death" (Ream, 1979, p. 153). Although intentional harassment of wildlife does occur, the major impact is caused by recreationists who unknowingly and innocently produce stressful situations for wildlife (Fig. 2). Photographers and bird watchers who seek out the nesting areas of secluded species, backcountry campers who camp within critical watering and feeding habitats of large mammals, and off-road vehicle users who seek a closer look are but a few examples of unintentional forms of wildlife harassment. Of course, chasing of winter-stressed wildlife by snowmobiles and certain forms of hunting are some extremes of intentional harassment. Harassment is such a common phenomenon in human-wildlife interactions that it has

Figure 2. Recreationists unknowingly and innocently often produce stressful situations for wildlife. (*Photo:* Bruce C. Hastings.)

led some authors to state that there is no such thing as "nonconsumptive" use of activities concerning wildlife (Weeden 1976; Wilkes 1977). Wilkes rejects completely the concept that certain passive outdoor recreational activities are nonconsumptive and points out several impacts on wildlife by naturalists, photographers, and hikers. Wilkes even suggests the need for a skills test to be associated with the licensing of wildland recreationists because of the damage caused by uninformed, unskilled people to wildlife resources.

Many factors influence the effects or severity that harassment has on animals. "Well-fed, healthy animals with ample refuges from disturbance can withstand more harassment than wildlife already under stress from severe weather, malnutrition, parasite loads, birth or nesting, or inadequate security areas" (Ream 1979, 153). Geist (1972, 1975) emphasizes the importance of physiological and psychological stresses to various wildlife, particularly bighorn sheep, and how stresses can compound the impacts of harassment. While some species seem to habituate to the presence of humans, others are very stress-prone toward humans. The location of human-wildlife interactions is also a critical factor. The presence of people at key locations such as wolf dens, desert bighorn waterholes, snowfields used by caribou to escape heat and insects, ungulate migration routes, and salt licks may present major impacts (Ream 1979). Locational harassment impacts can be managed, simply by protecting key areas from roads and trails, by locating campsites in appropriate areas, and by seasonally closing critical breeding habitats. Ream (1980, p. 7) suggests, "The primary targets of management should be critical times of the year and key locations of wildlife species vulnerable to harassment. Time and effort spent in alleviating harassment in other situations are wasted if habitat loss and wildlife mortality continue to occur at critical times and places."

The mere presence of people has been shown to be sufficient to cause harassment to some species whatever the recreational activity or number of people involved. Shore-nesting birds during the breeding season seem particularly susceptible to the presence of humans. The occurrence of even a few people inhibited the little tern (*Sterna albifrons*) in Great Britain from returning to its nest (Norman and Saunders, in Speight 1973). A survey of the breeding status of the species revealed a number of instances of breeding failure, apparently related to fishermen and sunbathers on the nesting beaches. Similar results have been reported for the ringed plover (*Charadrius hiaticula*). The red deer (*Cervis elephas*) of

Europe and the bighorn sheep (*Ovis canadensis*) of the United States have also been observed to be sensitive to the presence of people. The situation may be more aggravated if people are wearing brightly colored clothing (Speight 1973).

The documentation of animal movement and behavior, including that related to human-caused disturbances, has been greatly aided by radio telemetry studies. Telemetry has commonly been used to determine location and movement of radioed animals. It is now possible to distinguish feeding, resting or rumination, and walking activity in elk (Ward, Cupal, Lea, Oakley, and Weeks 1973). Johnson and Pelton (1979) have used telemetry to study the denning behavior of the black bear in Great Smoky Mountains National Park. Heart-rate telemetry is also used to determine the reaction of big game to disturbance from vehicles, recreationists, livestock, and other wildlife (Ward 1977). Future use of telemetry will allow scientists to measure alarm or harassment through increased heart rate of running animals and also in animals in which the flight reaction is inhibited. It can also be used to estimate energy expenditures and time required to recover from exertion and to facilitate testing of methods to mitigate fear and stress (Ream 1979).

Harvest

Although harassment may produce a considerable amount of stress on wildlife and may even lead to the death of individual animals, the stress is second to that produced by recreational hunting, fishing, and trapping. Entire populations of wildlife in heavily hunted and fished areas are influenced by these recreational activities. In addition, certain types of hunting with dogs and types of trapping may lead to additional stress beyond that caused by the normal processes of harvesting wildlife. Martinka (1979) stated that many wild animals display the ability to differentiate various human activities and react more intensively to those perceived as threats to their life based on past experience. Comparative studies of hunted versus nonhunted animals show that hunted wildlife are especially sensitive to humans during hunting seasons and tend to retreat from most forms of recreational activity at these times.

History has documented the elimination or near elimination of many game species, including the passenger pigeon, beaver, bison, and other big game species. However, it was market and subsistence hunting in the context of reduced and fragmented habitat rather than recreational hunting that primarily led to the removal of these species. Recreational hunting, fishing, and trapping may eliminate a species on a local basis, but it is unlikely that these activities alone could directly result in the extinction of wildlife species.

Recreational activities directly associated with the harvesting of animals can lead to three major changes in the size of wildlife populations that, in turn, affect the quality of these recreational activities. These changes are (1) near elimination of a game species on a local level, (2) reduction beyond a viable breeding population, and (3) reduction beyond a viable hunting or fishing population. In the first instance, heavy hunting and fishing pressures on local populations of wildlife can locally extirpate certain species. The strong tradition of raccoon hunting and year-around training of raccoon dogs in the Southern Appalachian Mountains of East Tennessee has caused the near extirpation of this animal in several counties. Similarly, the traditional hunting of black bear in the Southern Appalachians has eliminated the species from many local areas. Secondly, harvesting of wildlife may not extirpate a population, but it may reduce the number or sex ratio of individuals to such low numbers that the population can no longer breed successfully. Again, habitat loss is typically involved with harvest when this occurs. Finally, a population may have sufficient numbers to maintain a viable breeding unit but lacks an adequate surplus to provide a rewarding harvest yield to the majority of hunters and fishermen. Of course, wildlife management agencies have the ability to regulate and manage all three of these situations.

Habitat Modification

For every animal species affected directly by wildland recreational activities, many more must be affected indirectly by modification of habitat. Habitat modification is the primary impact of man on insect, amphibian, reptile, bird, and small mammal populations. Soil organisms have been shown to decrease by up to a hundredfold in compacted soils and under snowmobile trails. Mice, voles, and shrews depend on the insulating properties of snow, which are lost when compacted by snowmobiling and other winter recreational activities (Stace-Smith 1975). Tunnels and burrows of certain species are collapsed by off-road vehicles, particularly on beach dunes and desert lands (Bury, Wendling, and McCool 1976). Over a 10-year study of off-road vehicle impacts at Dove Springs within the California Desert, Berry (1973) documented loss of the desert tortoise, a protected and threatened species, and a reduction in both the density and diversity of small mammals and lizard populations. Not only do the tires of dune-buggies cause physical damage to animals through the collapse of animal burrows, but they also eliminate their means of escape from extreme desert temperatures and desiccation.

In campgrounds, removal of shrubs and hazardous trees eliminates sources of food and shelter for birds and small mammals (Webb 1968). In improving or creating aquatic recreational sites, the removal of large quantities of shallow-water vegetation is responsible for loss of spawning grounds for freshwater fish. Sedimentation, pollution, and eutrophication of lakes by recreational homes and activities that modify the habitat of many species are common in many recreational areas.

Although recreational activities cause primarily a negative impact on wildlife habitat, there are several examples of habitat gain as a result of wildland recreation. Speight (1973) summarized these, including (1) the increased availability of nesting sites for mallards and wood ducks and over-wintering sites for species that use open water lakes and reservoirs developed for recreation, (2) increased food source as a result of organic litter left around campsites and picnic areas and the planned food plots of wildlife management agencies, (3) habitat changes and population localization of bear and wild boar as a result of campground rubbish dumpsites, and (4) creation of habitat for ecotone species as a result of trail, campsite, and pond development.

From his review of the literature, Speight (1973, p. 19) summarized the effects of recreation on habitat modification as follows:

Increasing intensities of recreational use would seem to exert their most profound effects on microhabitats, by causing a progressive simplification of vegetation, ground surface, and soil structure. Invertebrate species particularly associated with soil or ground flora are in consequence perhaps more likely to be affected by trampling than vertebrates. In any event, the evidence suggests that a net decrease in animal species-diversity can be expected when an area is exposed to outdoor recreation, in parallel with any decrease in plant species-diversity that occurs, but offset to some extent by an influx of scavenging species. Species associated with ephemeral habitats such as bare ground might be expected to maintain their numbers or even increase in abundance at the expense of species associated with more stable ecosystem conditions like woodland.

Alteration of Behavior

The behavior of wild animals is often drastically altered by the frequent presence of humans. The behavioral changes can range from complete disappearance to slight modifications in habitat and daily use patterns to the habituation and taming of animals.

Habituation of wildlife in recreation areas is most often associated with food availability. Garbage dumps and litter at campsites have attracted bears, deer, birds, rodents, and insects, altering the natural feeding habits of these animals (Fig. 3). Skunks, chipmunks, and mice have become so dependent on human food sources at backcountry shelters and frontcountry campsites that they are a nuisance in many U.S. national parks. The number of birds in Yosemite National Park, California, was actually increased by the presence of campgrounds (Foin et al. 1977). However, most of the increase was attributed to an abundance of a few species, especially Brewer's blackbird (*Euphagas cyanocephalus*) and the mountain chickadee (*Parus gambeli*). Clark's nutcracker (*Nucifraga*

Figure 3. The natural feeding habits of animals are commonly altered by the availability of human food sources. (*Photo:* Jane Tate.)

columbiana) and various species of jays have demonstrated a similar attraction to campsites and trails. At the same time, most other species decline in campgrounds.

Several other species have been shown to alter their behavior in response to recreational activities. Eagles and waterfowl have been documented as not returning to feeding sites until several hours after human disturbance, and large mammals have had their movement and feeding patterns modified by park traffic and roads. Singer, Otto, Tipton, and Hable (1981) found that average daily movement was greater for disturbed wild boars in Great Smoky Mountains National Park than for those with no disturbance. In another study Singer (1978) documented five possible responses of mountain goats to disturbances associated with highway crossings in Glacier National Park: (1) unsuccessful crossing attempts, (2) separation of nannies from kids, (3) alterations of crossing routes, (4) apparent alteration of crossing times, and (5) alteration of normal behavior and posture of goats.

Species Displacement and Reproduction Level

Species displacement results in an animal being removed from a familiar environment and being placed in a new habitat. Often, the replacement environment is of poorer quality or has more competing elements than the original area. Because of these factors, displacement is more of a drastic change for wildlife than recreational harassment and habitat modification. The latter two impacts do not require that the animal move from a familiar environment. This may be a particular advantage in breeding success since familiar habitat and territory play a key role in wildlife reproduction. While reproduction levels of wildlife are affected by most recreation-caused impacts, species displacement is likely to have the most drastic effect.

Species of wildlife that are secretive and sensitive to the presence of humans may become permanently displaced from recreational areas. Bighorn sheep and mountain goats have been forced into smaller areas and poorer, more remote ranges because of human encroachment. In Colorado bighorn sheep were forced into higher elevation ranges during lambing season, resulting in weather conditions that caused 80 percent incidence of pneumonia and a resultant decline in population (Woodward, Gutierrez, and Rutherford 1974). Batcheler (1968) found that red

deer, when hunted and harassed in areas of good habitat, were displaced to poor habitat and did not return to the good habitat even after
prolonged cessation of hunting and harassment. In addition, deer displaced to the poorer habitat became nocturnal and experienced reduced
reproductive rates and lower fat deposition.

Hunting and fishing have led to species reduction and displacement.
Species eliminated by hunting and shooting tend to be predators at the
end of food chains. Elimination or displacement of predators has an
indirect effect on the population levels of other food chain members. In
addition, the management of fish and game animals has resulted in
some displacement impacts. In Great Smoky Mountains National Park,
rainbow trout (*Salmo gairdnerii*), introduced in the early 1900s by loggers,
have now out-competed the native brook trout (*Salvelinus fontinalis*) in
many of the streams. Several other introductions of exotic species for
recreational purposes have displaced original species, including native
flora as well as native animals.

Hobby collecting of rare butterflies is the most important single factor
contributing to the decline of two species of butterflies in Great Britain
(Speight 1973). The British race of the large copper butterfly is extinct in
Great Britain because of over-collecting. Certain plants like ginseng,
orchids, and wild ramps have been displaced locally in many parts of
the Southern Appalachian Mountains because of hobby collecting and
selling of the items.

Species Composition and Structure

The end result of the previously discussed impact parameters is an
alteration of species composition and structure among wildlife populations. Gains, losses, and modification occur in both habitat and types of
species. In general, the consequence of recreational activities in an area
results in an overall decrease in species diversity in all trophic groups in
all parts of the ecosystem (Speight 1973, p. 19). This follows a general
decrease in structural differentiation of the ecosystem (i.e., loss of a
proportion of the habitats present without their replacement by new
habitats) and increase in the degree of resource sterilization (i.e., human
simplification of site conditions). Certain populations of organisms increase as a consequence of recreational activities but usually at the expense of a decline in species diversity and richness.

IMPACTS ON WILDLIFE SPECIES

Large Mammals

Large mammals are mobile and difficult to study. However, three large animals that have received considerable attention are bears, bighorn sheep, and deer. Each presents a different type of major impact and set of management implications.

Black Bears

The black bear (*Ursus americanus*), because of its size, potential danger, and historical attraction to recreational sites, has been studied more than other animals. The major impact problem with the bear is the alteration of its natural behavior, more specifically, its habituation to human food sources. Black bears have learned to associate people and their camping equipment with food. This process is accelerated by the willingness of many recreationists to offer them handouts (Fig. 4). In Great Smoky

Figure 4. Panhandler bears in Great Smoky Mountains National Park visit backcountry shelters for food hand outs (*Photo:* Bruce C. Hastings.)

Mountains National Park, 5 to 10 percent of these bears, euphemistically known as panhandlers, forsake their shy and secretive nature and soon begin to beg along roadsides, raid picnic tables, tear open coolers and backpacks, and break into vehicles and tents (Tate and Pelton 1983). While panhandling behavior is not restricted to bears only, the size and strength of these animals make such encounters with people potentially dangerous. Singer and Bratton (1976) reported 107 incidents of human injury and 715 of property damage in Great Smoky Mountains National Park, Tennessee, in 1964 through 1976. Park records listed property damage at 83 incidents in 1977 and 189 in 1978, with injuries totaling eight and 16 for those years, respectively (Tate and Pelton 1983).

Similar injury and property damage impacts have been recorded in Yosemite National Park, California (Table 1). Interactions between bears and humans have occurred in Yosemite since the 1920s, leading to alterations in natural behavior, foraging habits, distribution, and population levels (Keay and VanWagtendonk 1983). Bears in marginal natural habitats appear more dependent on visitor foods than bears in prime natural habitat. Keay and VanWagtendonk also found a positive linear relationship between numbers of visitors and bear incidents, suggesting that visitor density reflects a level of food availability that attracts bears. After a certain level of bear/human interaction and/or food availability is reached, bears might more likely be drawn into a camp area and cause incidents than in sparsely used zones. As a result of the high incidence of bear/human interactions in Yosemite, an intensive management program was initiated in 1975. The program included public information and education, removal of artificial food sources, enforcement of regula-

TABLE 1. Visitor Use, Reported Bear Incidents, and Property Damage Estimates for the Backcountry, Yosemite National Park, 1976–1979

Year	Visitors	Visitor Nights	Bear Incidents	Dollar Damage
1976	71,066	186,526	165	4,758
1977	74,537	194,243	371	9,397
1978	70,909	172,472	277	9,398
1979	66,053	181,775	225	8,553
Mean	70,641	183,754	260	8,027

Source: Keay and VanWagtendonk, 1983. Copyright © by International Association for Bear Research and Management.

tions, control of problem bears, and research and monitoring. From 1975 to 1979, this program resulted in decreases of bear incidents and property damage from 879 to 161 incidents, and from over $100,000 to $13,000 in damages.

Habituating behaviors of black bears at a garbage dump was documented in Jasper National Park, Canada. At the park garbage dump bears exploited the resource by forming social aggregations, tolerating other bears at shorter distances when at the dump than when away (Herrero 1983). Social interactions between bears were characterized by tolerance, avoidance, and spacing. The dump was visited by 7500 to 10,000 park visitors during a 1968 study, and "despite hundreds of close approaches, including 57 situations in which people threw rocks or chased bears, a bear never struck, bit, or touched a person." Herrero observed that the average litter (2.67 offspring) was higher for bears that regularly visited the dump, suggesting that the food source contributed to reproductive success.

National parks that once contained open garbage dumps, and in some cases actually fed bears at the dump sites for public viewing, have now eliminated the dumps, forcing bears into natural feeding areas. Bear-proof trash cans in frontcountry campgrounds and the hanging of food out of the reach of bears in backcountry campgrounds have also decreased the incidence of bear/camper interactions. While these management actions return bears to a dependence on natural food sources, there is evidence that in some instances the practice has decreased the reproductive success, health, and number of bears in certain populations.

Bighorn Sheep

Bighorn sheep present a different type of impact conflict. Human encroachment on bighorn habitat has contributed to displacement and a decline in sheep populations (Dunaway 1970). In the Sierra Nevada Mountains of California where recreational use is heavy, backcountry hiking disrupts the local migration and movement routes of bighorns. In areas heavily used by campers, hunters, or off-road vehicles, use of high-value habitat by bighorns can be excluded completely. Light (1971) found that bighorns tolerate only limited human disturbance before being driven from home ranges. Ewes with young were less tolerant of human approaches than individual ewes and rams.

Most observational studies have stressed the intolerance of bighorns to human encroachment, resulting in strict management policies on recreational use in some areas. However, the need for such policies is not exactly clear. Wehausen, Hicks, Garber, and Elder (1977) report that when zoological areas were established in the Sierra Nevadas to protect bighorns from assumed adverse effects of human disturbance, the results suggested that human disturbance was not as significant a factor as supposed. An eight-year study of sheep in Death Valley National Monument, Nevada, showed that only "unchecked human encroachment appears to actually threaten bighorns." Deliberate attempts of humans to conduct themselves within limits acceptable to bighorn sheep led to tolerance of human presence. Even though the limits and specific effects of human encroachment on bighorns are not completely understood, most resource managers are recommending that prompt conservation action should be taken, with the alternative in mind that management policy can be altered if the actions are proven unnecessary.

White-Tail Deer

In a survey of professional resource managers, the majority of respondents "felt that white-tail deer were the most harassed species in their areas" (Huff, Savage, Urich, and Watlov 1972). Harassment and additional stress during winter months when deer are attempting to conserve metabolic energy are a major concern with winter recreational activities. Deer are naturally adapted to energy-conserving behaviors and mechanisms during snow seasons when range size is restricted. Energy conservation of up to 1000 Kcal/day for a 60 kg deer can result from reduced activity levels such as seeking level land, reducing snow depth, and walking slowly (Moen 1976). Winter harassment by hunting, snowmobiling, or skiing, whether intentional or not, is detrimental to the energy-conserving adaptations of deer. Moen, Whittemore, and Buxton (1981) reported that heart rate among captive deer in controlled tests increased an average of 2.5 times above normal rates when snowmobiles moved tangentially to the deer and 2.9 times above normal rates when circling the deer.

Research on the displacement of deer by snowmobile traffic has been mixed in its findings. During a test of 10 radio-collared deer in Wisconsin, results indicated that the deer did not significantly increase or decrease the size of their home ranges during three weekends of snowmobiling. Noise from the snowmobiles seemed to have little effect; snowmobiles had to be within sight of the deer before the animals would move away. While animals were displaced from the snowmobile trails, the displacement was very temporary. The deer returned to areas along trails within hours after snowmobiling ceased. The research also revealed that deer will change the location of home ranges markedly even if snowmobiles are not present (Bollinger, Rongstad, Soom, and Eckstein 1973).

Studies by Dorrance, Savage, and Huff (1975) in Minnesota indicate

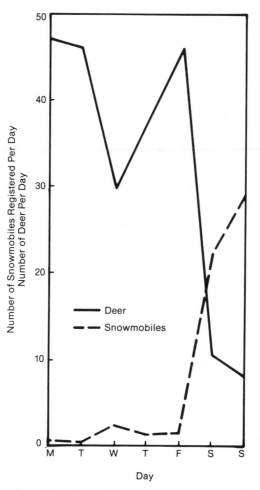

Figure 5. Mean number of deer observed per day, according to day of week, along a 10-km snowmobile trail in St. Croix State Park, Minnesota, 1973. (*Source:* Dorrance, M. J., P. J. Savage, and D. C. Huff, in *Journal of Wildlife Management,* Volume 39, Number 3, pp. 563–569. Copyright © 1975 by the Wildlife Society. Reprinted with permission.)

that deer in smowmobile use areas may become habituated to snowmobile traffic. Home range size, movement, and distance from radio-collared deer to the nearest trail increased with snowmobile activity at a wildlife management area where public snowmobiling was prohibited but remained unchanged at a state park where numbers of snowmobiles per day averaged 10 on weekdays and 195 on weekends. However, the number of deer seen immediately adjacent to trails decreased with snowmobile use in the state park (Fig. 5). The deer did return to areas along trails within hours after snowmobiling ceased. Dorrance et al. (1975) hypothesized that the subtle movements away from trails by deer result in little impact to deer, except during severe winters on poor ranges. In sensitive areas where some deer change their home ranges to entirely different locations, the authors believe that these effects could cause changes in the animal's energy budget that could be detrimental, especially during severe winters.

Deer are capable of habituating to the presence of man and vehicles. Deer often remain close to men working with chain saws and heavy equipment and are often attracted to established snowmobile trails that make walking easier in deep snow and browse more available. Research has also indicated that deer in areas open to snowmobile use react initially to the machines, but further snowmobile traffic has little effect on their movement.

Other Ungulates

Although Nordic skiers cannot travel as far and as fast as snowmobiles, they can have similar adverse impacts on wildlife during the stressful winter months. Ferguson and Keith (1982) studied the influence of Nordic skiing on the distribution of moose and elk in a park in central Alberta. They found that elk and moose both tended to move away from ski trails. Significantly, movement away from trails was caused by the first skier encountered; the passage of additional skiers did not result in additional disturbance. While there is little information on adverse consequences of such movements on reproduction and survival, we do know that this increases the necessary caloric intake of these animals. Where food is limited, this could adversely affect animals.

Medium-Sized Animals

Habituation to recreation-related food sources similar to that for black bears occurs among many medium-sized animals. Raccoons and skunks are a common element of many frontcountry campgrounds, particularly at night. Skunks in Great Smoky Mountains National Park have become so numerous and habituated to humans that they are a common occurrence during daylight hours, commonly meandering through campsites. Local populations in these recreation areas increase rapidly and can lead to population densities where wildlife disease epidemics can be a serious problem.

Foxes and wolves show more avoidance toward recreationists. This is more so for wolves than red fox as the latter has been shown to increase activity on and near snowmobile and snowshoe trails. This behavior may be because of easier walking on the compacted snow or of the presence of cottontail rabbits, snowshoe hares, and other prey of fox that commonly use compacted snow trails. Wolves have been extensively studied in Isle Royale National Park, Michigan, because movement of the wolves is confined to the island, and visitor use is heavy. Peterson (1977) found that wolf use of Isle Royale trails declines after visitors arrive in the spring. Selection of den and rendezvous sites indicates pronounced avoidance of humans. Management suggestions include limiting visitation, enlarging backcountry campsites rather than establishing new campgrounds, disallowing further trail development, and discouraging winter visitor use.

The impacts of snowmobiles on medium-sized animals is inconclusive. Snowshoe hares were observed to avoid snowmobile trails, but red foxes were more active near and in such trails (Neumann and Merriam 1972). Schmid (1971) also observed that red foxes and deer were commonly seen following snowmobile trails. Apparently, the animals penetrate the snow less in the tracks of snowmobiles and find it easier to travel in the tracks. Penetrometer readings and measurements of animal penetration in snow off trails indicate an increase of about 85 percent (Neumann and Merriam 1972).

The indirect impact on predator species such as foxes, wolves, coyotes, bobcats, owls, hawks, and eagles by lowering the population of small animals in snowmobile use areas is a concern that has not been investigated. Snowmobile activity can have a detrimental effect on the numbers of small mammals surviving under compacted snowcover.

Easier and accelerated harvesting of animals because of increasing access to remote areas by snowmobiles is a concern of resource managers. The overharvesting of beaver and other furbearers has been suggested but not conclusively documented (Malaher 1967; Usher 1972). There is also little evidence that the snowmobile is likely to lead to significantly increased hunting pressure on big game. This is not to say that incidence of illegal hunting and harassment by snowmobiles is not a concern, but rather that the overharvesting of animals as a result of snowmobiles has little support.

The popularity of river recreation has presented new levels of impact on many water-based species. Floating of whitewater and backcountry rivers has increased rapidly in the United States, increasing the incidence of human interaction with waterfowl, eagles, osprey, and similar species. On canoeing rivers and lakes where overnight camping is common, the impact on loon populations is a concern. Increasing use of loon nesting islands for camping by canoeists appears to be the primary cause of decrease in loon productivity in the Boundary Waters Canoe Area, Minnesota. Osprey in Minnesota were also observed to build nests farther from lake and river shores, presumably because of increased watercraft activity.

Small Animals

Because the niche and microhabitats of small animals are small, the habitat of these species is susceptible to destruction during the improvement and alteration of recreation sites. Clearing of both terrestrial and aquatic vegetation eliminates herbs, shrubs, and trees, which serve as sources of food and shelter for birds and small mammals. At the same time, human food sources attract rodents and certain species of small mammals and birds. Surveys of the riparian zone of the Colorado River showed abnormally high and unhealthy populations of rock squirrels, resulting from feeding by hikers. Lizard populations, which utilize driftwood for shelter and foraging, were reduced through the reduction of driftwood for campfires.

The effects of campgrounds on rodents are alteration of the feeding behavior and an increase in the population density of opportunistic feeders such as wood rats and deer mice. Backcountry overnight shelters along the 2000 mi long Appalachian Trail receive heavy visitation at night by mice, requiring proper storage of backpacker food. The same is true for food storage during daylight hours for chipmunks and ground squirrels.

The influence of recreation on birds has already been discussed to some extent. The major impacts to songbirds and small nongame species are related to modification of the structure of vegetation and harassment during nesting. However, the presence of vegetation changes, of humans, and of food debris in campgrounds leads to an increase in numbers among some bird species. Brewer's backbird, the brownheaded cowbird, and robins were significantly more abundant in campgrounds of Yosemite National Park, and Oregon juncos were less abundant than in surrounding areas (Garton, Hall, and Foin 1977).

The most dramatic impact on small animals is caused by off-road vehicles, particularly snowmobiles. The compaction of snow by snowmobiles causes a reduction or destruction of the subnivean space, resulting in a mechanical barrier to the movement of small animals. The tunnels of these animals are collapsed and the feeding area greatly reduced. The compacted snow also reduces the insulating qualities of the snow, causing stress and death to small mammals through reduced temperatures (Schmid 1971). Schmid (1972) further documents the effects by stating:

> Experimental manipulation of a snowfield has shown that the winter mortality of small mammals is markedly increased under snowmobile compaction. We recovered none of 21 marked animals from the experimental plot, whereas 8 of 18 marked specimens were captured at least once on an adjacent control plot. (p. 37)

Fish

Fish are not commonly thought of as wildlife by the general public, yet the recreating public can be an impacting agent on this specific form of wildlife. Lakes and streams concentrate recreational activities both from a water-based and shore-based perspective, leading to concentrated levels of impact on aquatic organisms (Fig. 6). Unfortunately, recreational impacts on fish populations are not well-documented.

Direct impacts in the form of displacement occur through removal by fishing and introduction of exotic game species. Wilderness camping at popular alpine lake areas have "fished-out" some lakes and reduced populations to numbers where the native populations are hardly viable. Accelerated harvesting as a result of ORV and snowmobile access to remote lakes has been documented, with one report indicating 556 lbs of fish being harvested from a remote lake on a single winter day. "This would have been an entire season's catch if snowmobile access had not been possible" (Cooney and Preston, in Bury et al. 1976). The introduc-

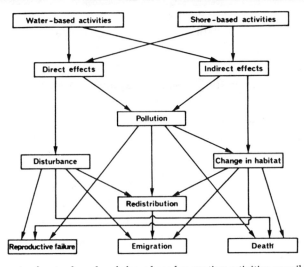

Figure 6. Impacts of water-based and shore-based recreation activities on wildlife. (*Source: Liddle and Scorgie 1980.*)

tion of rainbow trout to the streams of Great Smoky Mountains National Park by loggers before the area was designated a park has led to the displacement of the native brook trout from many of the streams. Fishing for the native brookies is no longer permitted in the park.

Most recreational impacts to fish result from indirect impacts to water quality and ecosystems. Eutrophication, pollution, and mechanical disturbance to aquatic vegetation as a result of wave action from boats all have the potential to disturb fish to varying degrees. Boating also contributes to increased turbidity, human-waste disposal, and the deposit of gasoline/oil mixtures on water surfaces. Concentrations of gasoline/oil mixtures have led to unacceptable levels of depleted oxygen supply for certain fish species and the off-flavoring of the flesh in fish.

SUMMARY

1. Different species of wildlife have different tolerances for interactions with humans. Even within a species, tolerance level for interactions will vary by time of year, breeding season, animal age, habitat type, and individual animal experience with recreationists.

2. Recreational impacts on wildlife may be *direct* or *indirect*. Direct impacts include the effects on animals by primary disturbances and interactions with humans. Indirect impacts are the secondary result of disturbance to habitat and other environmental parameters by recreationists. Larger game species are more affected by direct impacts while smaller species are more affected by indirect impacts of habitat modification.

3. The major impact to wildlife by recreationists is unintentional harassment, caused by individuals who unknowingly and innocently produce stressful situations for wildlife. Physiological and psychological stresses, particularly during winter, can greatly compound the severity of harassment impacts. The location and time of human/wildlife interactions are key elements in managing harassment impacts. Wildlife species vulnerable to harassment can be protected by protecting critical areas from roads and trails, by locating campsites in appropriate areas, and by seasonally closing critical breeding habitats.

4. The frequent presence of humans in wildland areas can alter the normal behavior of animals drastically. Slight modifications in habitat use and daily use patterns and the habituation and taming of animals are the most common behavioral changes. The availability of human food has led to altering the natural feeding habits of many animals in recreation areas.

5. In general, the consequence of recreational activities in an area results in an overall decrease in species diversity. A change in species composition and structure among wildlife populations is the ultimate result of human-wildlife interactions.

REFERENCES

Batcheler, C. L. 1968. Compensatory Responses of Artificially Controlled Mammal Populations. In *New Zealand Ecological Society Proceedings* 15:25–30.

Berry, J., ed. 1973. Preliminary Studies on the Effects of Off-road Vehicles on the Northwestern Mojave Desert: A Collection of Papers. Privately printed, Ridgecrest, CA. 100 pp.

Bollinger, J. G., O. J. Rongstad, A. Soom, and R. G. Eckstein. 1973. Snowmobile Noise Effects on Wildlife, 1972–1973 Report. Engineering Experiment Station, University of Wisconsin, Madison, WI. 85 pp.

Bury, R. L., R. C. Wendling, and S. F. McCool. 1976. Off-road Recreation

Vehicles—A Research Summary, 1969–1975. Texas Agricultural Experiment Station, College Station, TX. Texas A & M University System. 84 pp.

Dorrance, M. J., P. J. Savage, and D. E. Huff. 1975. Effects of Snowmobiles on White-Tailed Deer. *Journal of Wildlife Management* 39:563–569.

Dunaway, D. J. 1970. Status of Bighorn Sheep Populations and Habitat Studies on the Inyo National Forest. *Transactions of Desert Bighorn Council* 14:127–146.

Ferguson, M. S. D., and L. B. Keith. 1982. Influence of Nordic Skiing on Distribution of Moose and Elk in Elk Island National Park, Alberta. *Canadian Field-Naturalist* 96:69–78.

Foin, T. C., E. O. Garton, C. W. Bowen, J. M. Everingham, R. O. Schultz, and B. Holton, Jr. 1977. Quantitative Studies of Visitor Impacts on Environments of Yosemite National Park, California, and Their Implications for Park Management Policy. *Journal of Environmental Management* 5:1–22.

Fraser, D. F., and N. D. Eichhorn. 1969. Man and Nature in the National Parks: A Reflection on Policy. Conservation Foundation. Washington, DC.

Garton, E. O., B. Hall, and T. C. Foin, Jr. 1977. The Impact of a Campground on the Bird Community of a Lodgepole Pine Forest. In *Visitor Impacts on National Parks: The Yosemite Ecological Impact Study*. T. C. Foin, Jr., ed. University of California, Davis: Institute for Ecology. Publication No. 10. 99 pp.

Geist, V. 1972. On the Management of Large Mammals on National Parks. *Park News* 8(4):7–14, 8(5):16–24.

Geist, V. 1975. Mountain Sheep and Man in the Northern Wilds. Cornell University Press, Ithaca, NY. 248 pp.

Herrero, S. 1983. Social Behavior of Black Bears at a Garbage Dump in Jasper National Park. In E. C. Meslow, ed. *Bears—Their Biology and Management*. International Conference for Bear Research and Management 5:54–70.

Huff, D. E., P. J. Savage, D. L. Urich, and R. L. Watlov. 1972. Wildlife-Snowmobile Interaction Project—Preliminary Report. University of Minnesota and Minnesota Department of Natural Resources. 34 pp.

Johnson, K. G., and M. R. Pelton. 1979. Denning Behavior of Black Bears in the Great Smoky Mountains National Park. *Proceedings Annual Conference Southeastern Association of Fish and Wildlife Agencies* 33:239–249.

Keay, J. A., and J. W. VanWagtendonk. 1983. Effect of Yosemite Backcountry Use Levels on Incidents with Black Bears. In E. C. Meslow, ed. *Bears—Their Biology and Management*. International Conference for Bear Research and Management 5:307–311.

Kuss, F. R., A. R. Graefe, and J. J. Vaske. 1984. Recreation Impacts and Carrying Capacity: A Review and Synthesis of Ecological and Social Research. Draft Review Report, University of Maryland, College Park, MD. 180 pp.

Liddle, M. J., and H. R. A. Scorgie. 1980. The Effects of Recreation on Freshwater Plants and Animals: A Review. *Biological Conservation* 17(2):183–206.

Light, J. T. R. 1971. An Ecological View of Bighorn Habitat on Mount San Antonio. *Transactions of the North American Wild Sheep Conference* 1:150–157.

Malaher, G. W. 1967. Improper Use of Snow Vehicles for Hunting. In Transactions, 32nd North American Wildlife and Natural Resources Conference. Wildlife Management Institute, Washington, DC. pp. 429–433.

Martinka, C. J. 1979. Measuring Effects of Human Presence on Wintering Wildlife in National Parks. In *Proceedings of the Second Conference on Scientific Research in the National Parks*. USDI National Park Service. San Francisco, CA. 6:199–211.

Moen, A. N. 1976. Energy Conservation by White-Tailed Deer in the Winter. *Ecology* 57(1):192–198.

Moen, A. N., S. Whittemore, and B. Buxton. 1981. Snowmobile Effects on Heart Rates of Captive White-Tailed Deer. Unpublished Paper. Department of Zoology. Auburn University, Auburn, AL. 18 pp.

Neumann, P. W., and H. G. Merriam. 1972. Ecological Effects of Snowmobiles. *Canadian Field-Naturalist* 86:207–212.

Peterson, R. O. 1977. Management Implication of Wolf-Moose Research, Isle Royale National Park, Michigan. Report to the USDI National Park Service. Washington, DC. 14 pp.

Ream, C. H. 1979. Human-Wildlife Conflicts in Backcountry: Possible Solutions. In *Recreational Impacts on Wildlands*. R. Ittner, D. R. Potter, and J. K. Agee, eds. USDA Forest Service Pacific Northwest Region. Seattle, WA. pp. 153–163.

Ream, C. H. 1980. Impacts of Backcountry Recreationists on Wildlife: An Annotated Bibliography. USDA Forest Service General Technical Report INT-81. 62 pp.

Schmid, W. D. 1971. Modification of the Subnivean Microclimate by Snowmobiles. In *Proceedings of Snow and Ice Symposium*. Cooperative Wildlife Research Unit, Iowa State University, Ames, IA. pp. 251–257.

Schmid, W. D. 1972. Snowmobile Activity, Subnivean Microclimate, and Winter Mortality of Small Mammals. *Bulletin of Ecological Society of America* 53(2):37.

Singer, F. J. 1978. Behavior of Mountain Goats in Relation to U.S. Highway 2, Glacier National Park, Montana. *Journal of Wildlife Management* 42(3):591–597.

Singer, F. J., and S. P. Bratton. 1976. Black Bear Management in Great Smoky Mountains National Park. Uplands Field Research Laboratory Management Report No. 13. USDI National Park Service, Great Smoky Mountains National Park, Gatlinburg, TN. 34 pp.

Singer, F. J., D. K. Otto, A. R. Tipton, and C. P. Hable. 1981. Home Ranges, Movements, and Habitat Use of European Wild Boar in Tennessee. *Journal of Wildlife Management* 45(2):343–353.

Speight, M. C. D. 1973. Outdoor Recreation and Its Ecological Effects: A Bibliography and Review. Discussion Paper in Conservation 4, University College, London. 35 pp.

Stace-Smith, R. 1975. The Misuse of Snowmobiles Against Wildlife in Canada. *Nature Canada* 4:3–8.

Stebbins, R. C. 1974. Off-road Vehicles and Fragile Desert. *American Biology Teacher* 36(4):203–208, 220 and 36(5):294–304.

Tate, J., and M. R. Pelton. 1983. Human-Bear Interactions in Great Smoky Mountains National Park. In E. C. Meslow, ed. *Bears—Their Biology and Management.* International Conference for Bear Research and Management 5:312–321.

Usher, R. J. 1972. Use of Snowmobiles for Trapping on Banks Island. *Arctic* 25:170–181.

Wall, G., and C. Wright. 1977. *The Environmental Impact of Outdoor Recreation.* Department of Geography Publication Series No. 11. University of Ontario, Waterloo. 69 pp.

Ward, A. L. 1977. The Effects of Highway Operation Practices and Facilities on Elk, Mule Deer, and Pronghorn Antelope. Project No. 942-41-42-13-0088-33 F2-6-2580. Annual Report of the Federal Highway Administration, Office of Research and Development. Washington, DC. 53 pp.

Ward, A. L., J. J. Cupal, A. L. Lea, C. A. Oakley, and R. W. Weeks. 1973. Elk Behavior in Relation to Cattle Grazing, Forest Recreation, and Traffic. *Transactions of the 38th North American Wildlife and Natural Resources Conference* 38:327–337.

Webb, W. L. 1968. Public Use of Forest Wildlife: Quantity and Quality Considerations. *Journal of Forestry* 66:106–110.

Weeden, R. 1976. Nonconsumptive Users: A Myth. *Alaskan Conservation Review* 27(9):3–15.

Wehausen, J. D., L. L. Hicks, D. P. Garber, and J. Elder. 1977. Bighorn Sheep Management in the Sierra Nevada. *Transactions of the Desert Bighorn Council* 21:30–32.

Wilkes, B. 1977. The Myth of the Nonconsumptive User. *Canadian Field Naturalist* 91(4):343–349.

Woodward, T. N., R. J. Gutierrez, and W. H. Rutherford. 1974. Bighorn Ram Production, Survival, and Mortality in Southcentral Colorado. *Journal of Wildlife Management* 38(4):771–774.

5 Water

The impact of wildland recreation on aquatic ecosystems is seldom mentioned and understood among recreational activities, yet water quality is a major concern in recreation areas. It serves as both a medium for water-based activities, including body contact sports, and as a drinking source for users. Thus, water-related impacts are somewhat unique from soil, vegetation, and wildlife impacts in that water quality is more directly related to human health.

While water quality is sanctioned by law in highly developed recreation areas and has been researched fairly extensively at cottage-based lakes, far less is known about water-related impacts in remote wildland areas. Because of the lack of developed sanitation facilities in these areas, drinking water and human waste disposal are concerns. The problem is compounded by the concentration of backcountry users at alpine lakes and streams. This chapter reviews some of the major physical, chemical, and bacteriological problems of water sources in wildland recreation areas. Lake and river impacts related to high residential development (cottages) will not be considered.

BASIC WATER ECOLOGY

Aquatic ecosystems, like terrestrial ecosystems, have many parameters which interact to determine water quality. Some of these impact parameters are *direct*, occurring on or in the water. Other impacts to water systems are *indirect,* characterized by inputs that originate from actions that occur on-shore or in the watershed (Liddle and Scorgie 1980). Major impact parameters influencing water quality are: (1) nutrients, (2) suspended solids, (3) amount of dissolved oxygen, (4) temperature and flow, (5) pH, (6) fecal bacteria and pathogens, (7) dissolved solids, and (8) transparency (Kuss, Graefe, and Vaske 1984). Recreation-related impacts focus primarily on (1) nutrient enrichment of the water, (2) suspended solids (turbidity), (3) reduced dissolved oxygen, and (4) bacterial contamination in the form of fecal waste. Water temperature and flow as well as seasonal and site factors influence the importance of each of the variables.

Water Temperature and Flow

Water impacts reach unacceptable levels commonly under the conditions of warm temperatures and low flow rate. Dissolved oxygen levels often reach their lowest levels during warm summer evenings when water flow also is low. Warm temperatures tend to increase the growth of aquatic plants and bacteria, problems of warm water systems. Temperature also affects animal life. Recreational activities can indirectly increase the temperature of lakes and streams, affecting the species composition of fish populations. Some fish can tolerate temperatures as high as about 30°C (Newsom and Sherratt 1972) while trout can survive an absolute maximum of 25°C to 26°C for only a short period of time. As a rule of thumb, trout waters should never exceed 20°C. Removal of stream bank foliage may increase the temperature of trout streams above acceptable levels. In lakes, depletion of oxygen at lower depth (the hypolimnion) forces trout to move to upper layers with sufficient oxygen but higher temperatures, which may be fatal.

Water flow is related to dilution capacities, influencing the concentration of pollutants in water sources at any particular time. Restricted bays and inlets to lakes, as well as slow-flowing springs and streams, often contain the highest bacterial counts and lowest oxygen supplies. In water systems that show a rapid flushing rate or a high flow rate, the danger of water quality appears to be minimized. Precipitation patterns and the dilution capacity of a water system can greatly influence the degree of recreation-caused impacts. However, the influence of storms is mixed. The rapid flushing rate of storms can help in removing suspended and dissolved nutrients from streams, but at the same time storms are a major agent at flushing nutrients and soil from disturbed watersheds into lakes and streams. Nutrient influx and coliform bacteria are sometimes most prevalent just following a storm.

Nutrients

Nutrients in lakes are directly related to the aging of these water systems, a process known as eutrophication. The addition of nutrients, primarily nitrogen and phosphorus, stimulates the net productivity of water bodies. A lake normally undergoes natural successions from a young, nutrient-deficient, unproductive lake with high oxygen levels (oligatrophic) to increased nutrient levels, higher production, greater deposits of organic matter, and low oxygen levels (eutrophic). Eutrophication can be accelerated by recreational activities and actions that increase the rate at which nutrients are added to lakes. The additional nutrients increase the rate and amount of plant growth, and if excessive, lead to undesirable weed growth, algal blooms, or the replacement of sport fish by less attractive species. The excessive vegetation also leads to a depletion of the dissolved oxygen supply during decay of the organic plant materials.

For most recreational use, high water quality means low productivity so that lakes are clear, cool, and deep—suitable for swimming, boating, and good habitats for sport fish (Wall and Wright 1977). In alpine lakes even minute changes in nutrients can cause increases in algae populations. Heavy shoreline use of these lakes and streams accelerates soil erosion, leading to an influx of nitrates into these water bodies. Lake edge and stream bank erosion not only accelerate the rate of nutrient influx, but they influence water clarity, an important indicator of water quality for recreation purposes. Water clarity is conditioned by many factors, including productivity levels of the water as influenced by phytoplankton densities, turbidity, and water color.

Phosphorus, in the form of phosphate, tends to be the limiting factor in aquatic plant growth. It has a strong affinity for soil particles and tends to be tied up in the bottom sediments of lakes. However, swimming, wading, boating, and other activities that stir the bottom sediments of streams and shallow lakes may release concentrations of phosphate and other nutrients. Phosphates contained in motor boat oil and in detergents find their way into aquatic systems although not as much as in the past. Detergents, for example, contain fewer phosphates than in the past.

The response of lakes to nutrients and their vulnerability to accelerated eutrophication are based on many site factors. Size of watershed or drainage basin, shoreline configuration, mean depth, elevational position, and present trophic status are important (Sargent and Zayer 1976). Shallow lakes with numerous bays and inlets at low elevations with warm temperatures will show the most impact to recreational activities. The type of soils and geology surrounding the lake as well as type and extent of forest or vegetation cover will also have an influence on rate of eutrophication.

Dissolved Oxygen

Dissolved oxygen is necessary in respiration of most aquatic organisms. When the depletion of oxygen by respiring organisms occurs at a faster rate than it is being diffused in from the atmosphere or produced by photosynthetic organisms, a deficit in oxygen level may develop. If plant growth and decomposition are excessive, the dissolved oxygen supply of the bottom layer of lakes (hypolimnion) will be depleted by the decay of organic matter. With the increased decay of organic matter, bacterial respiration is high. The depletion is most pronounced in warm lakes because oxygen solubility varies inversely with temperature.

The depletion of oxygen in aquatic ecosystems has several impacts on aquatic animals and plants. The minimal requirements of species vary and often limit the spatial distribution of certain forms in aquatic communities (Reid 1961). Coldwater fish such as trout need a minimum of 6 to 7 parts per million (ppm) of dissolved oxygen; warmwater fish such as bass need a minimum of 5 ppm. Fish kills resulting from oxygen depletion have occurred in lakes, ponds, and streams (Hynes 1970). Many species of aquatic insects are typically replaced by less oxygen-demanding species as an oxygen deficit develops, causing further changes in aquatic populations positioned higher on the food chain. Availability of oxygen affects plants in primarily two ways: species composition and nutrient uptake. Some submerged species of aquatic plants are sensitive to low levels of dissolved oxygen and are replaced by more tolerant species. In terms of nutrient levels, phosphate increases under anoxic conditions and becomes more readily available for plant production in the surface layers of lakes. Thus, nutrient level, plant production and decomposition, and dissolved oxygen supply are all intricately related. In relation to recreational use, the impact can be summarized as follows: with recreational use, production in lakes can be quickly altered from acceptable rates to excessive growth rates with associated changes in oxygen supply and species composition of aquatic organisms (Vander Wal and Stedwill 1975).

Pathogens and Other Pollutants

The major concern with recreational aquatic impacts involves the presence of pathogens and pollutants that directly influence human health. Pathogens are disease-causing organisms that are transmitted by the feces of humans and other warm-blooded animals. The major source is raw or inadequately treated sewage, a particular concern in remote recreational areas. Pathogens at unacceptable levels are a serious health hazard, making water sources unfit for body-contact and drinking.

Human feces contains over 100 viruses, bacteria, and protozoa, which cause disease or death to infected humans (Cowgill 1971). The common indicator bacteria such as total coliforms, fecal coliforms (FC), and fecal streptococci (FS) are widespread in fecally contaminated environments and originate from diverse sources, including the intestinal tract of humans, other mammals, birds, and reptiles (Kabler and Clarke 1960). The presence of coliforms in a stream or lake usually indicates recent fecal pollution and the possible presence of enteric pathogens. Coliform bacteria themselves are nonpathogenic but are used as indicators since they are more easily measured than the pathogens with which they are associated.

The relationship of fecal coliform (associated with humans) to fecal streptococcus (associated with other animals) density (FC/FS ratio) is used to provide information as to sources of pollution.

> Based on per capita contributions of indicator bacteria from man and domestic livestock, FC/FS ratios greater than about 4:1 are usually indicative of man's body wastes. Ratios less than about 0.7:1 suggest contamination originated from livestock, wildlife, storm water runoff, and other nonhuman sources (Gary 1982, 5).

As will be documented later in this chapter, animal sources of coliform appear to be more prevalent in wilderness areas than are human sources.

Human wastes are also a source of nutrients. Feces of humans may contain as much as 1.5 g of phosphorus and 10.4 g of nitrogen per person per day (Kuss et al. 1984). In sterile, remote environments human and animal feces located around heavily used lakes can be two of the most common sources of bacterial influx to these aquatic systems (Merriam et al. 1973).

Other major sources of pollutants in wildland aquatic areas fall into the categories of oil products, solid wastes, and sediments. All three of these water quality impacts are greatly associated with motorboating. Muratori (1968) suggests that 500 million liters of unburned outboard fuel are discharged every year into the navigable waters of the United States. Litter, in the form of bottles and cans, finds its way to the bottom of lakes and streams. Finally, turbidity of streams and lakes, which is due to boat propeller action and aquatic activities, can influence light penetration through water and reduce photosynthesis.

IMPACTS ON WATER QUALITY

Nutrient Influx

Nutrients, primarily nitrogen and phosphorus, enter wildland water systems mostly as a result of shoreline and campsite erosion. However, seasonal data to indicate that wildland recreation activities are a major impact on nutrient balance in lakes and streams are generally lacking (Gosz 1982). Studies in campgrounds usually fail to show increased nutrient levels in associated waters (Brickler and Utter 1975; Gary 1982; Segall and Oakley 1975). In some cases moderately eutrophic conditions are found in streams in campgrounds, but analyses upstream indicate that the nutrients are primarily from natural sources. Potter, Gosz, and Carlson (1984) list natural sources to include precipitation, runoff, bottom sediments, decomposing plankton, transient waterfowl, falling tree leaves, bedrock type, and natural soils.

Gary (1982) surveyed over a three-month period the nutrient balance of a Colorado stream as water entered and left a small commercial campground. Levels of No_3-N did not exhibit any definite seasonal trend, and concentrations at three study sites were not significantly different. Other chemical and physical properties remained unchanged and were not significantly increased by campground use. Similar results have been obtained for campgrounds that are equipped with modern sanitation facilities (Gosz 1982).

In mountainous backcountry areas where lakes are normally oligotrophic and are popular recreation areas, the impact of nutrient influx is a particular concern. Algae populations in oligotropic lakes respond to only small changes in nutrients. Shoreline and campsite erosion and water contamination by campers are potential sources of nutrients in these systems. Silverman and Erman (1979) studied two lake basins, one receiving high visitor use and the other low use in Kings Canyon National Park, California, for differences in water quality. Visitor use was found not to affect the condition of the lakes; however, there were extreme differences between the basins because of natural sources. The basin lakes receiving low use had about 60 times more nitrates than the high-use lakes early in the summer. Phosphate concentration was similar for all lakes. Background levels and natural sources of nutrients are a major problem when relating recreational use to nutrient influx. In many cases natural sources contribute the largest quantities of nutrients, making comparative studies difficult to interpret (Barton 1969). Baseline studies of conditions before and after recreation occurs in an area are needed, rather than studies that compare areas of high and low visitor use. However, this procedure may not be the complete solution. Stuart, Bissonnette, Goodrich, and Walter (1971) found that a closed watershed, when opened for "limited recreation and logging," actually decreased in bacterial contamination.

Phosphate appears to be more of a nutrient input in wildland areas than nitrogen. Water quality studies carried out at nine campground sites and controls in the Boundary Waters Canoe Area, Minnesota, indicated that recreational use increased phosphate concentration and coliform bacteria in the lake water near campsites. Flushing of the bare, campsite impact zones and of fire pits is a common occurrence with each rain storm and contributes to the nutrient input of the lakes (Fig. 1). Even though phosphate and coliform levels increased at the BWCA campsites, other water quality parameters, including temperature, dissolved oxygen, pH, specific conductance, nitrate concentration, and nitrogen were not affected by recreational use.

Perhaps the most convincing data to date that shows a causal link between wildland recreation and nutrient influx is the work by Dickman and Dorais (1977). They found that human trampling of the shoreline and steep-sided basin of a semiwilderness lake in Canada led to an exceptionally high phosphorus loading of the lake. Over a 20-year period (1956–1976) recreational use of the small lake increased tenfold, significantly reducing plant cover in the lake basin and increasing erosion on its steep slopes. The trampling and resulting erosion caused a

Figure 1. Rain storms flush nutrients and pollutants from campsites and fire pits directly into the nearby lake, Boundary Waters Canoe Area, Minnesota. (*Photo:* W. E. Hammitt.)

phosphorus loading of 854 mg/m^2 of lake surface, placing Pinks Lake among the most eutrophic lakes of North America (Dickman and Dorais 1977). However, the lake receives no municipal, agricultural, or rural effluent discharge because of its location in a semiwilderness, forested watershed. A significant portion of the dissolved phosphorus is entering the eutrophic zone of the lake from apatite-rich rock, which has eroded following the destruction of ground cover as a result of human trampling. The causal link between human trampling and the high phosphate concentrations was further corroborated by leachate tests of the eroded apatite rock material near the edge of the lake. The tests independently supported the hypothesis that apatite-derived, dissolved phosphorus was the principal factor responsible for the high concentrations of phosphorus in the spring.

Coliform Bacteria

The major controversy over recreational use of water is based on a sanitation concern. Many studies suggest that recreational activity is a significant source of bacteria contamination. Likewise, many studies fail to show significant water quality degradation because of wildland recreation. Many results are site specific, and in a number of cases, conflict with each other. Thus, there is a divergence of opinion on the question of recreational impact on bacterial water quality levels (Aukerman and Springer 1975; Gosz 1982; Kuss et al. 1984; Wall and Wright 1977).

Studies conducted in wildland areas show that while sewage-flow rates may be the most significant source of bacterial contamination in developed recreational areas, this is not the case with wildland recreation. Campgrounds and other use areas in wildlands often have little or no water directly associated with sewage disposal (pit, vault privies, or no facility), as well as lower production (i.e., fewer individuals, as well as per capita production of sewage wastes in terms of laundry, dish water, etc.). The primary source of bacterial contamination in wildlands comes from surface soil, a result both of background levels of microorganisms and those associated with human and domestic animal waste products (Gosz 1982). Regardless of the presence or absence of man, natural bacterial densities in soils are high enough so that precipitation can be expected to increase the bacterial counts in nearby streams and lakes. No natural water source could consistently meet potable water standards because of the normal influx of bacteria (Potter et al. 1984; Silverman and Erman 1979).

One of the first backcountry studies to indicate that recreational use affects coliform bacteria was the work of King and Mace (1974) in the Boundary Waters Canoe Area, Minnesota. They found that coliform bacteria populations of water at canoe campsites were significantly higher than at control points (Table 1). The average coliform levels at the

TABLE 1. Coliform Populations for the Various Use Classes of Campsites: University of Minnesota, BWCA Campsite Study, 1970

Location	High[a]	Medium	Low
	(Number of Coliform/100 ml) Use Categories		
Campsite	4.61	6.63	5.83
Control	0.28	1.95	4.68
Difference	4.33	4.68	1.15

Source: Merriam et al. 1973.
[a] High use sites had over 1100 visitor days total use, medium use sites had over 500 visitor days total use, and low use sites had under 300 visitor days total use.

campsites were above the maximum (2.2. organisms/100 ml) considered safe for drinking water. The difference between campsites and controls was larger for the high- and medium-use campsites, suggesting a relationship between use level and coliform bacteria density. High bacterial counts were found only adjacent to the campsites, indicating that the effect on the lakes is generally small. Effluent from the pit toilet on each campsite was determined as the probable source of the bacteria (Fig. 2). Because the soils are shallow, effluents reach bedrock quickly and drain into lake basins. Shoreline activities at the campsites such as swimming, washing dishes, cleaning fish, and boat launching are other probable causes (King and Mace 1974). Such activities stir bottom sediments, shown to be a microbial habitat where the organisms from the fecal matter of warm-blooded animals can persist and concentrate (Van Donsel and Geldreich 1971).

In the heavily used backcountry areas of the White Mountains of the Northeastern United States, coliform levels have been a problem near shelters and huts. In untreated water supplies at shelters or major trails,

Figure 2. Pit toilets, if located on shallow soils and near water, can be a source of coliform bacteria and associated pathogens. (*Photo:* W. E. Hammitt.)

the presence of fecal and total bacteria was found to vary seasonally for most lakes, springs, and streams. Highest counts occurred in late July, with some counts in excess of recommended public health standards. However, by late August most waters sampled were nearly clear of bacteria.

At developed campgrounds in wildland recreation areas, Varness, Pacha, and Lapen (1978) and Johnson and Middlebrooks (1975) reported significant increases of coliform bacteria associated with recreational use. Varness et al. (1978) found higher bacteria densities downstream from heavily used camping areas without sanitary facilities, while Johnson and Middlebrooks (1975) found that sharp increases in fecal coliform counts coincided with peak recreational use at areas having toilets. The peak use levels of bacteria dropped sharply at the end of the recreation season.

Other investigations in both remote backcountry areas and at developed facilities in wildland recreation areas support the argument that recreational use has *no* significant adverse impact on the bacterial quality of water. Aukerman and Springer (1975) found no significant increases in coliform bacteria at heavily used developed campgrounds or at remote backcountry campsites in Colorado. In fact, they found an inverse relationship between cases of bacterial density increases and levels of campground utilization. The study is significant in that it involved three types of camping (i.e., campgrounds off paved roads, campgrounds off unpaved roads, and roadless backpacking sites), a number of campgrounds, and a heavily used recreational area. The authors concluded that "although campers are contributing to the bacterial pollution of the Cache la Poudre River watershed, the amount contributed at each campground is insignificant in terms of established water quality standards."

Similar results showing insignificant levels of coliform bacteria have been reported for alpine lakes in Kings Canyon National Park, California (Silverman and Erman 1977), for water sources in Great Smoky Mountains National Park (Silsbee, Plastas, and Plastas 1976), and for developed campgrounds in Colorado (Gary 1982) and Wyoming (Skinner, Adams, Richard, and Beetle 1974). In Kings Canyon National Park only 10 percent of the water samples had positive total or fecal coliform, and at most two per sample. Fecal streptococci levels were somewhat higher than coliform (52 percent positive samples and a maximum count of eight colonies per sample), indicating wildlife as the source. Skinner et al. (1974), studying a natural watershed only open to hikers and wildlife, found yearly means for fecal coliform in 1970, 1971, and 1972, to be 1.2, 0.6, and 0.2 organisms/100 ml, respectively. The fecal streptococci bacteria counts for the same years were 22, 2, and 3/100 ml.

An important issue concerning recreational areas that contain hazardous levels of bacteria is the source of the contamination. Many studies that have identified the source report the contamination to be from nonhumans. Livestock is responsible in some cases (Marnell, Foster, and Chilman 1978; Silsbee et al. 1976), while in many instances wildlife contaminate the water (Potter et al. 1980; Silsbee et al. 1976). In the Great Smoky Mountains National Park, European wild boars that root and wallow in springs and other water drinking sources are a major source of fecal streptococci bacteria. Bacteria in the feces of wildlife are as much a health hazard as that of humans. Therefore, reducing or managing the number of recreation users to an area may not necessarily reduce the bacterial levels to within safety limits. Also, drinking and cooking water may need to be boiled, even in areas receiving little or no recreational use.

There are some instances that suggest that in remote wildland areas light recreational use will improve the bacteriological quality of water sources because wildlife will avoid the areas (Stuart et al. 1971; Walter, Bissonnette, and Stuart 1971). Walter and Bottman (1967) compared a closed watershed and one open to recreational use. They found that bacterial counts (fecal coliforms and fecal streptococci) were higher for the closed watershed than for the open watershed, which in 1970 had been opened for "limited recreation and logging." Bacterial contamination decreased in the streams after the watershed had been made available for human use. The authors concluded that human activities had resulted in a reduced wildlife population, which had contributed substantially to the previous bacterial pollution.

Little is currently known about the accumulation of bacterial organisms and nutrients in the bottom sediments of wildland water sources. Most studies of bacterial contamination examine only the surface waters when, in fact, the bottom sediments may contain the larger concentrations of organisms and nutrients. Brickler and Tunnicliff (1980) found fecal coliform densities in bottom sediments to be significantly higher than for surface water of rivers and tributaries in Arizona. Surface water FC densities ranged from 2.1 to 8.0/ml in the Colorado River, while densities in bottom sediment reached 48,000/ml. Forty-three percent of the sediment samples exceeded 500/ml, and 34 percent of them exceeded 1000/ml. Bacterial levels in bottom sediments are of considerable importance since several recreational activities such as swimming and boating cause suspension of bottom sediments and direct contact of the microorganisms with recreationists. As more bottom sediment analyses are conducted, they may modify considerably our thinking about the status of water quality as represented by analyses of surface water alone (Gosz 1982).

Backcountry Camping and Drinking Sources

The previous discussion on coliform bacteria dealt with levels found in lakes and streams, with no specific attention devoted strictly to drinking sources in backcountry camping areas. Because water is not chemically treated in these areas and is often taken from springs or very small tributaries, bacterial contamination is a concern. Giardiosis, hepatitis, and other diseases are a constant potential threat in these situations (Fig. 3).

Silsbee et al. (1976) surveyed the fecal coliform and streptococci concentrations in four types of water sources in Great Smoky Mountains National Park: flowing springs, seepage springs, spring-fed streams, and tributary-fed streams. A flowing spring is a spring that flows from a localized source and can be sampled directly as it comes from the ground. A seepage spring seeps from the ground over a wide area and after it has flowed over the ground surface for some distance, drinking water can be obtained from it. Spring-fed or primary streams are fed mainly by a spring or by seepage. A tributary-fed or secondary stream is one fed by various tributaries.

Flowing springs tended to be the best drinking water sources, giving consistently low coliform counts (Table 2, page 117). Seepage springs were highly variable, giving both low and high counts. Small spring-fed streams also tended to be variable and gave high counts at times. Larger tributary-fed streams generally gave consistent levels of contamination although somewhat higher than flowing springs. These results indicate that flowing springs are the best drinking sources, followed by secondary streams. However, even in the secondary streams the coliform levels average in the danger zone.

Sources of bacteria in the four drinking sources were primarily wildlife. Most of the FC/FS ratios indicated animal sources of contamination. Data collected from above and below campsites and outhouses showed that they did not have a major effect on the bacteriological quality of the

Figure 3. Bacterial contamination is a constant concern with drinking sources in the backcountry. (*Photo:* W. E. Hammitt.)

water in the areas tested. The backcountry staff of Great Smoky Mountains National Park strongly recommend that campers boil all drinking water used in the backcountry. To date, Giardia has not been documented within the Park's backcountry, nor is human sickness often associated with its drinking water.

Solid Waste and Foreign Materials

Solid waste in the form of litter tends to accumulate at the bottom of streams and lakes. The amount of solid waste carried into backcountry

TABLE 2. Comparison of Different Types of Back-Country Water Source and Fecal Coliform Densities

Source Type	Range of Fecal Coliform Counts (Percent)					Number of Samples
	0	1–10	11–30	31–100	>100	
Primary stream	32	20	20	24	4	21
Secondary stream	15	77	7	1	0	72
Flowing spring	72	28	0	0	0	32
Seepage spring	33	40	15	8	4	21
All streams	20	62	10	7	1	93
All springs	57	32	5	4	2	53

Source: Silsbee et al., 1976.

areas is potentially greater for watercraft activities than for backpacking since the materials are more easily transported. During the summer of 1969, solid waste left behind by recreational users of the Boundary Waters Canoe Area, Minnesota, totaled an estimated 360,000 lbs of bottles, cans, and other nonburnable refuse (King and Mace 1974). This averages to about 3 lbs per recreation user. Barton (1969) estimates that the solid waste figure of 360,000 lbs is equivalent to 1 ton of phosphates and 13 tons of nitrogen. In addition, decomposition of the material provides an abundant supply of trace elements as well as some major ions (Barton 1969). Since the 1970s the Boundary Waters Canoe Area, and other areas, have prohibited bottles and cans on the backcountry lakes (Fig. 4).

Much concern has been expressed over the potential harm of oil and gasoline from outboard motors in aquatic ecosystems. Because outboard motors are two-stroke engines, the engine lubricant oil is mixed directly with the gasoline. The exhaust discharged into water by outboard engines contains oil and gasoline residues. Muratori (1968) and Stewart and Howard (1968) report that "as much as 4 gal of gasoline mixture out of every 10 may be discharged into the water from outboard motors." Modern motors should usually discharge between 10 to 20 percent of their fuels into the water. Besides the gasoline and oil being discharged into the water, the use of leaded gasolines has the potential of ejecting tetraethal leads into the water, which accumulate in bottom muds and may affect aquatic organisms (Barton 1969). English, Surber, and McDermott (1963) reported that outboard motor exhaust-water contains an average of 105 g/gal of nonvolatile oil, 57 g/gal of volatile oil, 0.53 g/gal of lead, and 0.60 g/gal of phenols.

Figure 4. Some heavily used water resource areas prohibit the use of bottles and cans in the backcountry. (*Photo:* D. W. Lime.)

The primary ecological effect of outboard motors is the deposition of oil on aquatic organisms. Oil in water attaches to the surface of unicellular plankton and other plants to interfere with air-gas exchange. Oil films also inhibit the growth of many forms of algae, disturbing the food chain of fish and other aquatic organisms. In addition to coating the surface of floating plants to interfere with gas exchange, oil can lead to oxygen depletion. One gram of oil in water requires 3.3 g of oxygen for complete oxidation (Barton 1964). Oil extracts also can stimulate bacterial growth, which is significant in that these organisms are competitors with algae for oxygen and nutrients found in water.

Phosphates and other chemicals contained in fuel-oil mixtures can also affect aquatic organisms, although little conclusive data exist (Jackivicz and Kuzminski 1973; Liddle and Scorgie 1980). Tainting of fish flesh occurs at a fuel-usage level of 8 gal of outboard motor fuel per million gal of lake water per season (English et al. 1963). Oil also has an adverse effect on fish growth and longevity. However, in experimental ponds, Lagler, Hazzard, Hazan, and Tomkins (1950) found no effects on populations of fish or plants that could be attributed to outboard motor exhaust.

Suspended Matter and Turbidity

Suspended matter may be the single most common factor influencing alterations in water quality in recreation areas. Anderson, Hoover, and Reinhart (1976) estimate that 80 percent of the deterioration in water quality is due to suspended solids. While in suspension, such solids cause waters to be turbid; reduced light penetration may restrict the photosynthetic activity of plants and the vision of animals. These finely divided materials at high concentrations are known to interfere with the feeding of filter feeder organisms and are abrasive to sensitive structures such as the gills of fish (Warren 1971). Reproduction of fish, particularly trout, and fish food are affected as these materials settle-out. Perhaps most important for recreation purposes, increased loads of suspended solids greatly reduce the clarity of water and the public's desire to enter it.

Turbidity, related to recreation, can originate in water bodies from primarily three zones: bottom sediments, shorelines and adjacent banks, and the surrounding watershed. The disturbance of stream and lake sediments by boats and swimmers has been reported. Liddle and Scorgie (1980) report numerous aquatic plants that are uprooted by the wash and turbulance resulting from outboard motor propellers in shallow waters. Narrow channels are a particularly sensitive area because of the repeated use of such areas. Boats propelled by oars and/or paddles impart relatively little impact to stream bottoms, except in shallow stream riffles where canoes commonly scrape periphyton from rocks. Although boating may increase turbidity in selected high use areas, there seems to be little quantitative evidence that it is a major impact factor (Hansen 1975; Lagler et al. 1950; Liddle and Scorgie 1980). For example, Lagler and colleagues found no recordable increase in turbidity because of outboard motors in their experimental ponds, even though there was considerable movement of the bottom sediments. There was some redistribution of benthic invertebrates, but no damage was recorded.

Swimming, wading, and fishing contribute to turbidity but only when concentrated in space and time. Gary (1982) recorded dramatic increases in suspended solids from waders near a small commercial campground on a few days when use was high. As soon as recreationists left the sampled area, suspended solid levels fell to almost predisturbance levels. Waders and swimmers in Great Smoky Mountains National Park also have an influence near campgrounds and heavy use segments of streams.

Streambank erosion and resulting suspended sediments are largely a result of trampling. Many wildland recreation activities concentrate at

Figure 5. Swimmers and innertube floaters are causing streambank erosion at the put-in and take-out locations in Great Smoky Mountains National Park. (*Photo:* W. E. Hammitt.)

Figure 6. Off-road vehicles can greatly disturb streambanks and bottom sediments when crossing streams. (*Photo:* W. E. Hammitt.)

one time or another near the edges of water bodies. Walking in and out of water and up and down streambanks can quickly destroy the vegetation that protects shoreline soils from erosion (Fig. 5). Marginal vegetation and soils may also be damaged by those walking parallel to the water's edge but not directly engaged in water activities. Larson and Hammitt (1981) found that onlookers were a dominant source contributing to streambank impacts near family campgrounds. The crossing of streams by ORV's and horses also disturbs streambanks and bottom sediments, but again the impacts are usually quite isolated (Fig. 6).

Turbidity impacts from watershed disturbances are associated primarily with certain multiple-use land management practices (e.g., logging) and some recreation-caused erosion. Off-road vehicle and hiking trails in the Southern Appalachian Mountains of the United States erode quickly where 80 to 90 in. of annual rainfall may be present. However, gravel roads, logging trails, and cutting practices in multiple-use recreational areas are probably a bigger contributor of watershed impacts than recreational use trails.

SUMMARY

1. Water quality is a major concern, but not prevalent impact, in wildland recreation areas. It serves as a medium for body contact sports and as a drinking source for users. Thus, water-related impacts are unique in that they are more directly related to human health than soil, vegetation, and wildlife impacts.

2. Nutrient level, aquatic plant production and decomposition, and dissolved oxygen supply in aquatic ecosystems are all intricately related. With recreational use plant production in warm lakes and streams can be quickly altered from acceptable rates to excessive growth rates with associated changes in oxygen supply and species composition of aquatic organisms.

3. While coliform bacteria and quality of drinking water are obvious concerns in wildland recreation areas, there is conflicting research evidence that backcountry recreation drastically impacts water quality. More studies have failed than have shown significant increases in coliform counts as a result of recreational use. In several situations wildlife have been the dominant source of bacteria contamination in drinking water sources.

4. Suspended matter and turbidity may be the single most important water quality factor in the eyes of recreationists. Increased loads of suspended solids greatly reduce the clarity of water and the public's desire to use it.

REFERENCES

Anderson, H. W., M. D. Hoover, and K. G. Reinhart. 1976. Forests and Water: Effects of Forest Management on Floods, Sedimentation, and Water Supply. USDA Forest Service General Technical Report PSW-18.

Aukerman, R., and W. T. Springer. 1975. Effects of Recreation on Water Quality in Wildlands. Final Report, Eisenhower Consortium Grant EC-105. 67 pp.

Barton, M. A. 1969. Water Pollution in Remote Recreational Areas. *Journal of Soil and Water Conservation* 24:132–134.

Brickler, S. K., and B. Tunnicliff. 1980. Water Quality Analyses of the Colorado River Corridor of Grand Canyon. College of Agriculture Paper 350, University of Arizona, Tucson, AZ. 134 pp.

Brickler, S. K., and J. G. Utter. 1975. Impact of Recreation Use and Development on Water Quality in Arizona: An Overview. In J. D. Mertes, ed., *Man, Lei-*

sure, and Wildlands: A Complex Interaction. Eisenhower Consortium Bull. 1, pp. 195–201.

Cowgill, P. 1971. Too Many People on the Colorado River. *The Environmental Journal* 45:10–14.

Dickman, M., and M. Dorais. 1977. The Impact of Human Trampling on Phosphorus Loading to a Small Lake in Gatineau Park, Quebec, Canada. *Journal of Environmental Management* 5:335–344.

English, J. N., E. W. Surber, and G. N. McDermott. 1963. Pollutional Effects of Outboard Motor Exhaust—Field Studies. *Journal of the Water Pollution Control Federation* 35:1121–1132.

Gary, H. L. 1982. Stream Water Quality in a Small Commercial Campground in Colorado. *Journal of Environmental Health* 45(1):5–12.

Gosz, J. R. 1982. Non-Point Source Pollution of Water by Recreation: Research Assessment and Research Needs. Eisenhower Consortium Bull. 13. 14 pp.

Hansen, E. A. 1975. Does Canoeing Increase Streambank Erosion? USDA Forest Service Research Note NC-186.

Hynes, H. B. N. 1970. *The Ecology of Running Waters.* Toronto: University of Toronto Press. 555 pp.

Jackivicz, T. P., and L. N. Kuzminski. 1973. A Review of Outboard Motor Effects on the Aquatic Environment. *Journal of Water Pollution Control Federation* 45:1759–1770.

Johnson, B. A., and E. J. Middlebrooks. 1975. Water Quality as an Approach to Managing Recreational Use and Development on a Mountain Watershed South Fork of the Ogden River-Ogden Valley Area, PRWA21-1. College of Engineering, Utah State University, Ogden, UT. 84 pp.

Kabler, P. W., and H. F. Clarke. 1960. Coliform Group and Fecal Coliform Group Organisms as Indicators of Pollution in Drinking Waters. *Journal of American Water Works Association* 52:1577–1579.

King, J. C., and A. C. Mace, Jr. 1974. Effects of Recreation on Water Quality. *Journal of Water Pollution Control Federation* 46(11):2453–2459.

Kuss, F. R., A. R. Graefe, and J. J. Vaske. 1984. Recreation Impacts and Carrying Capacity: A Review and Synthesis of Ecological and Social Research. Draft Review Report, University of Maryland, College Park, MD. 181 pp.

Lagler, K. F., A. S. Hazzard, W. E. Hazan, and W. A. Tomkins. 1950. Outboard Motors in Relation to Fish Behavior, Fish Production and Angling Success. *Transactions North American Wildlife Conference* 15:280–303.

Larson, G. L., and W. E. Hammitt. 1981. Management Concerns for Swimming, Tubing, and Wading in the Great Smoky Mountains National Park. *Environmental Management* 5(4):353–362.

Liddle, M. J., and H. R. A. Scorgie. 1980. The Effects of Recreation on Freshwater Plants and Animals: A Review. *Biological Conservation* 17:183–206.

Marnell, L., D. Foster, and K. Chilman. 1978. River Recreation Research Conducted at Ozark Scenic Riverways 1970–1977: A Summary of Research Projects and Findings. USDI National Park Service, Van Buren, MO. 139 pp.

Merriam, L. C., Jr., C. K. Smith, D. E. Miller, C. T. Huang, J. C. Tappeiner II, K. Goeckerman, J. A. Bloemendal, and T. M. Costello. 1973. Newly Developed Campsites in the Boundary Waters Canoe Area: A Study of Five Years' Use. University of Minnesota Agricultural Experiment Station Bull. No. 511.

Muratori, A. 1968. How Outboards Contribute to Water Pollution. *Conservationist* 22:6–8.

Newsom, G., and J. C. Sherratt. 1972. *Water Pollution.* J. Sherratt and Son, Altrincham.

Potter, L. D., J. R. Gosz, and C. A. Carlson. 1984. Forest Recreational Use, Water, and Aquatic Life: An Assessment of Research Results for Land-Use Managers in the Southern Rockies and High Plains. Eisenhower Consortium Bulletin No. 6, USDA Forest Service, Rocky Mountain Forest and Range Experiment Station.

Reid, G. K. 1961. *Ecology of Inland Waters and Estuaries.* New York: Reinhold. 375 pp.

Sargent, F. O., and F. Zayer. 1976. Land Use Patterns, Eutrophication, and Pollution in Selected Lakes. Technical Report, USDI Office of Water Research and Technology. 47 pp.

Segall, B. A., and S. M. Oakley. 1975. Development of a System for Monitoring the Physical and Chemical Characteristics of Forest Lakes. Final Report, Eisenhower Consortium Grant EC-90. 77 pp.

Silsbee, D., L. A. Plastas, and H. J. Plastas. 1976. A Survey of Backcountry Water Quality in Great Smoky Mountains National Park. Management Report No. 10. Uplands Field Research Laboratory, Gatlinburg, TN. 66 pp.

Silverman, G., and D. C. Erman. 1979. Alpine Lakes in Kings Canyon National Park, California: Baseline Conditions and Possible Effects of Visitor Use. *Journal of Environmental Management* 8:73–87.

Skinner, Q. D., J. C. Adams, P. A. Richard, and A. A. Beetle. 1974. Effect of Summer Use of a Mountain Watershed on Bacterial Water Quality. *Journal of Environmental Quality* 3:329–335.

Stewart, R. H., and H. W. Howard. 1968. Water Pollution by Outboard Motors. *The Conservationist* 22(6):6–8, 31.

Stuart, D. G., G. K. Bissonnette, T. D. Goodrich, and W. G. Walter. 1971. Effects of Multiple Use on Water Quality of High Mountain Watersheds: Bacteriological Investigations of Mountain Streams. *Applied Microbiology* 22:1048–1054.

Vander Wal, J., and R. J. Stedwill. 1975. A Lake Ranking Program Conducted on Forty-three Lakes in the Thunder Bay Area. ("Cited by") Wall, G., and C. Wright. 1977. The Environmental Impact of Outdoor Recreation. Dept. of Geography Publication Series, No. 11. University of Waterloo, Waterloo, Ontario.

Van Donsel, D. J., and E. E. Geldreich. 1971. Relationship of Salmonella to Fecal Coliform in Bottom Sediment. *Water Research* 5:1075–1087.

Varness, K. J., R. E. Pacha, and R. F. Lapen. 1978. Effects of Dispersed Recreational Activities on the Microbiological Quality of Forest Surface Water. *Applied and Environmental Microbiology* 36:95–104.

Wall, G., and C. Wright. 1977. The Environmental Impact of Outdoor Recreation. Dept. of Geography Publication Series, No. 11, University of Waterloo, Waterloo, Ontario.

Walter, W. G., and R. P. Bottman. 1967. Microbiological and Chemical Studies of an Opened and Closed Watershed. *Journal of Environmental Health* 30:157–163.

Walter, W. G., G. K. Bissonnette, and G. W. Stuart. 1971. A Microbiological and Chemical Investigation of Effects of Multiple Use on Water Quality of High Mountain Watersheds. Montana University Joint Water Resources Research Center, Report 17. 130 pp.

Warren, C. E. 1971. *Biology and Water Pollution Control*. Philadelphia: Saunders.

6 Impact Patterns

Chapters 2 through 5 described impacts of wildland recreation on soil, vegetation, wildlife, and water. These impacts often exhibit predictable patterns both in space and over time. Recreationists consistently tend to use the same places. Visitors to developed campgrounds concentrate on shaded sites near comfort stations and water sources, while backcountry campers congregate around spectacular lakes with good fishing. Such places tend to be more highly impacted than less popular places. Consistent use distributions result in characteristic patterns of impact on individual sites such as trails and campsites. Impacts on both trails and campsites generally decrease as one moves from the center to the edge of the site. Much of this chapter will explore the nature of spatial patterns of impact on trails and campsites.

Recreation sites and impacts are not static; they change over time. Temporal impact patterns are the second subject of this chapter. Impact generally occurs rapidly, with the rate of deterioration tending to taper off over time. However, rates of change differ with type of impact and between environments. For example, in forested areas, soil compaction and vegetation loss occur rapidly while loss of organic horizons occurs more slowly. In deserts, loss of organic horizons may occur more rapidly than soil compaction. Recovery rates vary greatly from place to place, although they are always slower than rates of deterioration.

SPATIAL PATTERNS OF IMPACT

One of the most distinctive characteristics of recreation use is its highly concentrated nature. Most use is restricted to a small number of travel routes and destination areas. Manning (1979) calls this the "node and linkage" pattern of recreation use and impact. Nodes of impact occur at destination areas; linkages develop along the routes between nodes. The table and firepit at a campsite, the edge of the cliff at a scenic overlook, and the riverbank at a boat put-in are examples of nodes where use is concentrated. Examples of linkages include hiking and equestrian trails, canoe portages, and the access trails between individual sites, the comfort station, and water sources in a developed campground. Concentration of use means that pronounced impacts, while locally severe, only occur in a small proportion of any recreation area. Wagar (1975) estimated that one European park, by restricting use to developed trails, has confined the direct impacts of use to only 0.1 percent of the park's 42,000 acres. In the Eagle Cap Wilderness, where users are free to travel where they will, Cole (1981) estimated that no more than about 0.5 percent of two popular drainage basins had been substantially disturbed by use of campsites or trails. Even around two very popular subalpine lakes, in the same wilderness, the proportion of the area that had been substantially disturbed was less than 2 percent (Cole 1982). Even in properly designed, developed campgrounds where camping pads are highly disturbed, much of the total campground may remain relatively undisturbed.

Many factors contribute to this concentration of use. Certain locations attract people over and over again. Waterfalls, lakes, and scenic viewpoints are all good examples. People also tend to be attracted to edges. Rivers, lakes, and cliff edges attract people as does the boundary between meadow and forest. Use also concentrates for reasons of safety and ease of use. Many people are more comfortable and feel safer camping or walking in places that obviously have been used before. It is also easier to walk on existing trails and to camp on sites that have already been cleared of brush and rocks.

The tendency for use to be concentrated within certain parts of a recreation area can be either good or bad. Situations where this is advantageous or not will be discussed in Chapter 12, along with techniques managers can use to encourage either use concentration or its counterpart—use dispersal.

Use is also concentrated within individual sites. Typically campers spend over three-quarters of their in-camp time close to the table, tent pad, and fire grill. This area is the most severely impacted. It is surrounded by a less intensively used area where wood may be gathered

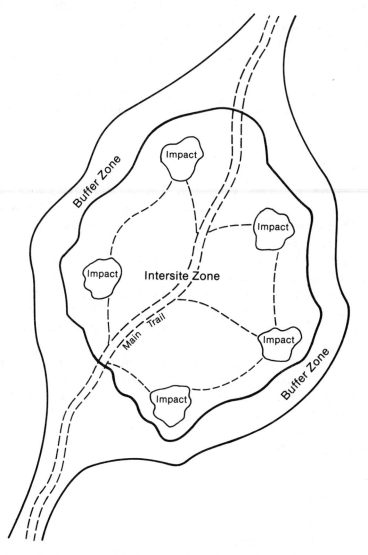

Figure 1. Impact, intersite, and buffer zones for a cluster of campsites in a backcountry recreation area. (*Source:* D. N. Cole.)

and people may walk to and from water or toilet facilities. Beyond this area is a zone that is rarely penetrated by the recreationist. On developed campsites McEwen and Tocher (1976) have called these three distinct areas the impact, intersite, and buffer zones, respectively (Fig. 1). They argue that these zones are a consistent and important feature of campsites. These zones should be recognized, their distinctive types and levels of impact should be understood, and management should be tailored to maintenance and enhancement of these zones. Because the concept of impact zones has such important implications for managing ecological impacts on campgrounds and other high-density recreation sites, McEwen and Tocher's summary of impacts and management implications for each zone is described in the following subsections.

Impact Zone

Deterioration of soil and vegetation is severe so impact zones quickly degenerate into hard, barren pads. Trampling pulverizes and scuffs away litter cover, eliminates herbaceous and small woody stems, and compacts soil. Soil compaction and loss of litter cover cause water infiltration rates to be severely reduced. This increases the severity of erosion. These changes occur within the first couple years of use, even with only moderate levels of visitor use. Moreover, recovery of impact zones will require long periods of time. High impact zones must be accepted, although problems can be minimized through site design to keep impact zones small and hardening of surfaces with gravel, sand, or woodchips (see Chapter 12). Encouraging continued, concentrated use of these impact zones is important. Therefore, it is critical to keep these areas attractive and clean. If they become trashy, dirty, dusty, or muddy, they are likely to be abandoned, and new areas will be impacted. Key objectives for management of impact zones are to keep them as small and as attractive as possible.

Intersite Zone

Vegetation and litter are lost and soil is compacted, but these impacts are only pronounced on informal trail systems. Elsewhere, the health and vigor of soil and vegetation are not seriously reduced. Species composition of vegetation and wildlife is likely to be altered, but this will not be evident to most visitors. Of particular importance, the capacity of vegetation to regenerate is not severely compromised. Intersite zones will be the nurseries for future generations of trees, and they provide screening between individual sites. Without them, one campsite tends to blend into the next. The greatest concern with intersite zones is that they will be eliminated through expansion of impact zones. This can be avoided by creating intersite zones during the initial site design phase and by maintaining impact zones so that they do not expand. Some planting of trees, shrubs, and placing of logs and rocks may be necessary both to minimize use of intersite zones and to provide protected regeneration sites, particularly for tree seedlings. Establishment and hardening of an "official" system of informal trails between impact zones, other sites, and conveniences such as water supplies and toilets are often necessary to avoid excessive trail proliferation.

Buffer Zone

Few impacts occur in the buffer zone, other than some firewood removal, a few hiking trails, and roadways. In most primitive campgrounds the buffer zone is simply a transition zone between the developed site and the surrounding natural community. As with intersite zones, buffer zones should be delineated and protected. Avoiding encroachment from expanding intersite zones is the major concern; no active management of vegetation or soil is needed because the zone is natural.

Although these three zones have been described for campgrounds where they are most useful, the concept can also be applied to other high-use sites. Trails exhibit parallel zones from the highly impacted trail tread through a less altered trailside zone to the undisturbed adjacent area. On most trails the tread is barren and compacted. Because it is often trenched below the local ground surface, the trail tread channels water and is subject to accelerated erosion. Where erosion is severe, roots and rocks are exposed, and the trail can become difficult to use. Hikers and stock may leave the tread to walk on easier ground, enlarging the area of impact. As with the impact zone on campsites, the trail tread is an inevitable—usually purposely constructed—zone of extreme impact. Management must strive to keep the tread functional so users stay in the tread and avoid widening the impacted zone. The goals are usually to avoid erosion by diverting running water off the tread and to provide a comfortable walking surface. This may require some type of paving or bridging, particularly in wet or boggy areas.

The adjacent trailside zone is similar to the intersite zone. It is not natural, but the impacts that have occurred are not evident to most users. Vegetation often grows along the trailside although its composition is usually very different from undisturbed environments (Cole 1981). Plants are usually low-growing, and many of the species growing here are exotic weeds inadvertently brought into the area. Soil compaction and erosion may occur, but it is less pronounced than on the tread. Perhaps the major source of impact is the initial construction of the trail. During construction, vegetation clearing opens up the trailside environment, increasing light intensities and changing moisture relationships. Moisture levels frequently increase along trails for several reasons. Fewer trees intercept less precipitation; fewer plants lose less water through evapotranspiration; and the compacted trail sheds water along its sides.

Trail construction also creates new habitats alongside trails. Rock faces are frequently either created or eliminated where trails are blasted out of rock outcrops. Flat, soil-covered surfaces are often created where trails cross steep boulder slopes on which soil and vegetation were minimal. Trails also interrupt drainages, leading to the development of boggy areas or to the drainage of areas that formerly were wet. Management of trailside zones should attempt to minimize disturbance by avoiding excessive alteration during trail construction. Thereafter, as with management of intersite zones on campsites, the most important thing is to avoid lateral expansion of the impacted tread into the trailside zone. One of the best ways to do this is to keep trailside zones rough and natural. This will tend to keep hikers and stock on the tread. The greater the contrast between the trail tread and the trailside zone, in terms of ease of walking, the easier it will be to avoid expansion of the highly-disturbed tread.

Impact patterns are less evident where use is more diffuse than it is on campsites and trails. This applies to cross-country travel by motorized or nonmotorized means and certain scenic areas, picnic areas, or places where stock are allowed to roam and graze. Even in such situations, however, there is usually a gradient from high impact zones to the natural community. Where concentrated use around nodes, edges, and facilities leads to pronounced impact, management will need to control use distribution in such a way that impact zones do not expand and proliferate over time. Recognition of these zones and spatial patterns is an important first step in devising management strategies for controlling impact. We will discuss this further in Chapter 12 on site management.

Spatial patterns are most pronounced and important when describing and managing impacts on vegetation and soil, components of the ecosystem that are stationary. Patterns are less distinctive when we consider animals and water, components that move around. Smaller animals are affected primarily by habitat alteration; as with vegetation and soil, such impact is highly concentrated. Larger animals, however, may be affected over very large areas. A grizzly bear or bald eagle population may be affected over its entire range, even though recreational use is highly localized and concentrated. This is especially true where recreational use is concentrated on an animal's preferred habitat or on critical feeding or breeding grounds. For many animals that live on or in the water, for example, it may be irrelevant that recreational use and impact are minimal a few yards from the water; if all of their habitat is subject to disturbance by recreational use, then they are likely to be highly disturbed. Bird populations, disturbed at their nesting sites, may show evidence of this disturbance in their wintering grounds, even if no recreational use occurs there. Impacts on water can also be felt far from the point where pollution occurs. Dilution of pollutants by water tends to reduce the severity of impact, but it increases the area affected. Because wildlife- and water-related impacts can spread far beyond the places where disturbance originates, management of these impacts provides challenges that vegetation and soil impacts do not.

TEMPORAL PATTERNS OF IMPACT

The rate at which impact occurs varies with type of impact. As mentioned before, herbaceous vegetation loss generally occurs more rapidly than loss of soil organic horizons. Rates are also dependent on use levels. Impact occurs most rapidly where use levels are heavy. Generally, however, impacts on vegetation and soil occur rapidly wherever use levels are even moderate. A number of studies show that the relationship between site impacts and the age of a site is asymptotic rather than linear (Fig. 2). That is, impacts increase rapidly during the first few years after a site is used and then increase more slowly, if at all, thereafter. In describing developed campsites, Hart (1982) distinguishes between a short break-in period, when the campsite is developed and initially used by campers—the period when most of the impact occurs—and a dynamic equilibrium period when changes are minimal. During the equilibrium period additional impacts caused by use tend to be offset

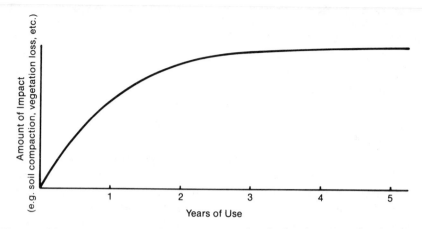

Figure 2. Most impact on recreation sites occurs within the first few years after the site is opened. (*Source:* D. N. Cole.)

by maintenance activities and natural rejuvenation processes. On forested campsites the final change is death of the overstory. This death may or may not be hastened by recreational use. When it occurs, the forested site will usually be replaced by an open campsite because there is usually no tree regeneration to replace the overstory.

The impacts resulting from development and initial use of campsites have been studied in wilderness by Merriam et al. (1973) and in a developed campground by LaPage (1967). After two years of use, soil penetration resistance (compaction) on campsites in the Boundary Waters Canoe Area Wilderness reached near-maximum levels that were not substantially surpassed in the following years. On car campgrounds in Pennsylvania, vegetation loss was most severe after the first year of use; vegetation cover actually increased in the following years, as trampling-tolerant non-native species replaced the original native occupants of the site.

Other impacts on campsites do not occur so rapidly with initial use and may continue to deteriorate with time. The most important of these types of impact are site expansion, damage to trees, and loss of organic matter. Site expansion occurs whenever a party either needs more space or prefers to use an unused portion of the site. Thus it is most likely to occur where sites are used by large parties or where impact zones are unattractive or undesirable (e.g., muddy or not flat). Over 5 years, 10 newly developed campsites in the Boundary Waters Canoe Area increased more than 50 percent in size, while the size of another four more than doubled. Figure 3 shows an example of how one of these Boundary Waters campsites doubled in size in just two years. Note the expansion to contiguous areas the first year, followed by development of a satellite site the second year. Some of the most serious problems with site expansion occur on campsites used by outfitters. Outfitted parties often consist of numerous unaffiliated groups of people, each seeking some privacy from the other groups. In seeking out private places to set up tents, a large area is affected.

Damage to trees is cumulative and, therefore, increases over time. Exposure of tree roots, physical damage to tree trunks, and sapling removal are long-term processes that may affect the vigor and growth rate of trees. Once a tree is felled or severely scarred, it will remain that way until it rots. Because old damage is slow to disappear, any new damage represents an increase in impact over time. Even though tree

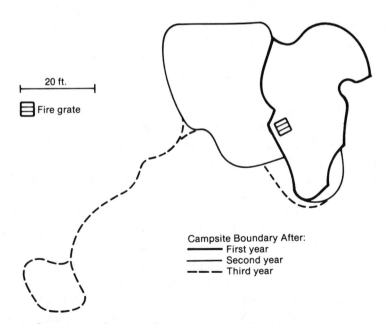

Figure 3. Campsites tend to expand in size over time. Development of satellite sites is a common pattern of site expansion. (*Source:* Adapted from Merriam et al. "Newly Developed Campsites in the BWCA: Study of Five Years Use," in University of Minnesota Agricultural Experimental Station Bulletin, 1973. Used with permission of the publisher.)

damage is one of those impacts that does increase over time, most tree damage occurs shortly after a site is opened.

Loss of organic matter over time is somewhat different. Loss of organic matter caused by scuffing and erosion of litter can be offset by the yearly leaf fall of hardwoods or the more continuous needle fall of conifers. However, loss of litter exceeds yearly litter fall on all but the most lightly used campsites. Consequently, a net loss occurs, and litter depth and cover decline over time. On forested sites, the decline is not as rapid as vegetation loss, so near-maximum levels of litter loss occur at a more advanced age than with vegetation loss. On Boundary Waters Canoe Area campsites mineral soil was not exposed until sometime between the second and fifth years of use, and it was still increasing 14 years after the campsites were first developed.

On trails the rate at which impact occurs may be even more rapid. Initial impacts associated with trail development include intentional felling of trees, removal of brush and ground vegetation, surface flattening, soil compaction, and drainage alteration. Once these changes have been initiated, those associated with trail use are usually of minor importance. Two impacts that can become more pronounced with time are trail widening and erosion. Trail widening is analogous to campsite expansion. It occurs where the trail tread is difficult to walk on, particularly where it is muddy or rocky. Widening can be continuous, or it can occur as a series of braided trails (Fig. 4).

Although trampling can cause erosion of some trails, its principal effect is to make the trail surface more susceptible to erosion, by churning up the soil, reducing infiltration rates, removing vegetation, and channeling water. The primary agent of erosion is running water from intercepted streams, snowmelt, springs, and even intense precipitation. Once water is channeled down a trail, erosion will occur and will probably increase in severity over time. Such erosion is likely to continue, with or without use, until water bars or some other drainage control device is installed to divert water off the trail.

Temporal patterns of impact on wildlife and water are less well understood. For wildlife they vary greatly between species and even within species. Some animals such as white-tailed deer can become habituated to disturbance. This creates a pattern of change over time that is analogous to vegetation loss on campsites. Initial impact is serious, but disturbance decreases over time as the animal develops a tolerance for disturbance. Many animals can develop a tolerance for predicta-

Figure 4. Trail widening in the form of multiple braided trails is a common impact pattern. (*Photo:* R. C. Lucas.)

ble disturbances, but are adversely affected by unpredictable types of disturbance.

Other animals can tolerate infrequent disturbance but become bothered by frequent disturbance. This pattern is the opposite of changes in vegetation and soil. In this case there is an initial resistance to impact, but once disturbance becomes frequent, a severe reaction takes place. Disturbance of certain types of nesting birds provides a good example. Parents may put up with the first few groups of visitors that come close to their nests. At some point, however, their tolerance of these intrusions will be exceeded, and they will abandon their nest.

Impacts on water also vary between the two extremes of rapid response to initial disturbance and initial resistance followed by a severe response. Fecal contamination at any place or time may be serious one day and gone the next, provided the input is not continuous. On the other hand, some pollutants accumulate over time. Initially, they may not present problems because they are diluted by water, but over time they may reach levels that present problems. For example, recreational use around alpine lakes in Kings Canyon National Park caused trace elements to accumulate to levels that eventually led to changes in biota. These changes have not been reversed by over a decade of reduced use levels (Taylor and Erman 1979).

RECOVERY RATES OF IMPACTS

Recovery rates are more variable than deterioration rates because they are more dependent on environmental factors. For example, 1000 people walking single file across wildflower fields on a mountain top and in a valley bottom would, in both cases, kill all plants in their path in one day; however, recovery of the mountain top vegetation might take many times longer than recovery of the valley bottom vegetation because the growing season on the mountaintop is much shorter.

Recovery rates for soils may be less variable than rates for vegetation. Although compaction levels are not consistent between studies, several studies report that compaction levels can return to normal after 6 to 18 years (Hatchell and Ralston 1971; Parsons and DeBenedetti 1979; Thorud and Frissell 1976). Recovery of organic matter levels may take longer. In Kings Canyon National Park, Parsons and DeBenedetti (1979) found that the depth of organic horizons and accumulation of woody fuels on campsites closed for 15 years had not returned to normal. Recovery from erosion will take even longer. Once it occurs, recovery will require centuries.

Recovery of vegetation on trails subjected to experimental trampling illustrates the variability of recovery rates. Some trails in the Southern Appalachians were almost completely revegetated just one year after trampling (Studlar 1983). In contrast, the vegetation cover of dry alpine meadows in Glacier National Park had only recovered 24 percent after six years (Hartley 1976). Rates can even be highly variable in different environments within the same general area. For example, five years after being experimentally trampled by horses, vegetation cover of a grassland was 100 percent of normal; cover in a nearby forest was only 26 percent of normal (Weaver, Dale, and Hartley 1979).

SUMMARY

1. Recreational resource impacts do not occur randomly in space, but exhibit concentrated and predictable spatial patterns. Most impacts, like

use patterns, are restricted to a small number of travel routes and distination areas.

2. In campsites, three distinct areas or zones of impact occur: (1) the impact, (2) intersite, and (3) buffer zones. Each zone of impact has distinct types and levels of impact and management implications.

3. Most impacts on vegetation and soil show an asymptotic rather than linear relationship over time. Vegetation disturbance and soil compaction increase rapidly during the first couple years after a site is used, but then increase more slowly thereafter. However, some impacts, such as site expansion, continue to increase over time.

REFERENCES

Cole, D. N. 1981. Vegetational Changes Associated with Recreational Use and Fire Suppression in the Eagle Cap Wilderness, Oregon: Some Management Implications. *Biological Conservation* 20:247–270.

Cole, D. N. 1982. Controlling the Spread of Campsites at Popular Wilderness Destinations. *Journal of Soil and Water Conservation* 37:291–295.

Hart, Jr., J. B. 1982. Ecological Effects of Recreation Use on Campsites. In D. W. Countryman and D. M. Sofranko, eds. *Guiding Land Use Decisions: Planning and Management for Forests and Recreation.* pp. 150–182. Baltimore, MD: Johns Hopkins Press.

Hartley, E. A. 1976. Man's Effects on the Stability of Alpine and Subalpine Vegetation in Glacier National Park, Montana. PhD dissertation, Duke University, Durham, NC.

Hatchell, G. E., and C. W. Ralston. 1971. Natural Recovery of Surface Soils Disturbed in Logging. *Tree Planters Notes* 22(2):5–9.

LaPage, W. F. 1967. Some Observations on Campground Trampling and Groundcover Response. USDA Forest Service Research Paper NE-68. 11 pp.

McEwen, D., and S. R. Tocher. 1976. Zone Management: Key to Controlling Recreational Impact in Developed Campsites. *Journal of Forestry* 74:90–93.

Manning, R. E. 1979. Impacts of Recreation on Riparian Soils and Vegetation. *Water Resources Bulletin* 15:30–43.

Merriam, Jr., L. C., C. K. Smith, D. E. Miller, C. T. Huang, J. C. Tappeiner II, K. Goeckermann, J. A. Bloemendal, and T. M. Costello. 1973. Newly Developed Campsites in the Boundary Waters Canoe Area—A Study of Five Years' Use. Agricultural Experiment Station Bull. 511, University of Minnesota, St. Paul. 27 pp.

Parsons, D. J., and S. H. DeBenedetti. 1979. Wilderness Protection in the High Sierra: Effects of a Fifteen Year Closure. In R. M. Linn, ed. *Proceedings of Conference on Scientific Research in the National Parks.* pp. 1313–1318. USDI

National Park Service Transactions and Proceedings Ser. 5. Washington, DC: U.S. Government Printing Office.

Studlar, S. M. 1983. Recovery of Trampled Bryophyte Communities near Mountain Lake, Virginia. *Bulletin of the Torrey Botanical Club* 110:1–11.

Taylor, T. P., and D. C. Erman. 1979. The Response of Benthic Plants to Past Levels of Human Use in High Mountain Lakes in Kings Canyon National Park, California. *Journal of Environmental Management* 9:271–278.

Thorud, D. B., and S. S. Frissell. 1976. Time Changes in Soil Density Following Compaction under an Oak Forest. Minnesota Forest Research Note 257. 4 pp.

Wagar, J. A. 1975. Recreation Insights from Europe. *Journal of Forestry* 73:353–357.

Weaver, T., D. Dale, and E. Hartley. 1979. The Relationship of Trail Conditions to Use, Vegetation, User, Slope, Season, and Time. In R. Ittner, D. R. Potter, J. K. Agee, and S. Anschell, eds. *Proceedings, Recreational Impacts on Wildlands.* pp. 94–100. USDA Forest Service, Pacific Northwest Region, R-6-001-1979, Portland, OR.

III FACTORS AFFECTING IMPACTS

7 Environmental Durability

Now that we have developed an understanding of recreational impacts on soil, vegetation, wildlife, and water and the patterns these impacts exhibit in space and over time, we will examine some factors that influence impact patterns. This is critical because it is through manipulation of these factors that managers can control recreational impacts. Many factors affect amount of impact and impact patterns on the land. Certain of these factors relate to environmental characteristics of the sites where recreational use is occurring. Both inherent site conditions and site durability during the season when use occurs can be important. These topics will be the focus of this chapter. Use characteristics, of course, are also highly influential. The importance of various characteristics of use will be the topic of Chapter 8.

Of all the topics in this book, environmental durability is probably the most difficult topic to do justice to in just one chapter; it is an extremely complex subject and a topic for which there is much suggestive information but few definitive answers. One characteristic may make a site durable while another makes it vulnerable. For example, a meadow may be resistant to vegetation loss, while its soils are highly vulnerable to erosion. There is also an important distinction between the properties of *resistance* and *resilience*. Resistance is the site's ability to tolerate recreational use without changing or being disturbed. It might be quantified in terms of the amount of use a site can absorb before some level of impact is reached. Resilience is the ability to recover from any changes that do occur. It might be quantified in terms of the number of years it takes for a site to recover from some level of impact to its predisturbance condition. Some sites such as many in desert areas are resistant but not resilient. They can tolerate use well; however, once impact occurs, it lasts for a long time. Other sites such as many riparian areas are resilient but not resistant. They are rapidly impacted, but recovery is also rapid. On sites designated for long-term recreation use such as developed campgrounds, resilience may be much less important than resistance because recovery from use is not an issue. Such sites are expected to be used and impacted for the foreseeable future. In areas of highly dispersed use, however, resilience is at least as important as resistance because management objectives in such places stress the avoidance of permanently impacted sites. Both resistance and resilience need to be considered, and their relative importance varies with management objectives.

Much more is known about the durability of vegetation and soil than about that of wildlife and water. Consequently, most of this chapter will deal with effects on vegetation and soil. Separate sections on wildlife and water are provided near the end of the chapter. It is convenient to group the environmental characteristics that influence vegetation and soil impact into vegetation characteristics, soil characteristics, and topographic characteristics. At a higher level of generalization, it is also possible to describe the importance of ecosystem-level characteristics. Durability is also affected by broad differences in regional climates, but regional climates will not be discussed because they cannot be influenced by management.

VEGETATIONAL RESISTANCE

Much of a site's durability can be assessed by examining vegetation characteristics. Influential characteristics include the resistance of individual species, species composition of the vegetation, total amount of vegetation cover, and vegetation structure (physiognomy). Characteristics that make individual species resistant were described in Chapter 3.

Attempts to generalize about the relative durability of various groups of plants provide useful guidelines for assessing the durability of different environments. Places where resistant plants are abundant will obviously be more resistant to vegetation loss than places where most plants are fragile. As mentioned earlier, mature trees and grasslike plants are generally resistant; mosses are neither highly resistant nor highly sensitive; and lichens and tree seedlings are highly sensitive. Shrubs vary from resistant to moderately sensitive, but their resilience is usually low once they are seriously damaged. Forbs vary from moderately resistant to highly sensitive, but resilience is usually greater than for shrubs. The likely response of shrubs and forbs, for which variation in resistance between species is high, can be predicted using the list of resistant characteristics in Chapter 3.

Despite these general trends, there are numerous exceptions. Even the response of two individual plants within the same species can be variable. Ecotypic differences—genetic differences between individuals that result from adaptations to different environments—can result in pronounced variations in resistance. High elevation ecotypes are often shorter and more matted than their low elevation counterparts; consequently, they are likely to be more resistant. Other species exhibit important phenotypic differences—differences in form and structure that are not genetically based. Bluegrass, for example, can abandon the erect form it exhibits in undisturbed environments and adopt a prostrate growth form in trampled areas. This increases its ability to tolerate trampling.

The relative resistance of plants also differs between seasons. Many forbs are particularly fragile early in the season when they are growing rapidly; shrubs are often more fragile late in the season, when their dry branches and stems are particularly brittle. The resistance of a species even depends on the other species with which it is associated. Holmes and Dobson (1976), working in subalpine meadows in Yosemite National Park, California, found that survival rates for the same species were generally about three times greater in communities of several species than when it grew in pure stands. Generally, resistance increases where there are several vegetation layers. Tall layers of plants absorb impact, protecting lower layers. Lower layers provide a cushioning effect that somewhat reduces impact to taller layers.

Many analyses of the relative resistance of entire species assemblages have been made. Commonly a researcher will experimentally trample several different vegetation types and compare responses to see which types decrease in cover most rapidly. Although many studies have examined the initial resistance of vegetation, few have followed recovery to evaluate resilience.

The graph in Fig. 1 provides some data from an experimental tram-

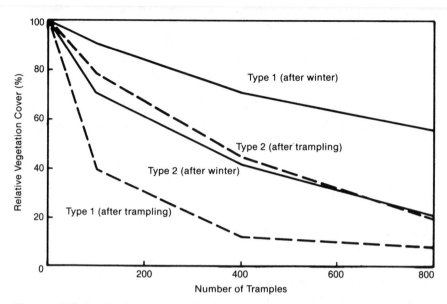

Figure 1. Relationship between surviving vegetation cover and number of experimental tramples for two vegetation types in western Montana. Type 1 is a forest with a ground cover dominated by lush forbs. Type 2 is a forest dominated by low-lying shrubs. One set of measurements, relevant to evaluating resistance, shows cover after trampling. Another set of measurements, relevant to evaluating resilience, shows cover after the winter following trampling. (*Source:* D. N. Cole.)

pling study undertaken in western Montana (Cole 1985). Two vegetation types are compared. Type 1 is a forest with an understory dominated by lush, erect forbs, species adapted to growth in heavy shade (Fig. 2). Type 2 is a forest with an understory dominated by shrubs that spread along the ground only a few inches off the surface. In each type people walked a given number of times back and forth across the vegetation; each one-way pass was a "trample." The low resistance of the forbs in type 1 is reflected in the "after trampling" graph in which over one-half of the cover is lost after fewer than 100 tramples. The low shrubs in type 2 are much more resistant; about 300 tramples are required before one-half of the cover is lost. This conforms to our expectations based on the relative resistance of these two growth forms. Although not presented in the graph, a grassland retained over one-half of its cover after 1600 tramples (Cole 1985), illustrating the much greater resistance of graminoids (Fig. 3). At the highest level of trampling reported—800 tramples—the difference in cover between types 1 and 2 is diminishing.

Figure 2. This vegetation type, with an understory dominated by lush forbs, has low resistance and high resilience. (*Photo:* J. L. Marion.)

Eventually all cover will be lost on even the most resistant vegetation type. The importance of differences in resistance between vegetation types is greatest at low to moderate use intensities. This fact has important management implications. There is little value to worrying about encouraging use of resistant vegetation when use levels are high. Where use levels are low, however, selection of durable sites can be quite effective in minimizing impact.

The two other lines on the graph show vegetation cover on each type after the winter, about nine months after trampling stopped. These data provide some idea about the ability of these vegetation types to recover from trampling. Type 1 recovered well; places that had been trampled 800 times recovered from less than 10 percent cover (after trampling) to over 50 percent cover over the winter. Although the aboveground cover of forbs was destroyed by trampling, the forbs were able to reproduce or initiate new growth from buds. Recovery was also improved by the abundant moisture in this vegetation type. The high resilience of type 1 is in marked contrast to the low resilience of type 2. Cover in type 2

Figure 3. Grasslands tend to be particularly resistant to damage from trampling. (*Photo:* M. E. Petersen.)

actually decreased slightly over winter. Stems and branches of the shrubs apparently were damaged during trampling but continued to provide cover until winter when they fell off. Very little regrowth or reproduction occurred over winter to offset this loss of cover.

The resistance of vegetation appears to be determined primarily by the growth form of the constituent species. Because growth form can be highly variable over short distances and within the same vegetation type, vegetation resistance can vary greatly over short distances. Resilience is also affected by growth form but is more dependent on environmental features such as soil fertility, length of the growing season, sunlight levels, and moisture levels. The importance of these factors will be discussed later in more detail.

The effect of amount of vegetation cover on durability is complex. Both sparsely and densely vegetated plant communities can be highly resistant; both can also be fragile. Perhaps the most important effect of vegetation cover is its ability to inhibit erosion. Vegetation acts to hold soil in place and reduce the erosive force of running water. Vegetation types that can retain a dense vegetation cover, despite being subjected to trampling, will resist damage from erosion more effectively than other types. Types with abundant graminoids and/or exotic, trampling-resistant species are particularly likely to retain a dense cover, as are highly resilient vegetation types.

The most significant aspect of vegetation structure is the effect of canopy closure on vegetation loss. As we have noted before, plants that grow in heavy shade tend to be more fragile than those that inhabit more open communities. This is well-illustrated in Table 1, which shows vegetation cover and loss on campsites in the Boundary Waters Canoe Area in relation to canopy cover. Mean cover is the mean vegetation cover on campsites. Absolute difference is an estimate of the vegetation loss that has occurred as a result of campsite use. It is obtained by calculating the difference in cover between campsites and neighboring undisturbed control sites. Both measures show much greater impact where tree cover exceeds 25 percent. Impact increases with each increase in tree cover; very little cover (only 3.5 percent) survives on the most shaded sites.

SOIL CHARACTERISTICS

Soil characteristics that have a pronounced effect on durability include soil texture, organic matter, moisture, fertility, and depth. The soil textures with the fewest limitations for campsites and trails are medium-

TABLE 1. Relationship Between Tree Canopy Cover and Vegetation Cover on Campsites in the Boundary Waters Canoe Area, Minnesota

	Vegetation Cover (%)	
Tree Cover (%)	Mean[a]	Absolute Difference[b]
0–25	52.4	−43.6
26–50	25.8	−60.7
51–75	14.9	−70.3
76–100	3.5	−77.1

Source: Marion 1984

[a] Means are for surviving vegetation cover on campsites.

[b] Absolute difference is the difference in cover between campsites and undisturbed control sites—an estimate of vegetation loss.

textured soils—sandy loams, fine sandy loams, and loams. Such soils usually have good drainage, are not highly erodible, and have a high potential for plant growth. Their major drawback is that their wide range of particle sizes makes them particularly susceptible to compaction. Coarse soils generally resist water and wind erosion because large particles are not easily moved by wind or water. However, structural instability makes coarse soils vulnerable to trail widening, and their low water holding capacity and cation exchange capacity (ability to hold cations that may be important nutrients) make them relatively impoverished environments for plant growth. Such drawbacks are likely to be more serious for trails than for campsites. In remote backcountry situations where use is low and dispersed, sandy soils may be particularly resistant sites for camping.

Coarse soils are clearly a better alternative than fine-textured soils. Silts and fine sands are highly erodible because soil particles are both readily detached and moved, the two requisites for erosion to occur. Moreover, silt is particularly prone to the formation of needle ice and to frost heaving, processes that increase erosion and make revegetation of bare areas difficult. Silt soils also become dusty when dry, making them undesirable trail locations. The permeability of clay is greatly reduced when compacted. This promotes increased runoff and erosion. Although clay particles resist detachment, they are readily moved by running water. Clays have a limited ability to support loads because they deform readily when wet. They also tend to be sticky when wet, and they dry slowly (Leeson 1979). All of these characteristics make clay soils particularly poor locations for recreational facilities.

The effect of stones and rocks on soil durability is variable. Leeson (1979) suggests, based on studies of trails in the Canadian Rockies, that it is advantageous for stones and rocks to comprise up to 25 percent of a soil's volume. They tend to inhibit severe compaction, and they increase the resistance of soil particles to being picked up by moving water. Above 25 percent, however, stones and rocks make footing difficult and construction and maintenance costly. Once stones are loose on the trail, they increase the turbulence of running water (increasing erosion) and erode the trail themselves when tumbled down the trail by water. Summer (1980) suggests not categorically removing all stones from trails because this sets up a never-ending cycle of deterioration. Removal of rocks leads to exposure and erosion of underlying fine particles which, once removed, expose more rocks at the surface.

Many of the most serious trail problems occur where soils are stone-free and homogeneous in texture. Such soils, which frequently occur in mountain meadows, are highly vulnerable to erosion. Deep and narrow, seasonally muddy trails force hikers and stock out of the rutted, muddy trail. New ruts develop alongside the old ones, quickly scarring scenic meadows with numerous parallel ruts (Fig. 4).

The advantages and disadvantages of organic matter are also complex, varying with amount and type of organic matter and with associated soil characteristics. Generally, organic matter is advantageous unless it is excessively abundant. Organic soils, those in which organic content exceeds 20 to 30 percent, tend to occur where drainage is or has been poor; they are particularly common at high elevations and latitudes where decomposition of organic matter is slow. Such soils have little ability to support heavy loads when they are wet. Recreational use of areas with organic soils rapidly creates wide, muddy quagmires. However, a thick organic horizon on top of mineral soil tends to shield the

Figure 4. Multiple trails are developing in this meadow. The main tread is deep, muddy, and wet, making it difficult to use. Hikers prefer to leave the tread, creating new parallel trails. (*Photo:* R. F. Washburne.)

mineral soil from compaction and inhibits runoff and erosion. Incorporated into the mineral soil, organic matter promotes good structural development, which enhances drainage, inhibits compaction, helps resist dispersion and detachment of particles, and promotes plant growth because of its tendency to increase water holding capacity and nutrient availability.

Soil moisture, as with most soil parameters, is most advantageous in moderate quantities, where it is sufficient to promote plant growth and recovery but not so abundant that it causes the problems common to poorly drained, wet soils. Soils with excessive moisture cannot bear loads without becoming muddy and greatly compacted. Moisture problems are most serious in fine-textured soils and are most likely to cause problems on trails. Such problems are particularly severe where stock use is heavy because of the great pressure stock exert on the soil. A majority of trail problems, other than erosion on steep slopes, result from locating trails in areas that are poorly drained or that have high water tables (Cole 1983).

Limited data suggest that the vegetation on moderately fertile soils is more resistant to impact than that on either highly fertile soils or infertile soils (Harrison 1981; Ripley 1962). There is insufficient data, however, to evaluate whether or not these results are generally applicable. Certainly the resilience of more fertile sites should be greater than that of sites poor in nutrients.

Finally, deep soils are often better suited to recreational use than shallow soils. This primarily reflects the high erodibility of very shallow soils and the vulnerability of vegetation established in pockets of thin soil. Another concern relates to the difficulty of disposing of human waste in environments where soils are shallow. On the other hand, some of the most resistant sites for low-use, dispersed backcountry camping are on bedrock, where the impacts of recreation use are likely to be minimal.

Table 2 summarizes, in very general terms, how soil properties influence site durability. As the preceding discussion suggests, there are exceptions to most of these generalizations. Still, they do provide some useful guidelines for locating facilities such as trails and campsites. The most serious and widespread problems occur where trails are located on soils with homogeneous textures (the usual problem is creation of a system of deeply-incised, braided trails in meadows) or locating any facility on wet mineral or organic soils (the usual problem is creation of a wide and muddy quagmire).

TABLE 2. Relationships Between Soil Characteristics and
Susceptibility to Impact

Soil Property	Level of Susceptibility		
	Low	Moderate	High
Texture	Medium	Coarse	Homogeneous; fine
Organic context	Moderate	Low	High
Soil moisture	Moderate	Low	High
Fertility	Moderate	High	Low
Soil depth	None	Deep	Shallow

TOPOGRAPHIC CHARACTERISTICS

Durability is often related to slope steepness and position, topography,
elevation, and aspect. Slope steepness and position are most important
in influencing impacts on trails and roads or in places where cross-
country travel occurs regularly. Generally, erosion potential increases
with slope. For example, Coleman (1981) studied the prevalence of erosion problems on trail segments of variable slope. On trails with a slope
no greater than 9 degrees, erosion problems were nonexistent; between
9 and 18 degrees erosion problems occurred, but most segments were
not eroding; above 18 degrees most trails were eroding (Fig. 5). She also
found that both trail width and depth increased as slope of the trail
increased. The increase in trail depth with slope reflects greater erosion
caused by the increased velocity of water running down steeper trails.
The increase in width may result from either people walking on the
sides of deeply eroded, steep trails to get better footing or the tendency
for people to spread out laterally when negotiating a steep slope. Bayfield (1973) found that more damage occurs on newly-opened trails
when hikers walk down rather than up a steep slope.

Where steep slopes cannot be avoided, problems can frequently be
averted by putting in water drainage devices such as water bars (see
Chapter 12). Problems also occur on trail segments where there is no
slope at all. Trail segments without any slope drain poorly. Poor drainage leads to the development of muddy quagmires that expand in width
as hikers and stock try to skirt the mud. Campsites with poor drainage
are undesirable when wet. Campers who do use such areas often end up
excavating trenches around their tents when rainfall is intense. Such

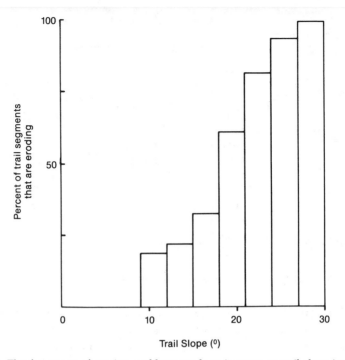

Figure 5. The frequency of erosion problems tends to increase as trail slope increases. Data are from footpaths in the Lake District of England. (*Source:* Adapted from Coleman, R. "Footpath Erosion in the English Lake District," in *Applied Geography.* Copyright © 1981. Used with permission of the publisher.)

impact could be avoided by locating sites where there is some slope and drainage.

Trails and roads located high on slopes have smaller watersheds from which they collect water than those located close to the base of slopes. This smaller watershed reduces erosion potential. Locations close to the base of slopes can also have problems with excessive moisture because springs may be intercepted by roads or trails cut into the slope.

Variable results are available concerning the effect of elevation on site durability. In the Great Smoky Mountains National Park, Bratton, Hickler, and Graves (1978, 1979) report that both trail and campsite deterioration increase with elevation. Higher rainfall and thinner soils occur at the higher elevations, contributing to more pronounced erosion and other soil impacts. Deterioration problems are also reported to be more severe at high elevations in the northeastern United States (Fay, Rice, and Berg 1977). In the Sierra Nevada in California, campsite alteration was greater at both high and low elevations than at moderate elevations (Dykema 1971).

The complexity of factors influencing environmental tolerance makes it unlikely for a variable like elevation to relate strongly to durability. Perhaps the most important effect of increasing elevation is a decrease in length of the growing season. This, along with locally variable factors such as frequent high winds and needle ice, often make resilience low at high elevations. Depending on the growth forms present, high elevation vegetation can be either resistant or fragile; however, because of the short growing season it will always recover slowly from what damage occurs. In desert regions, higher elevations receive more precipitation, which is likely to increase resilience. If the increase in resilience because of higher moisture levels compensates for the decreases in resilience related to a shorter growing season, then even resilience will increase with elevation.

Within a local area it may be possible to identify a relationship between the incidence of impact problems and elevation. This is what Bratton and her colleagues did for trails and campsites in the Great Smoky Mountains. However, such relationships are unlikely to be broadly applicable. Moreover, the effect of elevation on resistance may be different from its effect on resilience. Effects are also likely to differ between vegetation, soil, wildlife, and water and between types of facilities and activities. Guidelines relating elevation to durability, while useful, should be used cautiously.

The same is true for aspect. North-facing aspects may be more durable in one place and more fragile in another. One of the most common aspect-related problems occurs high in the mountains, where late snowmelt on north-facing aspects keeps soils water-saturated. Trails through water saturated soils become wide, muddy quagmires. They are also eroded by meltwater, channeled down the entrenched trail. Under droughty, low elevation conditions, however, north-facing aspects may be particularly resilient because of higher moisture levels that promote plant growth. In Iowa, Dawson, Hinz, and Gordon (1974) found that trails on north-facing slopes were less compacted and had lost less ground cover than trails on floodplains or south-facing slopes. As with elevation, such generalizations can be useful within localized areas, but they have little general utility.

ECOSYSTEM CHARACTERISTICS

Some researchers have proposed that vegetation durability increases with increases in an ecosystem's primary productivity (Liddle 1975) and is greater in more advanced successional stages (Goldsmith 1974). Primary productivity refers to the quantity of organic matter produced by plants through photosynthesis. It is dependent on many factors, from broad climatic characteristics such as temperature and rainfall, to soil characteristics such as nutrient availability. Liddle felt that productivity summarized, in one measure, potential for regrowth as well as the general ability of the environment to support growth. Resilience probably is strongly related to productivity. Resistance is not, however. For example, desert shrubs are resistant, despite their not being highly productive. A moisture rich, temperate forest is productive, but the vegetation is quickly eliminated by trampling. As we have seen before, resilience is related to general environmental factors, but vegetation resistance is dependent primarily on the growth forms of constituent species.

Communities and ecosystems change with time. Succession is the relatively orderly change from young, simple ecosystems to more diverse and specialized older ecosystems. The more advanced stages of succession may be more resilient because their higher productivity, diversity, and higher degree of specialization promote more rapid recovery following damage. However, resistance is not so clearly related to successional stage. Some early successional stages such as grassy fields and dry meadows are much more resistant than the later forested stage of succession. Again, growth form probably has more influence on vegetation resistance than successional stage, while individual soil characteristics such as texture have more influence on soil resistance.

There is no doubt that environmental factors profoundly influence amount of impact. The problem is that so many of the relationships between environment and impact are highly site specific. Relationships that apply in one place may not apply in another. In this chapter we have described some of the factors that are likely to influence durability. Ultimately, each area will have to develop its own guidelines for where to develop facilities. A good example is provided in Table 3. These guidelines specify likely problems in different vegetation types in the mountains of New England. They were developed over the years by observing where certain problems generally occur. They are useful in New England although they may not apply elsewhere.

TABLE 3. Vegetation Type and Plant Tolerance to Dispersed Recreation
Impacts in New England Mountains

Vegetation	Conditions to which Vegetation is Intolerant
Alpine plants	Trampling easily destroys these fragile plants. Due to the short growing season and other harsh conditions, alpine plants are very slow to regenerate.
Subalpine bog plants; sphagnum moss, sedges, dwarfed heath shrubs	Roots of bog plants are easily crushed by foot traffic though some species are adapted to colonizing disturbed denuded soils.
Krummholz	These trees are very slow growing. Clearing for tentsites rapidly destroys the krummholz and exposes them to wind damage.
Spruce-fir forests	Susceptible to windthrow where large openings have been cut. Compaction of soil around roots reduces tree vigor by reducing water and air infiltration and increasing their susceptibility to disease. Basal wounds make trees susceptible to fungal infections.
Mixed beech, sugar maple, birch forest	Can sustain a moderate amount of soil compaction and bark wounding.
Red maple trees	Can sustain a moderate amount of soil compaction and bark wounding.
Pure yellow or paper birch stands	Trees subject to bark peeling and cutting for firewood. This becomes visually unaesthetic and also reduces the vigor of the trees by increasing their susceptibility to disease. Openings cut in stands cause trees near opening edges to be subject to wind damage and dieback.
Pines, oaks, rhododendrons	Moderately durable vegetation.
Alders, willows	Moderately durable vegetation, though sites are generally unattractive to camping due to moist conditions.

Source: Adapted from Leonard, Spencer and Plumley, 1981. Copyright © 1981 by Appalachian Mountain Club, used with permission of publisher.

WILDLIFE IMPACTS

Much was said about the vulnerability of different wildlife species in
Chapter 4. For a given species, susceptibility also varies among different
environments. Unfortunately, very little work has been done on this

subject. Therefore, all we will be able to do here is present some relatively simple principles. Vulnerability to disturbance is usually greatest at certain key locations, particularly breeding areas, feeding areas, and watering holes. Disturbance of nesting birds has caused adults to fly off, leaving eggs and hatchlings open to predation (Hunt 1972). Severe or prolonged disturbance can lead to nest abandonment. Prolonged disturbance of animals in prime feeding and watering areas can force them to use poor habitat. In one study deer displaced to poor habitat had lower reproductive rates and less body fat. Moreover, they did not return to the better habitat even after disturbance had stopped (Batcheler 1968). Such disturbances can be particularly damaging to wildlife populations during periods of harsh weather or during unproductive years. Generally, sensitive environments are those key locations where the consequences of disturbance, flight, or displacement are particularly detrimental. Exactly which environments these are will vary between species, but certain habitats such as riparian areas are almost always critical for many species.

WATER IMPACTS

As was the case with wildlife impacts, there is little research on the susceptibility of different aquatic environments to recreation-related water impacts. Obviously, recreational activities undertaken in or near water have more potential for causing water pollution than those occurring far from water. On-land recreational activities are also more likely to adversely alter water quality where soils are highly erodible. For example, building roads and trails through areas of highly erosive material can greatly increase water turbidity, a change with negative effects on aquatic flora and fauna.

Water bodies themselves also differ in their ability to tolerate impact. Those that are frequently flushed out by large quantities of water or that have chemical properties that can buffer pollutants are less vulnerable to impacts than those without these properties. Lakes at high elevations commonly have low temperatures, few nutrients, and low levels of productivity. They often are in pristine areas where baseline disturbance levels are low. Recreational use on or around such lakes can cause pronounced deviations in biological, chemical, and physical properties from those found under baseline conditions. Lakes and streams at lower elevations tend to be more productive and less vulnerable to alteration than alpine lakes.

SEASON OF USE

The durability of the environment varies substantially between seasons. Vegetation and soil, for example, are protected from impact, to a great extent, when there is a thick blanket of winter snow. They may be particularly vulnerable in spring, however, when soils are saturated with snowmelt or spring rains. Young, tender herbaceous plants are particularly susceptible to trampling in the spring, causing early season loss of photosynthetic tissues, which means that plants must go an entire season without adding to their food reserves.

Season of use is particularly influential in determining the vulnerability of certain wildlife species and of water quality. Recreational activities can be highly disturbing to animals during the breeding season, while the same activity in the same place can have little effect the rest of the year. Animals are also vulnerable to disturbance during times of the year when they are weak. A number of animals, including deer, adapt to severe winter conditions by decreasing their level of activity and, thereby, conserving their energy. If encounters with recreationists cause them to flee, this strategy is undermined. Increased activity requires more food; if sufficient food is not available, it can lead to reduced vigor and reproductive capacity or even death. Harassment of wildlife species during winter months, when they are under physiological stress, is one of the most serious impact problems associated with snow recreation on skis or snowmobiles. Although winter is the season when the vulnerability of soil and vegetation is generally lowest, it is the season when wildlife vulnerability is often highest (Fig. 6).

Water is particularly sensitive to disturbance during the season when snowmelt keeps soils saturated with water. Vehicular travel on roads during this period can cause serious erosion because vehicles churn up the soil to the point where it can be easily moved by running water. Serious erosion of roads increases road maintenance costs; it also increases siltation of streams. This can have numerous adverse impacts, particularly on types of fish such as trout, that are sensitive to stream turbidity.

Other situations where vulnerability varies greatly between seasons are erosion of trails and trampling damage to meadows used by recreational packstock. In both cases, problems are most severe during the spring when snowmelt and spring rains keep soils saturated. The trail erosion problems are similar to the road erosion problems caused by motorized use. Wet soils are easily broken up, making them sensitive to

Figure 6. Wildlife disturbance can be particularly detrimental during winter when movement requires large amounts of energy and when animals have little energy to spare. (*Photo:* R. C. Lucas.)

movement where snowmelt is channeled down the trail. Trail use, particularly by stock, should be discouraged during snowmelt. Drainage devices, to divert water off the tread, are also important if severe erosion is to be avoided.

Meadow soil and vegetation can be rapidly disturbed when trampled during spring when soils are wet. Wet soils are more prone to compaction and more readily churned. This breaks up the meadow sod into a honeycombed topography, leading to both an increase in erosion and a lowering of the water table. In Sequoia and Kings Canyon National Parks, meadows dried out as water tables dropped, and this permitted trees to invade and replace meadows (DeBenedetti and Parsons 1979).

Vegetational tolerance varies between seasons, but differences are usually not very pronounced. Resistance of plants to trampling damage is often low during early spring when many herbs are succulent and during late season when plant parts are dry and brittle. However, resilience may be reduced more dramatically by trampling early in the season when perennial plants are still utilizing carbohydrate reserves for

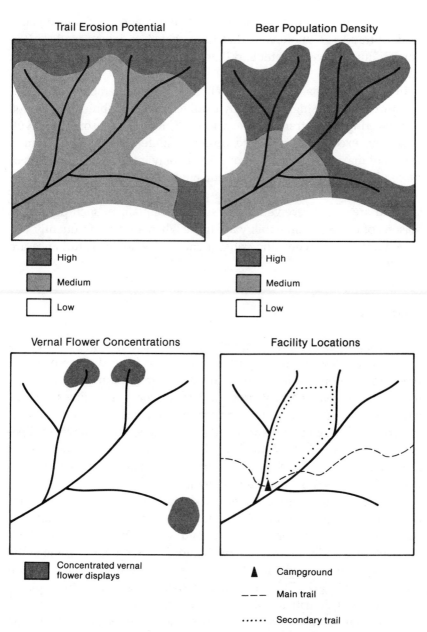

Figure 7. Maps of environmental factors that influence the placement of trails and camp-sites in Great Smoky Mountains National Park. (*Source:* Modified from Bratton 1977.)

growth and before annual plants have had a chance to produce viable seeds. Strand (1979) showed that the vegetation damage inflicted by horse trampling was greater and lasted longer in a wet meadow than in a dry meadow.

In the mountains, spring is usually the most vulnerable season; soil moisture levels are high and many wildlife species are breeding, as well as recovering their strength after winter. Winter is a season of low vulnerability, except for impact to certain wildlife species. The summer season of maximum recreation use is generally intermediate in terms of susceptibility to impact. These general guidelines break down, however, when applied to coastal areas, deserts, areas that do not receive snowfall, and areas that receive intense summer rainfall. In such places the seasons of highest vulnerability are those when soils are frequently water saturated and when the consequences of wildlife disturbance are particularly severe.

SUMMARY

The list of properties that either enhance or detract from site durability is long. Only a few of the important ones have been discussed in the preceding section. Understanding differences in site durability is critical to any impact management program because locating facilities and encouraging use of durable sites is an important means of limiting impact. Patterns of differential tolerance are highly site specific, however. Specific guidelines on site durability will have to be developed for each individual recreation area (although much information can be borrowed from other areas in similar environments).

Another technique that is useful in deciding where to build facilities or encourage use is to map locations that are particularly sensitive. A series of overlays of sensitive areas and attractions can identify both desirable and undesirable locations. Figure 7 shows maps of some of the factors to be considered when locating campsites in Great Smoky Mountains National Park. The campground was located away from places with high bear densities and flower concentrations, but close to water. The main trail stayed in areas with low erosion potential, except where it descended to the campground. Secondary trails were built up to the areas of flower concentrations but attempted to avoid areas where erosion potential was high.

REFERENCES

Batcheler, C. L. 1968. Compensatory Responses of Artificially Controlled Mammal Populations. *New Zealand Ecological Society Proceedings* 15:25–30.

Bayfield, N. G. 1973. Use and Deterioration of Some Scottish Hill Paths. *Journal of Applied Ecology* 10:635–644.

Bratton, S. P. 1977. Visitor Management. Unpublished report. Uplands Field Research Laboratory, Great Smoky Mountains National Park, Gatlinburg, TN. 22 pp.

Bratton, S. P., M. G. Hickler, and J. H. Graves. 1979. Trail Erosion Patterns in Great Smokey Mountains National Park. *Environmental Management* 3:431–445.

Cole, D. N. 1983. Assessing and Monitoring Backcountry Trail Conditions. USDA Forest Service Research Paper INT-303. 10 pp.

Cole, D. N. 1985. Recreational Trampling Effects on Six Habitat Types in Western Montana. USDA Forest Service Research Paper INT-350. 43 pp.

Coleman, R. 1981. Footpath Erosion in the English Lake District. *Applied Geography* 1:121–131.

Dawson, J. O., P. N. Hinz, and J. C. Gordon. 1974. Hiking Trail Impact on Iowa Stream Valley Forest Preserves. *Iowa State Journal of Research* 48:329–337.

DeBenedetti, S. H., and D. J. Parsons. 1979. Mountain Meadow Management and Research in Sequoia and Kings Canyon National Parks: A Review and Update. In R. M. Linn, ed., *Proceedings of Conference on Scientific Research in the National Parks*, pp. 1305–1311. USDI National Park Service Transactions and Proceedings Ser. 5; Washington, DC: U.S. Government Printing Office.

Dykema, J. A. 1971. Ecological Impact of Camping upon the Southern Sierra Nevada. PhD dissertation, University of California, Los Angeles. 156 pp.

Fay, S. C., S. K. Rice, and S. P. Berg. 1977. Guidelines for Design and Location of Overnight Backcountry Facilities. Unpublished report. USDA Forest Service, Northeast Forest Experiment Station, Broomall, PA. 23 pp.

Goldsmith, F. B. 1974. Ecological Effects of Visitors in the Countryside. In A. Warren and F. B. Goldsmith, eds., *Conservation Practice*, pp. 217–232. London: Wiley.

Harrison, C. 1981. Recovery of Lowland Grassland and Heathland in Southern England from Disturbance by Seasonal Trampling. *Biological Conservation* 19:119–130.

Holmes, D. O., and H. E. M. Dobson. 1976. Ecological Carrying Capacity Research in Yosemite National Park. Part I. The Effects of Human Trampling and Urine on Subalpine Vegetation, a Survey of Past and Present Backcountry Use, and the Ecological Carrying Capacity of Wilderness. U.S. Dept. of Commerce, National Technical Information Center PB-270-955. 247 pp.

Hunt, Jr., G. L. 1972. Influence of Food Distribution and Human Disturbance on the Reproductive Success of Herring Gulls. *Ecology* 53:1051–1061.

Leeson, B. F. 1979. Research on Wildland Recreation Impact in the Canadian Rockies. In R. Ittner, D. R. Potter, J. K. Agee, and S. Anschell, eds. *Proceedings, Recreational Impact on Wildlands*, pp. 64–65. USDA Forest Service, Pacific Northwest Region, R-6-001-1979, Portland, OR.

Leonard, R. E., E. L. Spencer, and H. J. Plumley. 1981. *Backcountry Facilities: Design and Maintenance*. Boston: Appalachian Mountain Club. 214 pp.

Liddle, M. J. 1975. A Theoretical Relationship Between the Primary Productivity of Vegetation and Its Ability to Tolerate Trampling. *Biological Conservation* 8:251–255.

Marion, J. L. 1984. Ecological Changes Resulting from Recreational Use: A Study of Backcountry Campsites in the Boundary Waters Canoe Area, Minnesota. PhD dissertation, University of Minnesota, St. Paul. 279 pp.

Moen, A. N. 1976. Energy Conservation by White-Tailed Deer in the Winter. *Ecology* 57:192–198.

Ripley, T. H. 1962. Recreation Impact on Southern Appalachian Campgrounds and Picnic Sites. USDA Forest Service Research Paper SE-153. 20 pp.

Strand, S. 1979. The Impact of Pack Stock on Wilderness Meadows in Sequoia-Kings Canyon National Park. In J. T. Stanley, Jr., H. T. Harvey, and R. J. Hartesveldt eds. *A Report on the Wilderness Impact Study*, pp. 77–87. Sierra Club Outing Committee, San Francisco, CA.

Summer, T. M. 1980. Impact of Horse Traffic on Trails in Rocky Mountain National Park. *Journal of Soil and Water Conservation* 35:85–87.

8 Visitor Use

Many characteristics of visitor use influence the degree, type, and distribution of ecological impacts in wildland recreation areas. The amount of use an area receives obviously has some effect on impact patterns in the area. This fact spurred the interest in the concept of carrying capacity that was discussed in Chapter 1. Beyond the amount of use an area receives, impacts are strongly influenced by other use characteristics— who the users are, where they go, and what they do. In wilderness, for example, Hendee, Stankey, and Lucas (1978) suggest ranking various groups in the following order of decreasing environmental impact:

1. Large parties of horse users
2. Small parties of horse users
3. Large parties of overnight campers
4. Small parties of overnight campers using wood fires
5. Large parties of day hikers
6. Small parties of overnight campers using campstoves and not building wood fires
7. Small parties of day hikers

From this it is clear that the potential to cause impact varies with party size (large vs. small), type of user (overnight campers vs. day hikers), behavior (using wood fires vs. campstoves), and mode of travel (horse users vs. hikers). The potential to cause impact also varies with where users go—use distribution—and various characteristics that can influence behavior, specifically knowledge of low-impact camping techniques, motivations, experience level, and social groups and structure. For example, impacts such as human litter, harassment of wildlife, and pollution of water sources are inappropriate or illegal behaviors that have a serious impact on recreational resources and experiences. In most situations a variety of visitor use and behavioral variables must be examined to accurately determine the consequences of recreational use on wildland park resources. In this chapter we will discuss these user characteristics.

AMOUNT OF USE

Conventional wisdom has often held that amount of use is the most important factor influencing amount of impact. Such thinking has been supported by describing the cause of impact with terms like "overuse" and proposing that solutions can be found by prescribing a "carrying capacity." Research shows such thinking to be oversimplified at best and erroneous at worst. The importance of amount of use varies between environments, between activities, with impact parameter, and with the range of use levels being examined. In addition, effects differ depending on whether concern is with rate, intensity, or areal extent of change.

Research on the relationship between use and impact began in the early 1960s with Frissell and Duncan's (1965) cross-sectional analysis of Boundary Waters Canoe Area campsites and Wagar's (1964) experimental trampling study. Both studies examined the effect of various use levels on amount of vegetation cover. Frissell and Duncan found that the most lightly used campsites (with use estimated at 0 to 30 nights/year) had lost 80 percent of their inferred original cover while heavily used sites (60 to 90 nights/year) had lost 87 percent. Impact increases as use increases, but lightly used sites are almost as highly impacted as heavily used sites. This asymptotic curvilinear relationship between amount of use and loss of vegetation has only been seriously contradicted by one of six similar studies in wilderness, five on developed campsites, and about 30 experimental trampling studies (Fig. 1).

The asymptotic curvilinear relationship between amount of use and vegetation loss demonstrated by so many studies suggests a number of generalizations. First, at very low use levels, differences in amount of

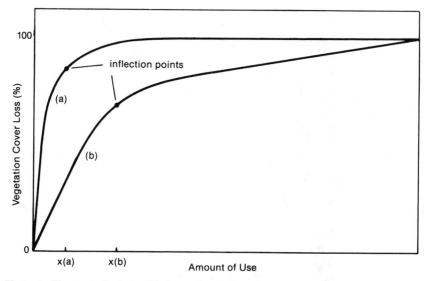

Figure 1. The general relationship between amount of use and loss of vegetation cover for (a) a fragile vegetation type and (b) a more resistant type. (*Source:* D. N. Cole.)

use are related to rapid changes in ground cover vegetation. Second, at higher use levels vegetation loss continues to gradually increase (toward a maximum possible limit of complete cover loss) as use increases, but differences in cover loss are seldom substantial, even when use levels of several orders of magnitude are compared. These two generalizations describe the curvilinear relationship between use and intensity of vegetation impact. Third, degree of curvilinearity increases as fragility increases. In fragile environments cover loss increases rapidly with increases in use at the very lowest use levels, and the inflection point, above which even substantial increases in use cause only minor increases in cover loss, comes at a low use level. In resistant environments cover loss increases more slowly with increasing use at the lowest use levels; the inflection point also comes at a higher use level. In Figure 2 differences in amount of use are likely to have a substantial effect on vegetation cover if at least one of the use levels is well below X(a) or X(b). Most studies have only examined sites with use levels beyond those that correspond to the inflection points on the curve; consequently, cover differences are not substantial.

The relevance of the relationship demonstrated in Fig. 1, particularly the location of the inflection points of the curves, is substantial to wildland recreation management. Attempting to minimize cover loss by

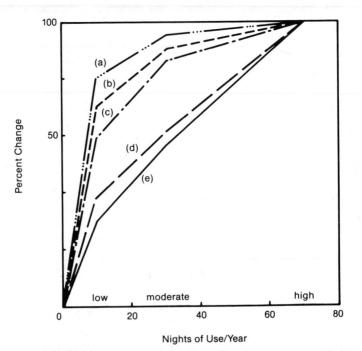

Figure 2. Relationship between amount of use and amount of impact in the Boundary Waters Canoe Area. (*Source:* Marion 1984). Numeric use levels are estimated from ordinal classes of low (0–12 nights/year), moderate (20–40 nights/year), and high (> 60 nights/year). Impact parameters are (*a*) tree damage, (*b*) loss of vegetation cover (*c*) increase in soil penetration resistance, (*d*) increase in exposed roots, mineral soil and rock, and (*e*) campsite area. Percent change is expressed as a percent of the change on high use sites.

keeping use levels low will only be effective where use levels can be kept substantially below the use thresholds that correspond to the inflection points. In several fragile subalpine forest vegetation types even use levels of no more than five nights/year exceeded threshold levels (Cole and Fichtler 1983). However, use thresholds are likely to be much higher on resistant vegetation types. For example, on developed campgrounds in the Atlantic Coastal Flatwoods region of South Carolina, Dunn, Lockaby, and Johnson (1980) found no significant loss of vegetation cover except on heavy use sites. As in most other studies, lack of adequate use measures makes it impossible to establish use thresholds for these South Carolina campsites. More research, employing better use estimates, and controlled experiments could enable us to establish use thresholds for important environments across the country.

Research does suggest a strong relationship between amount of use and the *rate* of vegetation loss. For example, in an experimental trampling study on alpine meadows in Mt. Ranier National Park, vegetation cover was reduced to 50 percent of control values in three weeks when trampled at 75 passes/week. At 18 passes/week, it took eight weeks of trampling for cover to be reduced to 50 percent of controls (Singer 1971). The areal extent of vegetation loss is also strongly related to amount of use (Bratton, Hickler, and Graves 1978; Cole 1982). The finding that most levels of increased use have little effect on amount of vegetation loss but a pronounced effect on area of loss suggests the value of concentrating and channeling use on a small proportion of any area (Cole 1981).

Many other impact parameters have been examined on campsites receiving different amounts of use. Those, like vegetation cover, for which a highly curvilinear relationship exists (Fig. 2), include bulk density, penetration resistance, macropore space, infiltration rate, changes in soil chemistry, loss of tree seedlings, and tree damage (Cole and Fichtler 1983; Dunn et al. 1980; Legg and Schneider 1977; Marion 1984; Young and Gilmore 1976). Loss of organic horizons, exposure of mineral soil, severe root exposure, and site enlargement are all changes related to use in a less curvilinear manner (Cole and Fichtler 1983; Coombs 1976; Marion 1984; Young 1978); there is more inherent resistance to these types of change, and use thresholds are higher. Changes in these parameters are easier to limit through manipulation of use intensities on campsites.

On trails, vegetation cover, bulk density, penetration resistance, and trail width relationships are highly curvilinear as they are on campsites (Crawford and Liddle 1977; Dale and Weaver 1974). Trail depth and the frequency of impact problems such as muddiness are generally not related to amount of use (Dale and Weaver 1974; Helgath 1975). Such situations relate more to location and design features although they obviously must be triggered by some use or construction.

In sum, these results suggest that there is little value, in terms of reduced impact, in limiting use of constructed trails. On campsites, limiting use is only likely to be effective if use levels can be kept very low. This is possible in some wildernesses but not in popular destination areas. In popular areas, channeling and concentrating use will have to be practiced to counteract the tendency for increased use to enlarge the areal extent of impact. Because the tipping point for each of these opposing strategies—dispersing use to keep levels low or concentrating use to minimize areal extent—varies greatly among environments, use thresholds need to be identified for major ecosystem types.

USE DISTRIBUTION

Visitors of wildland recreation areas often concentrate use in a few popular places, campsites, and trails. Such use behavior results in some zones of recreational areas being overused while other zones are seldom used. Because distribution of use is related to the distribution of resource impacts, use distribution is a major management concern for recreation resource managers. For example, if visitors are concentrating use on impact-resistant trails and campsites, management will want to encourage existing patterns of use. Also, use occurring on already heavily impacted sites does less damage than on new sites. However, in fragile areas or low use areas, management may want to disperse users from areas of concentrated use.

Numerous studies have documented the concentrated use patterns of wildland recreationists. In one of the most heavily used wildland areas, the Boundary Waters Canoe Area of Minnesota, nearly 70 percent of the use groups entered through only seven of the area's 70 entry points in 1974. Two entry points near population centers accounted for one-third of all user groups. Impacts are not only concentrated on these few entry points but also on the few portages and campsites near these entry points. In the Mission Mountains in Montana, over 90 percent of user groups entered at only two of the area's 19 trailheads (Lucas, Schreuder, and James 1971). When one considers that backcountry trips average only three to four days, there is little chance for these heavy concentrations of trailhead users to disperse. Visitor solitude and resource impacts are both concerns with these patterns of concentrated use.

Certain trails and lake routes within areas also show an uneven distribution of use. The Appalachian Trail within Great Smoky Mountains National Park (Tennessee-North Carolina) comprises only 12 percent of the Park's trail system yet receives 45 percent of the overnight use. In the Spanish Peaks Primitive Area (Montana) 10 percent of the trail system accounted for 50 percent of the trail miles hiked in 1970, and a third of the trail system accounted for three-fourths of trail use. Many other wildland recreation areas show similar patterns of concentrated trail use, particularly areas receiving large percentages of horse and day use. Both activities tend to concentrate use on main trails.

Although less concentrated than trails, campsites and scenic sites also show an uneven pattern of use. In the Desolation Wilderness (California) 50 percent of all use occurred on only 16 percent of the most popular campsites. Preferred sites for camping and hiking are often lake and stream edges, scenic overviews, and well-known physiographic attractions (i.e., peaks, gorges) of an area. Brown and Schomaker (1974) showed the most preferred and used campsites in the Spanish Peaks Primitive Area to have the following characteristics in common:

1. Proximity to both water and fishing opportunities
2. Scenic and lake views
3. Location within 700 ft of a trail
4. Availability of at least 500 ft^2 of level land
5. Availability of firewood within 300 ft

They found that about one-half of the campsites were within 50 ft of the shoreline of a lake or stream, almost two-thirds were within 100 ft, and 85 percent were within 200 ft. The shorelines of lakes and streams are considered to be particularly sensitive to ecological impacts although recent research by Cole (1982) suggests that lakeshore sites may have impacts little different from sites set back from lakeshores. In trampling experiments conducted in Waterton Lakes National Park (Canada), Nagy and Scotter (1974) found less vegetation change in a subalpine lakeshore meadow community than in the coniferous forests around the lake.

TYPE OF USER GROUP

Obviously, not all types of user groups produce the same type or amount of impacts. Certain types of users, because of length of stay, the activities they engage in, and the demands they place on wildland resources, cause more impacts than do other groups of users. Overnight campers produce more and different types of impacts than day hikers. Campers use wildland resources for a longer period of time, use a larger proportion of the resource (i.e., campsites), and use a greater diversity of the available resources (i.e., firewood, water). Because they stay over-night, they concentrate use on campsites, meaning that these nodes receive a proportionately larger amount of impact per person than do trails. Spatial patterns of impacts of overnight campers tend to be more nodal while those of day hikers are, for the most part, linkage-oriented.

In addition to length of stay, the type of activity the user group is engaged in influences environmental impacts. For example, canoe par-ties in the Boundary Waters Canoe Area and hunting parties in many of the Western wildland areas tend to be more destination-oriented and spend more time in camp than backpacking parties (Fig. 3). They also tend to carry more equipment and nonburnable materials, which serve as potential sources of litter, than hikers do into the backcountry. Many of these activities cause specific environmental impacts that are in addi-tion to those impacts directly related to backcountry camping. Campers fishing at alpine lakes often deposit fish entrails at the lake's edge and

Figure 3. Destination oriented use parties that spend several nights in the same camp (e.g., hunters) often manipulate the site, such as building campsite furniture. (*Photo:* D. N. Cole.)

cause more trampling impacts to the riparian zone of lakes than do nonfishing campers.

PARTY SIZE

Large parties of users are thought to cause greater impacts to certain aspects of the biophysical resource than smaller parties. Large parties are typically defined in wilderness areas as groups larger than 8 to 10 members. Although large parties tend to make up a small proportion of all parties visiting wildland recreation areas, they can contribute a disproportionate amount of certain environmental impacts. Expansion of campsite boundaries is a particular impact attributed to large groups. Large parties often expand campsites by clearing areas to facilitate additional tents, other equipment, eating space, and space for tying horses and storing canoes. Most backcountry campsites, like developed campsites, are designed for a capacity of one tent party per site. However, recreation parties often consist of more than one tenting subgroup. When multiple tenting parties want to camp together on a site, it is only natural that they expand the existing site or develop satellite sites adjacent to the boundaries of the existing site to facilitate their spatial needs.

Larger parties of users are also often associated with horseback, canoe, and vehicular modes of travel (Fig. 4). Both horses and vehicles, particularly when overnight use is involved, require additional space at campsite locations and lead to impacts beyond the specific campsite boundaries.

In addition to greater spatial needs of larger groups, they commonly exhibit behavioral use patterns that can lead to greater impacts. In the Boundary Waters Canoe Area large canoeing parties were found to characteristically stay longer, move camp more often, and penetrate farther into the backcountry than small parties (Lime 1972). This high mobility of larger groups suggests that they utilize more campsites and portages than small parties do and consequently have the potential for damaging more places. As pointed out by Lime (1972, p. 4):

Because more than half of the large parties kept moving, their impact on individual campsites was dispersed rather than concentrated. Staying in one location might be less damaging than using many sites, because the disturbance is increased by making and breaking camp several times.

Figure 4. Larger parties of users are often associated with horseback, canoe, and vehicular modes of travel. (*Photo:* R. C. Lucas.)

However, extended length of stay can often lead to greater amounts of impact to a given area.

Large parties are also capable of increasing the rate at which impacts occur. They concentrate a heavy amount of use in a short period of time on a site. Two nights of camping by a party of 30 individuals on a previously unused site in New York resulted in a 10 to 15 percent decrease in ground cover (Bogucki, Malanchuk, and Schenck 1975). The results of this study and others suggest that even a short-term use by large parties may severely alter the ground cover vegetation of fragile environments. Large parties are a particular problem in more pristine areas.

Large parties probably have no more resource impact on trails than many small parties as long as they remain on the trail tread. In the case of wildlife impacts, large parties may have less impact than several small parties if the frequency of disturbance is important, as is the situation with birdlife.

USER BEHAVIOR

In any setting the actions of individuals may be considered appropriate, inappropriate, and even illegal, depending on the normative behavior and conditions accepted for the situation and setting. In addition, these actions are determined by many behavioral factors. The motivating force behind one's actions, the group context within which an action is carried out, and one's education and past experience with a particular action all have an influence on whether the action will be conducted in an appropriate or inappropriate manner. In the case of resource impacts, all these factors affect the on-site behavior of recreationists, which in turn influences the appropriateness of their actions and the level of impacts that they can cause to wildland resources. Understanding the factors that determine user behavior and their relationship to resource impacts allows for management to modify the inappropriate actions of users and thus reduce resource impacts. Next, we will discuss these factors and their behavioral relationship to impacts.

Minimum Impact Knowledge

Many of the techniques involved in conducting wildland recreational activities can be performed in a number of ways that lead to differing levels of impact. As a result, most agencies involved with the management of wildland resources have informational programs aimed at educating users about how to reduce resource impacts (Fig. 5). Often, visitors are simply unaware of certain skills and techniques that result in minimum levels of resource disturbance. By educating visitors about wildland resources and their proper use, managers hope to create a minimum impact ethic that will eventually lead to a permanent behavioral change in visitors. Minimum impact camping techniques are a prerequisite if impacts are to be limited in wilderness areas where policy prohibits major site development practices.

Certain impacts can be greatly reduced or nearly eliminated through the practice of minimum impact techniques while other impacts are essentially inevitable if use occurs to any degree. The replacement of campfires with light-weight stoves, the nontrenching of tents, the packing out of all garbage, the proper disposal of human waste, and campsite landscaping on leaving a site can produce a backcountry campsite with the appearance of having been used minimally. Simply requiring

Figure 5. Minimum impact information, such as the proper use of lanterns in camp-grounds, is a useful management tool. (*Photo:* W. E. Hammitt.)

campstoves and educating users of proper firewood practices should eliminate some obvious campsite impacts. In the Eagle Cap Wilderness, Oregon, researchers observed that 95 percent of the overstory trees in campsites had been damaged by people collecting firewood and causing physical impacts to tree trunks (Cole and Benedict 1983). Particularly disturbing was the fact that over one-third of the trees had been cut down. Requiring the use of campstoves, along with a minimum impact education program, could modify inappropriate behavior of this nature among future users.

Experience Level

Experienced visitors, in terms of amount of on-site experience, have been found to be more sensitive to social impacts and to take more precautions to avoid social conflict situations (Heberlein and Dunwiddie 1979; Hendee et al. 1978; Vaske, Donnelly, and Heberlein 1980). The same should hold true for ecological impacts. While observing actual campsite selection behavior of wilderness users, Heberlein and Dunwiddie found that experienced visitors distinguished themselves from novices by selecting campsites that were (1) further from other visitors, (2) further from the nearest campsite, whether it was occupied or not, and (3) in an area with few other sites. It is usually the more experienced visitor that is displaced from crowded or heavily impacted areas. In a study of visitor perception of river environmental impacts, Hammitt and McDonald (1983) found that the more experienced users were, the more perceptive they were of river impacts and the more willing they were to support management controls aimed at correcting the problems. More experienced users often have an earlier "frame of reference" and set of norms of what an area "used to be like" and use this frame of reference when evaluating impacts.

Because experienced visitors are more aware and sensitive of social impacts, it follows that they are also likely to be more sensitive about causing ecological impacts to recreational resources. Certain forms of visitor behavior, such as littering, trenching around tents, hanging lanterns on trees, or camping in fragile meadows may not be considered inappropriate behavior by novice campers, yet experienced campers are likely to recognize the potential impacts caused by each of these actions.

User Motivation

The *reasons* why recreationists engage in certain activities or why they are motivated to visit certain recreational environments can influence the impacts they contribute to a recreational area. For example, the individual who is motivated to visit an area for solitude and a passive form of recreation is likely to produce fewer impacts than the individual who is motivated to visit by a desire to affiliate with others in a motorized form of recreation. Similarly, the person *attracted* to wildland areas to experience and observe nature is likely to produce fewer impacts than the individual who visits wildland areas as simply a means to *escape* the home and work environment. However, caution is necessary when speculating on the influence of user motivations on resources impacts, for little research has been conducted in this area, and visitor behavior is a complex phenomenon, seldom determined by one variable.

Considerable research has been conducted on user motivations from a psychological and visitor management perspective in outdoor recreation (Driver, 1976; Knopf 1983; Knopf, Driver, and Bassett 1973; McDonald and Hammitt 1983; Schreyer and Roggenbuck 1978). This research has demonstrated that (1) visitors engage in different activities for different reasons and in different ways, (2) visitors participate in the same activities for different reasons, and (3) they utilize recreational environments in different ways to achieve the experiences they desire. The information generated from these and similar studies has been quite useful in planning recreational areas and in managing visitors for the different recreational opportunities and experiences desired (Brown, Driver, and McConnell 1978; Driver and Brown 1978). However, all of the motivational studies have involved the experience outcomes desired by visitors, with little emphasis devoted to the influence of user motivations on the impacts to resource settings. Clark and Stankey (1979) have come as close as anyone in applying user motivations and resource settings to impacts through an application of the "recreation opportunity spectrum" concept. Others have suggested many vandalism-associated impacts are related to the moods and motivational forces underlying individual behavior while on site. For example, the need for excitement may lead to the chopping of trees while the need for skill development and achievement may lead to the building of furniture within backcountry campsites.

Application of user motivation in managing site impacts can be illustrated through use of campground data reported by Hendee and Campbell (1969). They found that many of the campers of developed campgrounds desired to camp with two or more other families or their extended family (e.g., grandparents) on the same campsite. Seven out of 10 campers preferring developed sites thought all campgrounds should have several units so two families could camp together. For these campers the desire to affiliate with another family is a major motive for their camping, and they require a double-sized site if resource impacts are to be restricted to the designed campsite and to a minimum. This same phenomenon applies to multi-unit backcountry groups that are motivated to share their backcountry experience with others on the same site.

Social Group and Structure

Almost all activities that occur in wildland recreation areas occur in the context of a group. Even in wilderness use where solitude is particularly important, we find that less than 2 percent participate alone. Most individuals participate as members of a family, friendship, mixed family and friendship, or organized group. The group in which one participates and the structure of members within the group are determinants of outdoor recreation behavior and can influence the amount and type of impacts occurring to the resource base.

As an example, two backcountry camping parties made up of eight members each, one consisting of two families and the other of early aged teenagers, would function as two distinctly different groups. Peer pressure and sanctions toward certain behaviors in the two groups of users would likely be different. Disposal of human waste, size of fires, and activities beyond the boundaries of the campsite impact zone are more likely to be a problem among the teenagers. Vandalism, which can greatly impact wildland resources, is particularly prominent among groups of pre- and young teenagers (Clark, Hendee, and Campbell 1971). Nonsupervised children are the headache of many campground managers, with many of their inappropriate actions leading to resource impacts.

In a study of innertube floaters of National Park Service and U.S. Forest Service rivers, we observed that organized groups of users (e.g., church, clubs) utilized the river resource in a gregarious fashion, necessitating more area use of resources than the resource base was physically capable of or designed to accommodate (Hammitt and McDonald 1981; McDonald and Hammitt 1981). Because organized and friendship groups often utilize resources differently than family groups, areas sensitive to impacts may need to be designed for these user groups or restricted from their use.

MODE OF TRAVEL

The means by which recreationists travel in wildland recreation areas also has an important effect on both ecological and sociological impacts. For example, the impacts associated with motorized travel are very different from those caused by horses which, in turn, are very different from those caused by recreationists on foot. Even for motorized travel, there are pronounced differences among those impacts caused by terrestrial off-road vehicles, snowmobiles, and motor boats. In Chapters 2 through 5 we described what is known about the impacts associated with these different modes of travel. Managers will need to understand differences between these modes of travel because an important management strategy is to restrict the means of travel. Wilderness areas by definition, with a few minor exceptions, prohibit all motorized recreational use. In other areas, certain modes of travel can be completely prohibited, prohibited in certain areas, allowed only in certain areas, or regulated in some other way. In this section we will compare impacts caused by common sets of travel modes a manager may face. These are (1) snowmobiles and skis, (2) motor boats and nonmotorized boats (e.g., rafts, canoes, row boats, and kayaks), and (3) off-road vehicles, stock, and recreationists on foot.

Snowmobiles/Skis

Impacts caused by travel over snow are different from those caused by travel on land. When snow depth is great, impacts on soil, vegetation, and water are minimal. When the snow is shallow, impacts on these ecosystem components can be as severe as when use occurs on snow-free ground. Generally, the most significant impacts are those associated with disturbance of wildlife. This has been described in some detail in Chapter 4.

Unfortunately, there is little research into differences in the disturbances caused by snowmobiles and skis. We can offer a few speculations, however. On roads and well-established trails, differences are probably not pronounced. The major difference is that snowmobiles can travel farther more easily. Therefore, more remote portions of an area are more likely to be affected frequently by snowmobiles than by skiers. Off roads and trails, differences become more pronounced. Because snowmobiles cover more ground in a shorter period of time, they can disturb more wildlife and compact snow over a larger area. Compaction of snow is particularly significant, since this can kill small mammals and destroy the subnivean layer, between snow and the ground, where many small mammals live. This may also have an effect on species that prey on small mammals such as owls, eagles, hawks, foxes, coyotes, and bobcats (Bury, Wendling, and McCool 1976). (Figs. 6 and 7).

Figure 6. Snowmobiles extend recreational impacts into the winter season, reaching remote areas that normally receive little recreational use during this time of the year. (*Photo:* R. C. Lucas.)

In general, then, snowmobiles have more potential to cause impact, particularly if they are not confined to established roads and trails. Differences between motorized and nonmotorized travel appear to be considerably less pronounced than for travel on land or over water, however. Differences in the impact each mode of travel has on the experience of other recreationists in the area may be more serious than differences in ecological impact.

Motor Boats/Nonmotorized Boats

Motor boats have more potential than nonmotorized boats for causing impact, primarily because they pollute water with fuel and oil. As described in Chapter 5, considerable quantities of oil and gasoline residue are discharged by outboard motors. This affects water quality and aquatic life. Nonmotorized craft obviously do not have such an effect. Nonmotorized craft are able to reach more remote parts of wildland areas, however. This can result in more pronounced impacts to remote

Figure 7. Tour and cross-country skiing are increasing in popularity as wildland recreation sports. (*Photo:* D. N. Cole.)

portions of recreation areas. For example, the use of rubber rafts to float people down the Grand Canyon and other remote desert canyons has greatly increased the amount of impact occurring in these areas.

In areas that are used primarily by nonmotorized craft, the most prominent impacts are usually along the banks of the lakes and streams in places where recreationists camp, picnic, fish, and take their boats in and out of the water. These impacts are little different from those caused by recreationists on foot. Impacts to water quality and aquatic life will usually be more serious in places where most use is by motor boats. There are exceptions to this generalization, of course. For example, groups traveling in motorized canoes in the Boundary Waters Canoe Area, Minnesota, or in motorized rafts through the Grand Canyon probably have more effect on land than on the waters.

Off-Road Vehicles/Stock/Foot Travel

For several reasons, the potential for off-road vehicles to cause substantial impact is particularly high (Webb and Wilshire 1983). Because distances can be covered rapidly, they are able to impact large areas on single trips. If the terrain is conducive to ORV travel, remote areas can be reached, even on day trips (Fig. 8). This is certainly the case in large dune and desert areas where remote places are likely to be inaccessible on foot or horseback. The forces that result from spinning wheels, in association with the effect of cleated tires, dislodge soil and vegetation particularly rapidly. This damage is compounded by the tendency for many ORV users to seek out steep, unstable slopes where erosion is easily triggered (Fig. 9). Other modes of travel tend to avoid steep and unstable slopes. Consequently, problems with erosion—one of the most significant of impacts because of its irreversibility and its tendency to get progressively worse even without continued use—are much more serious with ORVs than with nonmotorized use. Motorized recreational use can be damaging to water quality as well. Eroded soil, deposited in streams, increases sediment loads and turbidity; this can be particularly detrimental to certain fish species such as trout.

Horses, mules, and other types of recreational stock have less potential for causing erosion. The potential is still much higher than for foot travelers, however. Stock are much heavier than humans, and their

Figure 8. Trail bike use impacts both the wildland recreation resource and the experience of other user types. (*Photo:* D. N. Cole.)

Figure 9. Off-road vehicle impacts are compounded by the tendency of many ORV users to seek out steep, unstable slopes, where erosion is easily initiated. (*Photo:* D. N. Cole.)

weight is concentrated on a smaller surface area. Thus they exert much more pressure on the ground surface. Problems resulting from this high potential for trampling disturbance are compounded by the tendency for shod hooves to loosen the soil (McQuaid-Cook 1978), making it more susceptible to erosion. Thus equestrian trails are more prone to erosion and more likely to require hardening. In forests in the Rocky Mountains in Montana, Dale and Weaver (1974) found that trails used by horses and hikers were 2.5 times deeper than trails used only by hikers. Stock are also damaging to the banks of streams and lakeshores.

In an experimental study in Montana, Weaver and Dale (1978) examined the effects of horses, hikers, and a lightweight, slowly driven motorcycle. Trails produced by 1000 horse passes were two to three times as wide and 1.5 to seven times as deep as trails produced by 1000 hiker passes. Impacts caused by the motorcycle were intermediate in severity. Bulk density increased 1.5 to two times as rapidly on horse trails as on hiker trails. The effect of motorcycles, again, was usually intermediate in severity. Vegetation loss occurred much more rapidly on horse and motorcycle trails than on hiker trails. They also found that motorcycle damage was greatest when going uphill, while horse and hiker damage was greatest when going downhill. Thus they concluded that trail wear can be minimized if motorcycle trails ascend gentle slopes and descend steep slopes, while horse and hiker trails should ascend steep slopes and descend gentle slopes.

On campsites, differences between impacts caused by motorized users, stock parties, and hikers are pronounced. Ground cover disturbance and soil compaction are particularly severe where vehicles drive across campsites. More gear can be carried in vehicles, and this is also often translated into higher impact. Campfire impacts are often more pronounced; tree damage is more severe; lengths of stay are longer; and party sizes are larger, so campsites are larger and more highly developed.

Two studies have compared impacts on horse and hiker campsites—both in wilderness areas in Montana. In the Lee Metcalf Wilderness, campsites used by stock were 10 times as large and had seven times as much exposed mineral soil as sites used by backpackers. Cole (1983) found the same thing on sites in the Bob Marshall Wilderness. Stock sites were six times as large, with a bare area four times larger than backpacker sites. Stock sites had more than 10 times as many damaged trees, had been much more severely compacted, and had many more introduced plant species (Fig. 10).

The larger size of stock sites is primarily a result of the requirement for an area adjacent to the campsite to keep stock. The animals are frequently tied to trees, and this accounts for the more serious tree damage on stock camps (Fig. 11). Trees are also more likely to be cut down for tent poles, hitchrails, corrals, or firewood. The greater compaction is a result of the stock being heavier than humans, with their weight concentrated on a smaller surface area. Introduced plants are spread by seeds in horse manure or feed or by being stuck to the horses' bodies; this accounts for the greater amounts of these species on stock camps.

A further impact caused by stock results from their need to graze. Where this is allowed (where horses are not confined to corrals and only fed pelletized feed), grazing areas are trampled and plants are defoliated. This leads to further increases in the size of disturbed areas. In a portion of the Eagle Cap Wilderness, the area disturbed solely by stock amounted to three-fourths of the entire area disturbed by recreational use, although stock use accounted for only about 20 percent of the total

Figure 10. In the Bob Marshall Wilderness, Montana, campsites used by horse parties had more than 10 times as many damaged trees as sites used only by hikers. (*Photo:* D. N. Cole.)

use of the wilderness (Cole 1981). Grazed areas experience decreased vegetation cover, changes in vegetation composition, soil compaction, and in many cases accelerated erosion.

Horse manure is another unique impact associated with stock. This is a major source of exotic plant seeds. It can find its way into streams and pollute waters. Its major impact, however, is social, reflecting the objection of many hikers to its presence on trails and campsites. In many areas, horseback use is separated from hiking use, on different trails, to avoid problems of conflict between stock and hiking parties.

Because foot travel is the most common mode of travel, its impacts are particularly pronounced and widespread. In addition, wildlife are often more readily disturbed by hikers than by motor vehicles (MacArthur, Geist, and Johnston 1982). Hikers are more unpredictable, more likely to approach animals, and may be considered more of a threat by animals. Hikers may also be somewhat more disturbing to wildlife than recreationists on horseback, although this has not been studied. Impacts

Figure 11. Horses tied to trees are a major source of damage to tree trunks and root systems. (*Photo:* R. C. Lucas.)

on soil, vegetation, and water, however, are much less severe, per capita, for hikers than for other types of recreationists.

Several writers have postulated that the type of shoe recreationists wear has a great effect on amount of impact. The popularity of the lug-soled boot has been blamed repeatedly for reported increases in trail wear (Harlow 1977; Ketchledge and Leonard 1970; Zaslowsky 1981). Nobody has been able to demonstrate, under realistic conditions, that this is the case, however. Kuss (1983) found no significant differences between two types of hiking boot when comparing loss of organic matter and soil from experimentally trampled trails. There were no significant differences in amount of loss after either 600 or 2400 passes, although both boot types caused significant disruption of the soil surface. This study substantiated the results of earlier studies by Whittaker (1978) and Saunders, Howard, and Stanley-Saunders (1980). Neither of these studies found significant differences in impact related to type of footwear.

All footgear, regardless of type, will cause substantial impact to vegetation and soils. Heavily worn trails are common in nature areas and urban parks where lug-soled boots are uncommon. More research may still uncover important differences under circumstances that have not yet been studied. For now, however, there appears to be little gained by asking hikers to wear any particular type of boot.

SUMMARY

1. Recreational resource impacts are determined as much by visitor use as by the durability of the resource site. For example, impacts vary with party size (large vs. small groups), type of user (overnight campers vs. day hikers), user behavior (using wood fires vs. campstoves), and mode of travel (horse users vs. hikers). The potential to cause impact also varies with where users go. Various user characteristics that can influence behavior are knowledge of low impact techniques, motivations, experience level, and social groups and structure.

2. The amount of use is not directly related to the amount of impact. Amount of use varies among environments, between activities, with impact parameter, and with range of use levels being examined. Effects also differ depending on whether concern is with rate, intensity, or areal extent of resource change.

3. Dispersal of concentrated campers in wildland areas is not always a good management practice. For example, if visitors are concentrating use on impact resistant trails and campsites or on very popular and already heavily impacted sites, management will want to encourage existing patterns of use. However, in fragile areas of low use areas, management may want to disperse users from areas of concentrated use.

4. Certain types of users because of length of stay, activities they engage in, and the demands they place on wildland resources, cause more impacts than do other groups of users. Horseback parties typically tend to be large, require additional space for horses at campsite locations, and lead to impacts beyond the specific campsite boundaries.

5. The motivating force behind one's recreation, the group context within which behavioral acts are carried out, and one's education and past experience with a particular activity all have an influence on whether wildland recreation is conducted in an appropriate manner that leads to minimal levels of resource impact.

6. Different modes of travel in wildland areas cause different types and levels of impact. Off road vehicles can travel a much farther distance than hikers, and cause large areal impact in a short period of time. Snowmobile impacts can greatly compact snow and influence the wildlife/soil environment under it. Horse trails and campsites have been shown to be 10 times as impacted as sites used by only backpackers.

REFERENCES

Bogucki, D. J., J. L. Malanchuk, and T. E. Schenck. 1975. Impact of Short-term Camping on Ground-level Vegetation. *Journal of Soil and Water Conservation* 30:231–232.

Bratton, S. P., M. G. Hickler, and J. H. Graves. 1978. Visitor Impact on Backcountry Campsites in the Great Smoky Mountains. *Environmental Management* 2(5):431–442.

Brown, P. J., and J. H. Schomaker. 1974. Final Report on Criteria for Potential Wilderness Campsites. Institute for Study of Outdoor Recreation and Tourism, Utah State University, Logan, UT. Supplement No. 32. 50 pp.

Brown, P. J., B. L. Driver, and C. McConnell. 1978. The Opportunity Spectrum Concept and Behavioral Information in Outdoor Recreation Resources Supply Inventories: Background and Application. In *Integrated Inventories of Renewable Natural Resources: Proceedings of the Workshop.* USDA Forest Service General Technical Report RM-55.

Bury, R. L., R. C. Wendling, and S. F. McCool. 1976. Off-road Recreation Vehicles—A Research Summary, 1969–1975. Texas Agricultural Experiment Station Publication MP-1277. 84 pp.

Clark, R. N., and G. H. Stankey. 1979. Determining the Acceptability of Recreational Impacts: An Application of the Outdoor Recreation Opportunity Spectrum. In R. Ittner, D. R. Potter, J. Agee, and S. Anschell, eds., *Recreational Impacts on Wildlands.* USDA Forest Service Conference Proceedings, No. R-6-001-1979.

Clark, R. N., J. C. Hendee, and F. L. Campbell. 1971. Depreciative Behavior in Forest Campgrounds: An Exploratory Study. USDA Forest Service Research Note PNW-161. 12 pp.

Cole, D. N. 1981. Vegetational Changes Associated with Recreational Use and Fire Suppression in the Eagle Cap Wilderness, Oregon: Some Management Implications. *Biological Conservation* 20:247–270.

Cole, D. N. 1982. Wilderness Campsite Impacts: Effect of Amount of Use. USDA Forest Service Research Paper INT-284. 34 pp.

Cole, D. N., and J. Benedict. 1983. Coverups—How to Pick a Campsite You Can Leave Without a Trace. *Backpacker* 11(5):40, 44, 87.

Cole, D. N. 1983. Campsite Conditions in the Bob Marshall Wilderness, Montana. USDA Forest Service Research Paper INT-312. 18 pp.

Cole, D. N., and R. K. Fichtler. 1983. Campsite Impact on Three Western Wilderness Areas. *Environmental Management* 7(3):275–288.

Coombs, E. A. K. 1976. The Impacts of Camping on Vegetation in the Bighorn Crags, Idaho Primitive Area. MS Thesis, University of Idaho, Moscow. 64 pp.

Crawford, A. K., and M. J. Liddle. 1977. The Effect of Trampling on Neutral Grassland. *Biological Conservation* 12:135–142.

Dale, D., and T. Weaver. 1974. Trampling Effects on Vegetation of the Trail Corridors of North Rocky Mountain Forests. *Journal of Applied Ecology* 11:767–772.

Driver, B. L. 1976. Quantification of Outdoor Recreationists' Preferences. USDA Forest Service Mimeograph Paper, Rocky Mountain Forest and Range Experiment Station, Ft. Collins, CO. 22 pp.

Driver, B. L., and P. J. Brown. 1978. The Opportunity Spectrum Concept and Behavioral Information in Outdoor Recreation Resource Supply Inventories: A Rationale. In *Integrating Inventories of Renewable Natural Resources: Proceedings of the Workshop.* USDA Forest Service General Technical Report RM-55. pp. 24–37.

Dunn, A. B., B. G. Lockaby, and E. E. Johnson. 1980. Camping and Its Relationship to Forest Soil and Vegetation Properties in South Carolina. Department of Forestry, Forest Research Series No. 34, Clemson University, Clemson, SC. 20 pp.

Frissell, Jr., S. S., and D. P. Duncan. 1965. Campsite Preference and Deterioration in the Quetico-Superior Canoe Country. *Journal of Forestry* 63:256–260.

Hammitt, W. E., and C. D. McDonald. 1981. Use Patterns and Impacts of Innertube Floating on a Mountain Stream. *Southern Journal of Applied Forestry* 5(3):119–124.

Hammitt, W. E., and C. D. McDonald. 1983. Past On-site Experience and Its Relationship to Managing River Recreation Resources. *Forest Science* 29(2):262–266.

Harlow, W. M. 1977. Stop Walking Away the Wilderness. *Backpacker* 5(4):33–36.

Heberlein, T. A., and P. Dunwiddie. 1979. Systematic Observation of Use Levels, Campsite Selection and Visitor Characteristics at a High Mountain Lake. *Journal of Leisure Research* 11(4):307–316.

Helgath, S. F. 1975. Trail Deterioration in the Selway-Bitterroot Wilderness. USDA Forest Service Research Note INT-193. 15 pp.

Hendee, J. C., and F. L. Campbell. 1969. Social Aspects of Outdoor Recreation—The Developed Campground. *Trends* (October):13–16.

Hendee, J. C., G. H. Stankey, and R. C. Lucas. 1978. Wilderness Management. USDA Forest Service Miscellaneous Publications No. 1365. 381 pp.

Ketchledge, E. H., and R. E. Leonard. 1970. The Impact of Man on the Adirondack High Country. *The Conservationist* 25(2):14–18.

Knopf, R. C. 1983. Recreational Needs and Behavior in Natural Settings. In I. Altman and J. Wohlwill, eds. *Behavior and the Natural Environment*. New York: Plenum, pp. 205–240.

Knopf, R. C., B. L. Driver, and J. R. Bassett. 1973. Motivations for Fishing. Transactions of the 38th North American Wildlife and Natural Resources Conference. Washington, DC. pp. 191–204.

Kuss, F. R. 1983. Hiking Boot Impacts on Woodland Trails. *Journal of Soil and Water Conservation* 38:119–121.

Legg, M. H., and G. Schneider. 1977. Soil Deterioration on Campsites: Northern Forest Types. *Soil Science Society American Journal* 41:437–441.

Lime, D. W. 1972. Large Groups in the Boundary Waters Canoe Area—Their Numbers, Characteristics, and Impacts. USDA Forest Service Research Note NC-142. 4 pp.

Lucas, R. C., H. T. Schreuder, and G. A. James. 1971. Wilderness Use Estimation: A Pilot Test of Sampling Procedures on the Mission Mountains Primitive Area. USDA Forest Service Research Paper INT-109. 44 pp.

MacArthur, R. A., V. Geist, and R. H. Johnston. 1982. Cardiac and Behavioral Responses of Mountain Sheep to Human Disturbance. *Journal of Wildlife Management* 46:351–358.

Marion, J. L. 1984. Ecological Changes Resulting from Recreational Use: A Study of Backcountry Campsites in the Boundary Waters Canoe Area Wilderness, Minnesota. PhD Dissertation, University of Minnesota, St. Paul. 279 pp.

McDonald, C. D., and W. E. Hammitt. 1981. Use Patterns, Preferences and Social Impacts of Floaters on River Resources in the Southern Appalachian Region. Final Report, USDA Forest Service, Southeastern Forest Experiment Station, Asheville, NC. 241 pp.

McDonald, C. D., and W. E. Hammitt. 1983. Managing River Environments for the Participation Motives of Stream Floaters. *Journal of Environmental Management* 16:369–377.

McQuaid-Cook, J. 1978. Effects of Hikers and Horses on Mountain Trails. *Journal of Environmental Management* 6:209–212.

Nagy, J. A. S., and G. W. Scotter. 1974. A Quantitative Assessment of the Effects of Human and Horse Trampling on Natural Areas, Waterton Lakes National Park. Unpublished Report, 145 pp. Canadian Wildlife Service, Edmonton, Alberta.

Saunders, P. R., G. E. Howard, and B. A. Stanley-Saunders. 1980. Effect of Different Boot Sole Configurations on Forest Soils. Department of Recreation and Park Administration, Extension/Research Paper RPA 1980-3, Clemson University, Clemson, SC. 11 pp.

Schreyer, R., and J. W. Roggenbuck. 1978. The Influence of Experience Expectations on Crowding Perceptions and Social-Psychological Carrying Capacity. *Leisure Sciences* 1(4):373–394.

Singer, S. W. 1971. Vegetation Response to Single and Repeated Walking

Stresses in an Alpine Ecosystem. MS Thesis. Rutgers University, New Brunswick, NJ. 69 pp.

Vaske, J. J., M. P. Donnelly, and T. A. Heberlein. 1980. Perceptions of Crowding and Resource Quality by Elderly and More Recent Visitors. *Leisure Sciences* 3(4):367–381.

Wagar, J. A. 1964. The Carrying Capacity of Wildlands for Recreation. *Forest Science Monograph*, No. 7. 23 pp.

Weaver, T., and D. Dale. 1978. Trampling Effects of Hikers, Motorcycles and Horses in Meadows and Forests. *Journal of Applied Ecology* 15:451–457.

Webb, R. H., and H. G. Wilshire, eds. 1983. Environmental Effects of Off-road Vehicles: Impacts and Management in Arid Regions. New York: Springer-Verlag, 534 pp.

Whittaker, P. L. 1978. Comparison of Surface Impact by Hiking and Horseback Riding in the Great Smoky Mountains National Park. USDI National Park Service, Management Report 24, Southeast Region, Atlanta. 32 pp.

Young, R. A. 1978. Camping Intensity Effects on Vegetation Ground Cover in Illinois Campgrounds. *Journal of Soil and Water Conservation* 33:36–39.

Young, R. A., and A. R. Gilmore. 1976. Effects of Various Camping Intensities on Soil Properties in Illinois Campgrounds. *Soil Science Society American Journal* 40:908–911.

Zaslowsky, D. 1981. Looking into Soles and Other Weighty Matters. *Audubon* 83(2):60–63.

IV MANAGEMENT ALTERNATIVES

9 Strategies and Concepts of Management

In the chapters on impacts to resource components, we developed an understanding of how recreational use alters elements of the natural environment. Then, in Part III we explored factors that influence the nature, magnitude, and geographic distribution of impacts. Now it is time to apply this knowledge to management. Management cannot—and indeed should not—eliminate impact. Cleared trails and campsites, for example, are desirable environmental changes in many recreation areas. Management should control impacts, however, by manipulating the factors that influence impact patterns. In this chapter we will start with some general principles that summarize what we have learned in earlier chapters. Then we will turn to discussions of some planning concepts and frameworks and management strategies that can be useful in guiding management. This should set the stage for the more detailed descriptions of management techniques that follow in Chapters 10, 11, and 12.

GENERAL PRINCIPLES

The following are the general principles discussed in previous chapters.

1. Change is an all-pervasive characteristic of natural environments. The norm in undisturbed wildlands is continuous change—*succession*—to use the ecological terminology. When people are introduced into the natural scene, particularly when they come in large numbers, the natu-

ral direction and rate of change are often altered. In many cases ecosystem processes are accelerated. Erosion provides a good example. Many streambanks are constantly being worn away by the action of running water. Where canoeists beach their boats at a picnic spot, erosion can be increased greatly, accomplishing in a few years what would have taken decades or centuries. In a case such as the suppression of fire, ecosystem processes—in this case, natural disturbance by fire—are slowed down. This, too, represents a serious impact. In other cases the entire direction of successional processes is diverted. Clearing and constructing a trail, where an undisturbed forest floor environment is replaced by a flat, compacted, barren, sunlit surface, represents a radical departure from the natural course of events.

Change is natural; thus management will generally not seek to halt change; rather, it will seek to halt undesirable change. How do we agree on what is an undesirable change? In wilderness and many national park environments, where preservation of natural conditions is an important goal, most but not all human-caused change is undesirable. Elsewhere human-caused changes that improve recreational opportunities are often considered desirable.

One important criterion for deciding whether or not an impact is undesirable relates to whether it tends to be self-limiting. Certain impacts tend to stabilize over time as they approach some limit of maximum change. Well-built trails, for example, are far from being in a natural state, but they deteriorate little over time. Other impacts get progressively worse over time. Trails that ascend steep slopes and lack drainage devices to divert water off the tread will continue to erode until all soil is gone. Impacts that are not self-limiting are generally more serious than those that are.

The desirability of change and, therefore, whether or not an impact should be attacked by management, depends on a recreation area's objectives and also, perhaps unfortunately, on the personal biases of whoever is managing the area. Consequently, it is critical to set some objective limits on the types and amounts of change that are either desirable or acceptable. A first task for management, as was mentioned in Chapter 1, is to set limits of acceptable change.

2. Impacts are the inevitable result of recreational use. All forms of outdoor recreation will inevitably lead to some compaction of soils and disturbance of vegetation. Moreover, the fragility of most natural environments is such that very little use causes substantial amounts of im-

pact. The asymptotic or curvilinear nature of the relationship between amount of use and amount of impact is an important, consistent conclusion of impact research. Therefore, it is not realistic to try to eliminate impact unless one is willing to prohibit all use. Instead, management should strive to *control* impact. Since low levels of use can cause significant impact, it is particularly important to control the areal extent of use and impact.

3. Impacts exhibit relatively predictable patterns both in space and over time. Impacts are highly concentrated around attractions and recreational facilities (nodes) and along travel routes (linkages) (Manning 1979). Although impacts can be severe in these places, they are usually minimal throughout the vast majority of most wildland areas. This is a fortunate situation that can be reinforced through planning and site design. A second pattern is for impact to occur rapidly once an area is opened to recreational use. After a few years, further impact is usually minor with one important exception. That exception is the tendency for sites to expand in area as they continue to be used. Again, planning and site design should recognize this tendency and move to actively counteract it.

4. Impacts vary greatly between environments, along with differences in the tolerance of each environment. Both resistance and resilience vary. Most environments have both low resistance and low resilience. Consequently, impact occurs rapidly and recovery is slow. However, all combinations exist except perhaps for high resistance and high resilience. These differences can be used to advantage in planning, such that the negative consequences of recreation use are minimized.

5. Impacts vary greatly with type of use and mode of travel. This was discussed in depth in Chapter 8. Both the nature and magnitude of impact vary with type of use. For example, horses cause more trail erosion than hikers; their need to graze will also cause types of impact not found in areas without horse use. From this it follows that the greatest impact should occur where the greatest mix of different uses occurs. This suggests that there are likely to be situations where zoning is a good strategy for minimizing impact.

6. All elements of the environment are interrelated. This is perhaps the highest principle in ecology. Everything is connected to everything else. This applies not only to the natural environment but to the recreationists in the environment as well. Actions taken to control one type of impact can affect another type of impact or another place. Moreover,

actions taken to reduce impacts can affect user experiences and vice versa.

In summary, it is critical to establish specific objectives—limits of acceptable change—to determine at what level impact becomes a problem demanding management action. Because impact varies with amount of use, type of use, and environment, these are the variables that management can change to control impact. Finally, because everything is connected to everything else, it is important to consider the likely consequences of any potential management action to all other parts of the system.

PLANNING FOR MANAGEMENT

A number of approaches could be taken to plan for recreational use in such a way that undesirable impact is minimized. Two that we find particularly useful are the Recreation Opportunity Spectrum (ROS) and a simple planning framework called the Limits of Acceptable Change (LAC) System for Planning.

Recreation Opportunity Spectrum

The ROS is a formal planning framework, currently used by both the U.S. Forest Service and the Bureau of Land Management. In its most basic form, it is a system for promoting recreational diversity. Different recreationists participate in various activities in different physical-bio-logical-social-managerial settings in order to realize various experiences. For example, one recreationist may choose camping (activity) in the natural, low-human-density, minimally restricted environment of a remote backcountry area (setting) to contemplate nature and get away from urban life for awhile (experience); another may choose downhill skiing in a developed, high-density environment to seek thrills and meet people. The same person may desire each of these recreational opportunities at different times. To serve all legitimate recreationists, it is best to provide a diversity of recreational opportunities. Not every area can provide a wide range of opportunities, but diversity should be promoted, and at least regionally a wide range should be provided.

In its current formal usage, the ROS recognizes six opportunity classes. They are defined in terms of setting characteristics—access, nonrecreational resource uses, onsite management, social interaction, acceptability of visitor impacts, and acceptable regimentation. Table 1 provides written descriptions of appropriate settings in each of the six types. In this book we are primarily concerned with the four more primitive types, not the rural or urban setting classes. In attempting to manage recreational impacts, these settings should be kept in mind.

In wildland recreation it is important to consider what recreational opportunities are being provided, whether several classes can be provided, and how these classes should be distributed (allocated) on the ground. Each class will have distinct objectives and will be managed in a unique manner. Toward the primitive end of the opportunity spectrum, recreational impacts are less acceptable, and objectives are more likely to stress low-impact conditions. At the same time, regimentation is more undesirable at the more primitive end of the spectrum. This has important implications for the appropriateness of various management styles. Subtle management techniques are preferable to extensive use of regulation and persuasion. Thus the recreation opportunity class (or range of classes) provided by any recreation area will determine, to a great extent, both limits of acceptable change for impacts and the most appropriate means of mitigating impact problems.

This also points out why management of impacts is particularly difficult toward the primitive end of the spectrum—in wilderness for example. Toward that end, impacts are least acceptable but management has the least amount of leeway in using restrictive techniques. Access is also difficult, making enforcement, patrol, and other management activities more troublesome. For all these reasons, management of more primitive wildlands is especially complex and will be discussed in considerable detail in the following chapters.

A Planning Framework

Figure 1 diagrams a simple but powerful framework for planning. In very simple terms it involves stating the conditions management will provide (how much impact and where), inventorying conditions to see how they compare to desired conditions, as stated in objectives, and then instituting management where existing conditions do not meet objectives. The final step, monitoring, involves periodically returning to the inventory stage of the process. Each of these steps needs to be looked at in more detail. Refer to Stankey, Cole, Lucas, Petersen and

TABLE 1. Appropriate Setting Descriptions for Each of the Six Classes in the Recreational Opportunity Spectrum

	Recreational Opportunity Spectrum Class				
Primitive	Semi-Primitive Nonmotorized	Semi-Primitive Motorized	Roaded Natural	Rural	Urban
Area is characterized by essentially unmodified natural environment of fairly large size. Interaction between users is very low and evidence of other users is minimal. The area is managed to be essentially free from evidence of human-induced restrictions and controls.	Area is characterized by a predominantly natural or natural-appearing environment of moderate-to-large size. Interaction between users is low, but there is often evidence of other users. The area is managed in such a way that minimum on-site controls and re-	Area is characterized by a predominantly natural-appearing environment of moderate-to-large size. Concentration of users is low, but there is often evidence of other users. The area is manged in such a way that minimum on-site controls and restrictions may be present, but	Area is characterized by predominantly natural-appearing environments with moderate evidences of the sights and sounds of man. Such evidences usually harmonize with the natural environment. Interaction between users may be low to moderate, but with evidence	Area is characterized by substantially modified natural environment. Resource modification and utilization practices are to enhance specific recreation activities and to maintain vegetative cover and soil. Sights and sounds of humans are readily evident, and the	Area is characterized by a substantially urbanized environment, although the background may have natural-appearing elements. Renewable resource modification and utilization practices are to enhance specific recreation activities. Vegetative cover is often exotic and mani-

Motorized use within the area is not permitted.

strictions may be present, but are subtle. Motorized use is not permitted.

are subtle. Motorized use is permitted.

of other users prevalent. Resource modification and utilization practices are evident, but harmonize with the natural environment. Conventional motorized use is provided for in construction standards and design of facilities.

interaction between users is often moderate to high. A considerable number of facilities are designed for use by a large number of people. Facilities are often provided for special activities. Moderate densities are provided far away from developed sites. Facilities for intensified motorized use and parking are available.

cured. Sights and sounds of humans, on-site, are predominant. Large numbers of users can be expected, both on-site and in nearby areas. Facilities for highly intensified motor use and parking are available with forms of mass transit often available to carry people throughout the site.

Source: USDA Forest Service, ROS User's Guide.

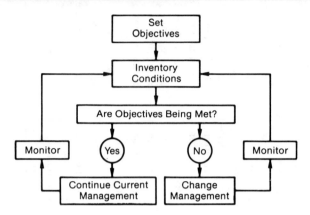

Figure 1. A simple planning framework. (*Source:* D. N. Cole).

Frissell (1985) for further detail on Limits of Acceptable Change planning.

Set Objectives

It is a relatively simple matter to determine the *magnitude* of an impact. Although not perfect, well-developed techniques are available for measuring, in quantitative terms, the increase in bulk density on a recreation site. Using similar techniques, several independent investigators could each determine that bulk density increased, say, 0.10 g/cm³. Where disagreement comes is in evaluating the *importance* of this amount of impact. Depending on one's point of view, an increase in compaction of 0.10 g/cm³ might constitute either disastrous damage or an insignificant change. Moreover, it might be highly desirable on a constructed nature trail or totally unacceptable in a remote trailless setting. Only where specific objectives have been established for specific places can one consistently determine whether or not an impact of a given magnitude constitutes a problem that demands management attention. Again, this relates to the notion of limits of acceptable change.

One might argue that all impacts should be minimized. As mentioned before, however, some impacts are desirable in certain situations. Moreover, all management actions entail costs, both to the visitor and management. Given both budgetary constraints and a concern for avoiding unnecessarily restricting recreation use and behavior, it is best to attack not impacts but impact *problems*—situations where impacts exceed levels specified in objectives.

Objectives could be written to limit every possible type of recreation impact. However, this is not reasonable or even desirable. Fortunately, actions taken to avoid certain impacts are likely to also protect against other types of impact. For example, reducing use to limit campsite disturbance is also likely to reduce wildlife disturbance. Therefore, it may only be necessary to set objectives for a few particularly important and sensitive types of impact. There may also be unique situations such as for rare or endangered species for which objectives are also needed. As mentioned before, objectives for dealing with impacts that are not self-limiting are particularly important. Some of the elements for which objectives might be written include trail condition, campsite density and condition, water quality, and wildlife populations and their distribution. Within each of these broad categories it is important to be even more specific. For example, objectives for campsite condition might be written for soil compaction, ground cover condition, tree damage, campsite area, or a combination of these factors, depending on the local significance of these impacts.

One place where specific objectives intended to limit impact are being developed is in the Bob Marshall Wilderness Area in Montana. This large (over 1 million acres), remote, and spectacular area has been heavily used by large parties travelling with stock. As a result of a long history of such use, many campsites have been highly impacted. Managers of the area feel that such high levels of impact detract from the values for which the area was designated as wilderness. Consequently, they have decided to limit impact and have proposed objectives for the area based on (1) a maximum devegetated area and number of damaged trees on campsites in any 5-acre area, (2) a maximum number of campsites in any square mile, and (3) maximum amounts of range utilization and specified standards for range condition and trend.

For each of these measures of impact, quantitative objectives have been proposed. Moreover, to incorporate diversity into the system, as discussed in the previous section on ROS, these quantitative limits vary between different zones established within the wilderness. Currently, the area contains considerable diversity. Some areas are pristine and trailless while others are heavily used and show considerable evidence of disturbance. To preserve, enhance and, in some cases, redirect this diversity, the Bob Marshall Wilderness has been divided into four zones. In the most pristine zone proposed objectives state that no 5-acre area will contain more than 100 ft² of devegetated area or more than 15 damaged trees on campsites; there will be no more than one campsite in any square mile; range utilization will not exceed 20 percent; range condition will be good; and range trend will be static or improving. If these objectives are met, environmental impact in this zone will be low. Elsewhere, more impact is tolerated. For example, the allowable number of campsites in any square mile increases to two, three, and six in the three successively less primitive zones. The allowable devegetated area on campsites in any 5-acre area increases to 500, 1000, and 2000 ft^2.

Inventory Conditions

Once objectives have been established it is time to go out and inventory conditions on the ground to see where objectives are and are not being met. In many cases some initial inventory will be necessary before realistic objectives can be set. It does not do any good to set objectives that are so stringent they can never possibly be met. It also does little good to set objectives so lax that their attainment does little to avoid impact problems. Thus, it is helpful to do a little sampling of conditions, before quantitative objectives are established, to help set meaningful but realistic objectives.

Inventorying is the first phase of a long-term monitoring program. Monitoring is merely periodically repeating the inventory and comparing current conditions both to objectives and previous inventory data. Monitoring is covered in much more detail in Chapter 10. At this stage, two points should be made. First, the most important things to monitor (inventory) are the elements addressed in objectives; other data can be collected, but first priority must go to elements addressed in objectives. For example, in the Bob Marshall Wilderness, objectives dictate that managers must collect information on campsite devegated area and damaged trees. They are also collecting information on size of the campsite, but this is less important because it is not specified in the objectives. Second, inventory must be conducted in an objective and systematic fashion. Techniques must be well documented so that successive inventories are comparable.

Compare Conditions to Objectives

Once the inventory is completed it is a relatively simple matter to identify places where conditions are not being met. These are problem areas that demand management attention. It may also be possible to identify places where conditions currently are in line with objectives, but there is reason to believe they may not be in the near future. This ability to predict will improve greatly as monitoring progresses and some trend data become available. Places where the trend is downhill may also require management attention. Even in places where objectives are being met, it may be appropriate to change or strengthen management if it is not too burdensome to the visitor. For example, promoting low-impact camping techniques and a pack-it-in, pack-it-out litter policy are desirable even where campsite impact and litter are not problems. Such programs are not burdensome to visitors. However, greatly restricting numbers of users or prohibiting certain activities is hard to justify if objectives are being met.

There are usually a number of alternative management actions that can be taken to mitigate any single problem. In the following section, we discuss how to decide on an appropriate course of action. Chapters 11 and 12 will provide specifics on alternative techniques and some of their pros and cons.

MANAGEMENT OF PROBLEMS

Although our concern is with management of ecological impacts, it is important to remember that an equal concern must be given to the provision of quality recreational experiences. The simplest, most effective means of minimizing recreational impact is to prohibit all use. This obviously defeats the purpose of a recreation area. It is not possible to optimize both provision of recreational opportunities and protection from environmental impacts; a compromise is always necessary. In thinking about how to manage impact, then, it is important also to consider how any action affects the recreational experience.

Given many alternative courses of action, it is imperative that managers carefully consider all possible actions. Too often there is a tendency to select techniques that are familiar or administratively expedient but not ideally suited to the situation at hand. Among the factors to consider, when trying to decide on a course of action, are effectiveness, costs to administer, costs to the visitor, and likely side effects. Supporting actions are often necessary if a given course of action is to be successful. These should be considered as well. Ultimately, the best programs will consist of carefully selected sets of actions that maximize effectiveness and minimize costs. Often attacking a problem from several different angles will be the best course to follow. This is why it is worth considering the strategic purpose of actions.

Strategic Purpose

As we noted in the chapters on factors that influence impact, amount of impact is a function of amount of use, type of use, and environment. Each of these variables offers a unique strategic approach to controlling impact problems. The most obvious—but seldom the most desirable—approach to reducing impact is to reduce use. Everything else being equal, less use should cause less impact. However, one party that builds a campfire or that travels with horses can cause more impact than several parties of backpackers using a portable stove. Another approach to reducing impact, then, is to leave amount of use constant but reduce the amount of impact each visitor causes. This can be accomplished in several ways:

1. *Use Dispersal.* Use can be spread out, so that areas of concentrated use and impact are avoided.
2. *Use Concentration.* Conversely, use can be concentrated in space so that only a small proportion of the resource is altered.
3. *Type of Use.* Type of use can be managed in such a way that particularly destructive uses are minimized.
4. *Site Location.* Use can be directed to particularly durable places that are able to tolerate heavy use.
5. *Site Hardening or Shielding.* A site's capacity to tolerate use can be increased by either hardening it or shielding it from impact.

All of these strategies attack the cause of impact problems. Another strategy is to attack the symptoms through site maintenance and rehabilitation. Generally, this approach is costly and never-ending so it should be complemented with attacks on the causes. However, there are situations where attacking symptoms must be the core of a management program. A good example is dealing with human waste in areas of concentrated use. Use can be concentrated, and the resource can be shielded by building outhouses and convincing visitors to use them. However, there is little alternative to establishing a flushing system, a composting system, or hauling the waste out. Examples of how each of these strategies might be employed in a program to reduce impact on campsites are provided in Table 2.

Most of these strategies can be implemented through management of

TABLE 2. Strategies and Actions for Reducing Impact on Campsites

Strategy	Possible Actions
Reduce Amount of Use	Limit number of parties entering the area
Reduce *per capita* impact	
Use dispersal	Persuade parties to avoid camping on highly impacted campsites
Use concentration	Prohibit camping anywhere except on designated sites
Type of use	Teach low impact camping techniques
Site location	Teach parties to choose resistant sites for camping
Site hardening/shielding	Build wooden tent pads on campsites
Rehabilitation	Close and revegetate damaged campsites

visitors or through site manipulation, the subjects of Chapters 11 and 12, respectively. For example, use concentration can be promoted either by requiring visitors to camp at designated sites (visitor management) or by using railings or rocks and shrubbery to confine traffic flow (site manipulation). Only the site hardening/shielding and site maintenance/rehabilitation strategies are entirely within the domain of site manipulation. Distinctions between visitor and site management are not as clearcut as is often assumed because site manipulation is often done for the purpose of managing visitors. A useful general principle is that the best management approach will utilize a combination of visitor and site management, as well as a combination of strategic approaches.

A final important point about strategies is that any single strategy can be used to attack a number of different problems. This is a reflection of the interrelatedness of everything. The problem is that some of the effects of implementing any course of action may be undesirable. As Manning (1979) puts it, "The various strategic uses of park management tools should be explicitly recognized before they are implemented so as to gain multiple benefits where possible and avoid unwanted side effects where potential."

Types of Undesirable Visitor Actions

Several management responses to impacts caused by undesirable visitor behavior have been suggested by Lucas (Hendee, Stankey, and Lucas 1978). He recognized five types of visitor actions:

1. Illegal actions with adverse impacts
2. Careless or thoughtless violations of regulations with adverse impacts
3. Unskilled actions with adverse impacts
4. Uninformed behavior, which intensifies use impacts
5. Unavoidable minimum impacts

Examples and appropriate management responses to each of these types are presented in Table 3. The important point here is that different responses are required for different types of users. What is necessary in one place may be overkill in another, where the users are more skilled or more likely to obey regulations.

Direct vs. Indirect Approaches

An important distinction has been made between direct and indirect management of visitors (Gilbert, Peterson, and Lime 1972). Direct management attacks human behavior directly, usually through regulation. An example would be allowing camping in only one area. The visitor must either camp there or break the law; free choice is extremely limited.

TABLE 3. Types of Visitor Actions and Appropriate Management Responses

Type of Visitor Action	Example	Management Response
Illegal actions	Motorcycle violation	Law enforcement
Careless actions	Littering, Nuisance activity (e.g., shouting)	Persuasion, education about impacts, rule enforcement
Unskilled actions	Ditching tent	Primarily education about low-impact use practices, some rule enforcement
Uniformed actions	Concentrated use	Education-information
Unavoidable impacts	Human waste, physical impact of even careful use	Reduction of use levels to limit unavoidable impacts; relocation of use to more durable site

Source: Hendee et al. 1978.

Indirect management attacks decision-making factors in an attempt to indirectly influence rather than force behavior. Visitors retain the freedom to choose their course of action. This is usually accomplished through information, persuasion, or site manipulation. For example, visitors could be told that a certain area (where managers want them to camp) is the nicest place to camp; visitors could be asked to camp in that area; or facilities could be built in the area to attract visitors.

Much of the debate about whether direct or indirect approaches are preferable revolves around considerations of each approach's effectiveness and the burden each approach places on visitors. It is commonly assumed that direct approaches are more effective and also carry more visitor cost. Both of these assumptions are oversimplified and can be misleading. For example, shortcutting switchbacks continues even in places where it has been prohibited. Trail design, such that shortcutting is extremely difficult, an indirect approach, can be more effective.

There are also cases where direct techniques are less costly to visitors than indirect techniques. For example, we would prefer a regulation prohibiting camping in a certain area that we were aware of before entering the area (direct regulation) to having a ranger walk into our camp and ask us to move out of a fragile or overused area (indirect persuasion). There are a number of important dimensions that must be considered when choosing between direct and indirect approaches to management. These dimensions are freedom of choice, subtlety, and where and when (in terms of the visitor's recreational experience) the management occurs.

Freedom of Choice
The distinction related to freedom of choice is between regulation and manipulation of human behavior. As Lucas (1982) points out, recreation and regulations are inherently contradictory because freedom and spontaneity lie at the core of most wildland recreational pursuits. Regulations are particularly undesirable toward the primitive end of the recreational opportunity spectrum where regimentation is supposed to be low. An objective of recreation management in wilderness, for example, is to provide opportunities for an "unconfined type of recreation." Freedom of choice is important and should be preserved where possible.

There are situations, however, where regulation plays an important and legitimate role. Several such situations mentioned by Lucas (1983) include safety (e.g., regulations keeping motorboats out of swimming areas), reducing interference with other visitors (e.g., regulations requiring quiet after 10:00 P.M.), and situations where a few individuals use more than their share of recreation resources (e.g., limits on numbers of fish or game). Generally, regulations are appropriate where it is imperative that most visitors comply with the regulation and where there is law enforcement available to back it up. Where regulations are instituted, it is important to:

1. *Explain Reasons for Regulations.* This should help to improve visitor compliance. Visitors are more inclined to respect rules and also to be hassled less by them if they recognize that they are necessary.

2. *Be Sure That Visitors Understand How They Are Expected to Behave.* In some cases visitors may be left unaware of regulations, or the rules may be ambiguous. This is likely to reduce compliance and increase confusion and frustration.

3. *Enforce Regulations.* It is not fair to law-abiding visitors to not enforce regulations. If enforcement is impossible, it is probably better just to ask people to behave in a certain manner.

4. *Regulate at the Minimum Level Possible.* Do not overattack the problem with restrictions that unnecessarily burden visitors.

There may be situations where the same objectives can be accomplished without establishing a regulation. Persuasion—asking visitors not to build campfires, for example—is usually preferable to prohibiting campfires. Effectiveness may be comparable, and visitors still retain final choice. Even with persuasion, however, visitors are still likely to feel pressured to conform to what the manager wants, and this is a burden. Persuasive approaches lack subtlety and if the contact between management and the visitor occurs within the area, it may be even more obtrusive and disturbing than a regulation. This can be a particular problem where conscientious visitors give up something important to them such as campfires and have to watch unconscientious visitors enjoy them.

Subtlety

Perhaps as important as freedom of choice is subtlety. Subtlety refers to the extent to which a visitor is aware of being managed. The example of a ranger walking into camp and asking a camper not to build a fire is an extreme example of a nonsubtle manipulative action, not substantially preferable to a regulation prohibiting campfires. Freedom of choice is retained, but the burden of guilt, should the camper choose to defy the wishes of the ranger, makes this of little importance. Education/information, without telling visitors what they should do, and physical manipulation are more subtle approaches to management. For example, when trying to keep people from camping in a particular place, such as on a lakeshore, visitors could be educated about the fragility of lakeshores, or trails could be developed that avoid lakeshores and lead to other places where attractive campsites are located. These actions could be effective and would avoid the loss of freedom that comes with regulation. It is subtlety, as much as lack of regulation, that is the preferred approach to management of recreation use.

Where and When Management Occurs

Particularly toward the primitive end of the opportunity spectrum, it is preferable to regulate or influence behavior outside of rather than inside the recreation area. This allows the visitor to adjust to restrictions early and to not be encumbered greatly while engaging in recreational activities. For example, where entry to an area is controlled, it is preferable to limit trailhead entry rather than limit movement within the area. In our ranger example, it would be more acceptable to be asked not to build a fire before entering the area. The best time to communicate restrictions or attempt to influence behavior is when visitors are in the planning phase of their trip. At this stage they can change their plans, if the impact of management programs is unacceptable to them, and they have time to accept and adjust to restrictions.

A final concern is with the number of visitors affected by an action and the importance of the freedoms visitors are asked or required to forego. For the majority of backcountry users, a regulation limiting party size is much less bothersome than being asked not to build a campfire. This follows from the fact that fewer parties are affected by a party size limit. Similarly, asking visitors to pack out their litter should be less costly than asking them not to build campfires. Most visitors place more importance on being able to have a fire than on being able to leave their trash, so denial of the campfire is more burdensome. The cumulative weight of a number of restrictions must also be considered. Many people have said that reducing use should be the last option a manager exercises. It may be much worse, however, to keep visitors from doing many of the things they want to do, than it would be to occasionally deny them access to the area.

In sum, it is a complicated matter assessing the cost of an action to visitors. Everything else being equal—which it never is—preferred approaches would be those that are nonregulatory and subtle and that confront the visitor outside the area during the planning phase of the trip. Few actions combine all of these desirable elements. Where other combinations exist, managers will need to balance pros and cons. All of these concerns need to be weighed against an evaluation of likely effectiveness.

Toward the primitive end of the opportunity spectrum, subtlety is probably the most important concern. It is not possible, however, to make simple rules about whether or not an internal nonregulatory approach is preferable to an external regulatory approach. Toward the more developed end of the spectrum, regulation and nonsubtle approaches are to be expected. The important concerns here are usually the number of visitors affected and the importance of the freedoms visitors are asked to forego. In all areas it is important to maximize freedom and spontaneity because these are critical elements of most wildland recreational experiences.

REFERENCES

Gilbert, G. C., G. L. Peterson, and D. W. Lime. 1972. Towards a Model of Travel Behavior in the Boundary Waters Canoe Area. *Environment and Behavior* 4:131–157.

Hendee, J. C., G. H. Stankey, and R. C. Lucas. 1978. Wilderness Management. USDA Forest Service Miscellaneous Publication 1365. 318 pp.

Lucas, R. C. 1982. Recreation Regulations—When Are They Needed? *Journal of Forestry* 80:148–151.

Lucas, R. C. 1983. The Role of Regulations in Recreation Management. *Western Wildlands* 9(2):6–10.

Manning, R. E. 1979. Strategies for Managing Recreational Use of National Parks. *Parks* 4:13–15.

Stankey, G. H., D. N. Cole, R. C. Lucas, M. E. Petersen, and S. S. Frissell. 1985. The Limits of Acceptable Change (LAC) System for Wilderness Planning. USDA Forest Service Research Paper INT-176. 37 pp.

USDA Forest Service. No date. ROS User's Guide. 38 pp.

10 Monitoring Recreational Impacts

In the last chapter we discussed the importance of inventory and monitoring within a planning framework. Inventory provides a means of evaluating the current condition of the resource in relation to management objectives so that problems can be identified. Over time, monitoring allows trends in condition to be recognized. Information about current conditions and trends aids in the selection of limits of acceptable change. It also permits the effectiveness of management programs to be assessed and suggests places where changes in management are needed. Places where problems are particularly pronounced or where conditions are rapidly deteriorating can be identified as areas of concern. This can be useful in budgeting, allocating manpower, and establishing project priorities.

Reliable data are needed to manage recreation just as reliable inventory data are needed to manage other natural resources, such as timber. Unfortunately, they are seldom available. In recreation, management has too frequently had to rely on guesswork or the personal experience and intuition of managers. While a manager's professional opinion is important, it is no substitute for reliable and systematically collected inventory and monitoring data. This is particularly true where turnover in personnel is frequent, as it is in many governmental land-managing agencies.

In this chapter we will examine some of the techniques available for monitoring three important types of recreational facilities and resources: campsites, trails, and water bodies.

CAMPSITES

Camping is among the most popular of all recreational activities. Usually it involves highly concentrated use; consequently, impacts are often pronounced. Campsites vary greatly, from highly developed sites in large campgrounds that cater to travellers in recreational vehicles to remote, isolated, lightly impacted sites in the backcountry. As objectives vary among these different situations, appropriate monitoring techniques also vary. A monitoring program, to be efficient, must be developed with specific objectives in mind. Otherwise, important information may not be collected, and time and money may be wasted in collecting nice-to-know but marginally useful data.

Despite great variability in which monitoring techniques are appropriate in different situations, there are some characteristics that are generally desirable to all monitoring systems. A campsite monitoring system should provide accurate and meaningful information about how much impact has already occurred on campsites. This tells a manager how serious current problems are. It should also provide a reliable baseline for subsequent monitoring so that trends can be identified. A good system will have four characteristics:

1. Meaningful measures of impact are utilized.
2. Measurement techniques are reliable and sensitive.
3. Costs are not too high to prohibit an inventory of all campsites.
4. Measurement units can be relocated precisely.

The value of the information collected will depend on how carefully impact parameters—measures of impact—are selected. Some parameters measure current conditions, but not how much impact has occurred on the site. For example, some monitoring systems have measured vegetation cover on campsites. By itself, this is not a measure of impact because vegetation cover is dependent on many environmental factors as well as recreational use. Fifty percent vegetation cover may be perfectly natural, or it may represent a loss of as much as 50 percent of the natural vegetation. It is much more meaningful to compare the vegetation cover on a campsite with the cover of a similar undisturbed site. The difference provides a good estimate of how much vegetation has been lost.

Deciding on just one variable to measure can be difficult. It is usually cost-effective and easier to base a monitoring system on several different parameters. Sometimes it is convenient to aggregate these parameters into a single index of site condition. This can be done by rating each parameter, say on a scale of 1 to 3, and then taking the mean rating as an overall index. If this is done, it is important to retain the ability to disaggregate data. This will make it possible to evaluate change in individual parameters over time.

A second desirable characteristic of any monitoring system is reliability. Assessment techniques must be sufficiently precise to allow independent observers to reach similar conclusions about site condition. Monitoring is of little value if different people give widely divergent assessments of site condition. Precision depends on the use of well-documented techniques and consistent training of evaluators. Assessment techniques must also be sensitive enough to detect managerially relevant differences between sites and changes over time.

There is always a trade-off between reliability/sensitivity and cost. More precise methods take more time and cost more money. This may be prohibitive in large backcountry areas with numerous, remote, dispersed sites. For example, in Sequoia and Kings Canyon National Parks, over 7400 backcountry campsites have been inventoried (Parsons and McLeod 1980). As the objectives of inventory are to characterize both the distribution and condition of sites and how they change over time, it is best to use as precise techniques as possible while retaining the ability to inventory *all* sites. Only by inventorying all sites is it possible to characterize the number and distribution of sites—a critical concern in dispersed use areas. Where relatively imprecise rapid survey techniques must be used in order to inventory all sites, it may also be desirable to take more precise measurements on a subsample of sites. This permits subtle changes to be detected, changes that can be related to differences in characteristics such as use levels, environmental characteristics, and other variables that might affect amount of impact.

Finally, to monitor change over time it is important to document the exact location of all areal units on which measurements were taken. This might apply to the entire campsite or to square plots, line transects, or any other sampling units that were used.

Existing campsite inventory techniques can conveniently be grouped into three classes: measurements, rapid estimates of conditions, and photographs. The ideal program will use all three of these types to some extent.

Measurements

The best way to get accurate, replicable data is to take careful measurements in the field. Rapid estimates and photographs are less costly, but the data collected is less precise. Where they can be afforded, measurements are best. Keep in mind, however, that it is still important to inventory all sites. Therefore, a system based on measurements will only be feasible where there are a small number of campsites. This may be the case in a developed campground or in backcountry areas with designated sites. For example, measurements were used in the backcountry at Great Smoky Mountains National Park where there were only 113 legal sites and 289 illegal sites (Bratton, Hickler, and Graves 1978). Compare this with the situation in Sequoia and Kings Canyon National Parks where there are more than 7400 backcountry campsites.

Numerous impact parameters could be measured on campsites. Appropriate parameters vary with both type of campsite and environmental conditions. The numerous research studies of campsite conditions that have been conducted (Cole and Schreiner 1981) provide a good source for selecting measurement techniques. It is important that meaningful measures of impact are selected. Accurate and precise measurements are of little use if they are not managerially relevant. Therefore, each individual recreation area should tailor a system to its own particular needs rather than blindly copy an existing system.

Let's look at two methodologies that have been used successfully. The first was used to examine impact on individual sites in the Eagle Cap Wilderness, Oregon (Cole 1982). The second was used on backcountry campgrounds in Great Smoky Mountains National Park (Bratton et al. 1978). Sites in the Great Smoky Mountains vary greatly in level of development from shelters to user-constructed sites; many are occupied simultaneously by more than one party.

In the Eagle Cap each sample site consisted of both a campsite and a similar undisturbed site in the vicinity. This undisturbed site serves as a control, a measure of what the campsite was like before it was camped on. On each campsite, linear transects were established, radiating from an arbitrarily established center point, in 16 directions. Distances were measured from the center point to both the first significant amount of vegetation and the edge of the disturbed part of the campsite (Fig. 1). This defined the area of the barren central core of the site (bare area) and the entire disturbed area (camp area). Both are important indicators of

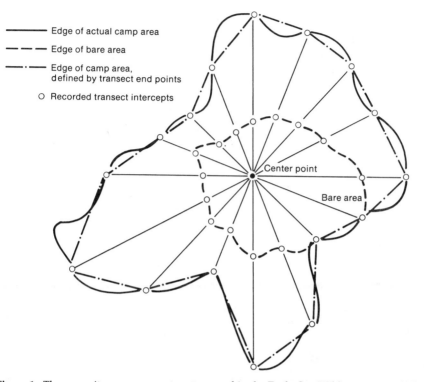

Figure 1. The campsite measurement system used in the Eagle Cap Wilderness recorded bare area, camp area, number of damaged trees, and number of tree seedlings. (*Source:* D. N. Cole 1982.)

impact. Tree seedlings and mature trees were counted within the entire disturbed area. Any human damage (e.g., ax marks, initials, etc.) was noted. Tree seedlings were also counted on a 50 m^2 control plot close by. Differences between campsite and control, in the density of seedlings (the number per m^2), are attributed to recreational impact. Measures of impact for tree damage are the number of damaged trees and the percent of all trees on the campsite that are damaged.

On each campsite, approximately 15 quadrats, 1-m by 1-m, were located along four transects that ran from the center point to the edge of the site and that were oriented perpendicular to each other. The distance between successive quadrats decreased with distance from the center point so that the central part of the campsite was not over sampled. In each quadrat the coverage of total vegetation, of exposed mineral soil, and of each plant species was estimated (Fig. 2). Coverages were estimated to the nearest percent if under 10 percent or in 10 percent coverage classes between 10 and 100 percent. The midpoints of each coverage class were used to calculate mean percent cover for each of these types of ground cover. These cover estimates were compared with similar estimates on controls. Again, differences are considered to be measures of the amount of recreational impact that has occurred on campsites. For example, mean vegetation cover was 55 percent on controls and 8 percent on campsites. Therefore we infer that camping removed vegetation from 47 percent of the average site.

On both campsites and controls, four soil samples were collected to measure bulk density, organic content, and chemical composition. Water infiltration rates were measured, as were pH and the depth of surface organic horizons. Soil samples were systematically distributed to avoid bias and oversampling of any part of the site.

Figure 2. Estimates of the percent coverage of vegetation and other ground cover parameters are often made with the aid of a quadrat. (*Photo:* D. N. Cole.)

Measurements on campsites in the Great Smoky Mountains were different, consisting primarily of length and width measurements for different types of impact. The conditions that were examined were bare rock, mud, slope erosion, bare soil, leaf litter (in places where vegetation had been removed by trampling), trampled vegetation, firewood clearing, tree damage, and trash dispersal. For bare rock, mud, slope erosion, bare soil, leaf litter, and trampled vegetation, the total area on the site in each of these ground cover types was measured. For trash dispersal, tree damage, and firewood clearing, the maximum distance from the center of the site along at least two axes was used to calculate area. The number of firepits was counted as were other types of development (Bratton et al. 1978).

This monitoring system provides accurate measures of the areal extent of impact. They found, for example, that on legal campsites the mean area of vegetation damage and of bare soil was 800 m^2 and 405 m^2, respectively. This is a particularly valuable way of estimating impact in the Great Smoky Mountains, where many parties cluster together, creating large, multiple tent-site campgrounds. It will also be possible to follow changes in the area of these disturbances over time. However, the technique does not provide much information on the severity of impact—how much impact has already occurred on these sites. To provide this information, campsites would have to be compared with controls. If managers are primarily interested in change over time and not too concerned with an estimate of how much change has already occurred, this is a less time-consuming system than that used in the Eagle Cap. Systems similar to either of these have also been applied to developed campgrounds.

Rapid Estimates of Condition

Where it is not feasible to spend more than 5 to 10 minutes per campsite, rapid estimates must be substituted for measurements. This is usually the case in large, dispersed recreation areas, such as most backcountry areas and many roaded areas where people are allowed to camp wherever they want. Two alternatives are available: condition class and multiple parameter systems. Condition class systems consist of a series of site condition descriptions. Frissell (1978) suggests the following five classes:

1. Ground vegetation flattened but not permanently injured. Minimal physical change except for possibly a simple rock fireplace.

2. Ground vegetation worn away around fireplace or center of activity.

3. Ground vegetation lost on most of the site but humus and litter still present in all but a few areas.

4. Bare mineral soil widespread. Tree roots exposed on the surface.

5. Soil erosion obvious. Trees reduced in vigor or dead.

Each campsite is assigned to whichever class best describes its condition. A variation on this system has been used with Code-A-Site, a popular inventory system utilizing edgepunch cards to facilitate data storage and retrieval (Hendee, Clark, Hogans, Wood, and Koch 1976).

Frissell's system was developed from experience in the Boundary Waters Canoe Area, Minnesota, and what is now the Lee Metcalf Wilderness, Montana. It applies well in coniferous forests in cool climates where growing seasons are short, litter accumulation is great, and ground vegetation is highly sensitive to disturbance. In other environments, such as mountain grasslands or deserts, the system does not work well. Different descriptions that reflect the impacts that occur in these other environments can be developed, but for several reasons multiple parameter rating systems are generally preferable.

With multiple parameter rating systems, information is collected on a number of separate impact parameters. For example, in Sequoia and Kings Canyon National Parks, information is collected on vegetation density, vegetation composition, campsite area, area of the barren core, campsite development, presence of organic litter and duff, number of access (social) trails, and number of tree mutilations. Each of these is estimated or counted; time-consuming measurements are not required. Each parameter is assigned a rating, depending on amount of impact, and these ratings are totaled to obtain an overall impact rating (Parsons and MacLeod 1980). The advantages to such a system are:

1. It accounts for sites where one type of impact is high and another is low—in a condition class system such a situation results in a site partially matching several of the class descriptions.

2. It contains much more information, so that it is possible to track

change in individual parameters such as amount of tree damage over time.

3. It retains the flexibility to change parameters or reevaluate the importance of parameters without having to reexamine every site. With the condition class system, managers cannot change their condition criteria without redoing the entire inventory.

Cole (1983a) refined the system developed by Parsons and MacLeod (1980). In his system each parameter was recorded separately, and the objectivity of some of the rating descriptions was increased. To illustrate how the system works, Fig. 3 shows a campsite that managers might want to monitor. Figure 4 shows a completed form for that campsite. The following detailed instructions explain how the form is used.

Item 19, Vegetation Cover
Using the coverage classes on the form, estimate the percent of the campsite covered with live ground cover vegetation—not dead vegeta-

Figure 3. The condition of this campsite in the Eagle Cap Wilderness, Oregon, has been recorded on the form in Figure 4. (*Photo:* D. N. Cole.)

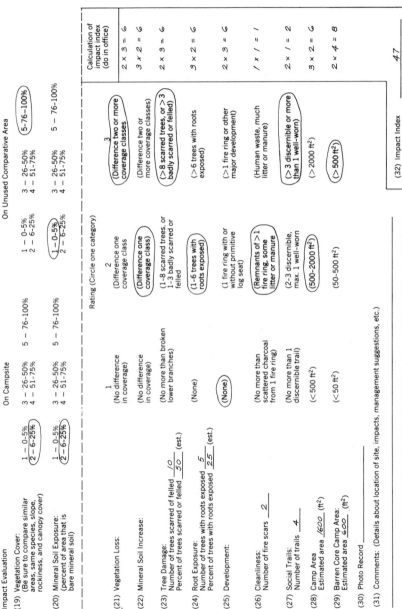

Figure 4. This form records information on the condition of the campsite shown in Fig. 3. (*Source*: D. N. Cole).

tion or trees or shrubs taller than a person. (Note the need to define what is meant by *ground cover vegetation*). Circle the appropriate coverage class. Do this for the campsite and do it for a nearby, unused site similar (except for the recreational impact) to the campsite.

Item 20, Mineral Soil Exposure
Using the same coverage classes, estimate the percent of the campsite and the same undisturbed comparative site without either live ground cover vegetation or duff—that is, the percent with exposed mineral soil.

Item 21, Vegetation Loss
Utilizing the information in Item 19, record the difference, in number of coverage classes, between vegetation on the campsite and the comparative area. If there is no difference (e.g., both the campsite and comparative area are class 4, 51 to 75 percent), circle rating 1. If coverage on the campsite is one class lower than on the comparative area (e.g., the campsite is class 3, 26 to 50 percent and the comparative area is class 4, 51 to 75 percent), circle 2. If the difference is more than one class, circle 3. (Note that this is similar to the measurements in the Eagle Cap Wilderness. Vegetation loss on the campsite is inferred by comparing a campsite and a control. In this case a single estimate replaces numerous quadrat measurements; the results are less precise but can be estimated rapidly.)

Item 22, Mineral Soil Increase
Utilizing the information in Item 20, record the difference in mineral soil exposure class between campsite and comparative area. In this case ratings of 2 and 3 are given when mineral soil cover is one, or more than one class higher on the campsite, respectively.

Item 23, Tree Damage
Count the number of trees with nails in them, ax marks, initials, and other human-caused scars. Also include stumps and/or cut-down trees. Do not count the same tree more than once and do not count trees on which the only damage is branches broken off for firewood. After recording this number, estimate very roughly what percentage of all the trees on the site have been damaged. If no trees are damaged, give the site a rating of 1. If one to eight trees are damaged or if one to three trees

have been felled or have bad scars (scars larger than 1 ft^2), give the site a rating of 2. If more trees are damaged, give the site a 3.

Item 24, Root Exposure
Count the number of trees with exposed roots and assign a rating based on this number.

Item 25, Development
Assign the site a rating of 1 if there are no facilities—not even a fire ring. A fire site is considered a ring only if the ring of stones is there; if they have been scattered, it is a fire scar. If there is only one fire ring, primitive log seats, or both, assign the site a 2. If there is more than one fire ring or more elaborate facilities, assign the site a 3.

Item 26, Cleanliness
Count the number of fire scars on the site, including any fire rings as fire scars. Assign the site a 1 if there is only one scar and essentially no evidence of litter, stock manure, or human waste. Assign the site a 2 if there is more than one fire scar or if litter or stock manure is evident. If litter or stock manure is "all over the place" *or* if there is any evident human waste, assign the site a 3.

Item 27, Social Trails
Social trails are the informal trails that lead from the site to water, the main trail, other campsites, or satellite sites. Discernible trails are trails that can be seen but that are still mostly vegetated. Well-worn trails are mostly devegetated. Count the total number of trails. Assign the site a rating based on the number of discernible and/or well-worn trails.

Item 28, Camp Area
Estimate the total area disturbed by camping and assign the site a rating based on this area.

Item 29, Barren Core Camp Area
Estimate the area within the camp without any vegetation. Bare area may or may not be covered with duff. Areas with scattered vegetation are not counted as barren area. Give the site a rating based on this area.

After the form has been filled out in the field, it is possible to calculate an overall impact index (Item 32). The ratings for each parameter are multipled by a weight. The weights for each parameter are decided on by managers based on their opinion of the relative importance of each parameter. The products of each rating and weight are then summed to give the impact index. In the Bob Marshall this index varied from 20 (minimal impact) to 60 (maximum impact). This range was then divided into four classes: light (ratings 20 to 29), moderate (30 to 40), heavy (41 to 50), and severe impact (51 to 60). These ratings were used to map the distribution of sites in each of these impact classes, to give a graphic display of where campsite impacts are most numerous and pronounced (Fig. 5).

The keys to such a system are selecting meaningful parameters, developing very specific definitions so that interpretations are consistent, developing ratings that adequately differentiate between campsites (if 90 percent of the campsites are rated 1, this does not provide much information), and then investing in training. Each area will do well to modify existing systems to its particular needs. In the Eagle Cap Wilderness, Oregon, where sites are smaller than in the Bob Marshall and where sites have less tree damage on account of less stock use, the same impact parameters were used, but some of the rating definitions were more stringent. For example, in the Eagle Cap, the boundary between ratings of 2 and 3 were 1000 ft^2 for camp area and one badly scarred or felled tree (Cole 1983a). This compares with 2000 ft^2 and three trees in the Bob Marshall.

In the Boundary Waters Canoe Area the same parameters were used, but an additional parameter has been added—length of shoreline disturbed by boat landings. In Grand Canyon National Park there are few trees, only patchy vegetation and organic matter, and campfires are prohibited. Several different parameters were selected to monitor sites there. Rangers in Grand Canyon are estimating barren core area, soil compaction, social trails, vegetation disturbance around the perimeter of the site, tree damage, litter, and campfire evidence.

Photographs

Photography has frequently been used for monitoring, sometimes systematically and sometimes not, sometimes to enhance field data and sometimes as the only monitoring tool. As with field data, photographs must be taken systematically, and their locations must be carefully documented or they are likely to be of little value. In our opinion, photo-

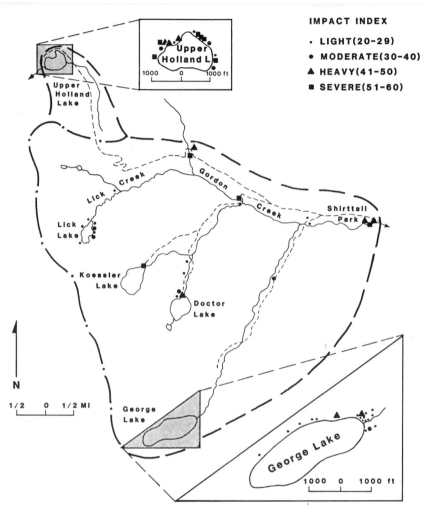

Figure 5. This map displays the condition (impact index) of all campsites in a portion of the Bob Marshall Wilderness, Montana. (*Source:* D. N. Cole.)

graphs are best used as a supplement to—rather than a replacement for—data collected in the field. It is unlikely that all of the information that should be collected can be captured on film. However, photographs can convey certain information not measured in the field. They can be used to validate field assessments and, of particular importance, they provide a visual means of conveying information on site condition quantified in field measurements.

Three photographic techniques that have been used as part of campsite monitoring programs are photopoints, quadrat photography, and campsite panoramas. More detail on each of these techniques can be found in Brewer and Berrier (1984).

Photopoints

This technique involves taking photographs from a location that can be reestablished at a future date. Establishing and documenting the location of the photopoint is critical. Photopoint locations can be referenced to landmarks, such as unique rocks, or to permanent metal markers, star drill marks in rocks, or marks on trees. All locations should be referenced in terms of distance and direction from trees and other landmarks. Reference points and photopoints should then be noted on sketch maps and photographs.

The location of the photopoint is important. Elevated points can provide good overviews. However, photos from a distance lose detail. When photographing forested sites, it is best to work on cloudy days when the contrast between shade and sunlight is reduced. Record the camera make and model, focal length of lens, height of the camera above the ground, filter type, and film type of each photograph. These should be replicated as closely as possible, as should time of day and year. Carrying copies of the original photos with you will facilitate accurate replication.

Quadrat Photography

This technique is a replacement for cover measurements taken in the field such as those employed in the Eagle Cap study. The advantage to photographs is that professional analysts do not have to go into the field; they can analyze the photographs in the lab. The disadvantage is the greater difficulty of making certain measurements such as coverage of individual species from photographs. As the height of the vegetation and the complexity of the ground cover increase, these interpretational problems become more serious. There are few situations where quadrat photographs provide an accurate replacement for field measurements.

Brewer and Berrier (1984) describe the quadrapod, a device that holds a camera at a set distance above the ground. A series of replicable quadrat locations are laid out and, using the quadrapod, photographs are taken of each quadrat. Prints or slides are enlarged, and the area of each ground cover type (e.g., vegetation, bare ground, or individual species) is traced onto paper for areal measurement. Individual quadrats can be followed over time or mean percent coverage of each ground cover type can be calculated and compared over time.

Campsite Panoramas

The campsite panorama technique involves piecing together a series of photographs that provides a full 360-degree view of the campsite (Fig. 6). A camera is mounted on a tripod at a point that can be readily relocated, usually the center of the site. Camera height needs to be constant (and documented for repeat photos), and the camera must remain level. A series of photographs is taken by rotating the camera. Each photo should overlap the preceding one by at least 25 percent. In the lab, trim adjoining photos in the middle of the overlap area and mount the photos on mat board.

It is not feasible to take accurate measurements on these panoramic photos on account of distortion and problems with precise replication. They do provide a means of counting newly fallen trees or changes in facilities, and they provide a good overview of site change. They are also effective means of visually communicating quantitative data collected in the field.

TRAILS

Monitoring of trail conditions can be useful for the same reasons that campsite monitoring is useful. Information on trail condition and trend can be used to evaluate the acceptibility of current conditions and whether or not trail management programs, including maintenance and reconstruction, are working. With trails, it is particularly important to establish specific objectives for trail conditions. Most trail impact (soil compaction, vegetation loss, etc.) is planned and desirable. Therefore, it is critical to define what conditions will be considered problems and to monitor these conditions.

Trail monitoring can also provide useful information about the relationship between trail condition and environmental conditions and design features. Often most of the trail segments that are deteriorating are located in just a few environmental situations (e.g., in highly erosive soils or in locations with seasonally high water tables) or in places where trail design is inadequate (e.g., where trails exceed a certain slope or lack

Figure 6. This 360-degree panoramic photograph of a campsite in the Selway-Bitterroot Wilderness, Idaho, has been used to monitor change on the site. (*Photo*: U. S. Forest Service.)

229

a sufficient number of water bars to divert water off the tread). Monitoring can be used to correlate trail problems with these conditions, and the knowledge generated can be used to guide the future design and location of new or reconstructed trails.

Available techniques can be conveniently grouped into three types: replicable measurements of a small sample of trail segments, rapid surveys of a large sample of trail segments, and complete censuses of trail problems and conditions.

Replicable Measurements

Detailed quantitative methods, using replicable measurements, permit subtle changes to be detected. However, the need to accurately document and relocate permanent measurement locations makes this a time-consuming process that may not always be worth the increased ability to detect subtle changes. Consequently, replicable measurements will often be less useful to managers than more rapid survey techniques.

Two schemes for locating replicable sample locations can be used. First, sample points can be distributed in a random or systematic fashion along the trail. This sampling design permits an unbiased assessment of the condition of the trail system as a whole. Repeat measurements, at a later date, allow managers to evaluate how much change has occurred on the entire trail, as well as on the individual sample locations. Alternatively, sample points can be located purposively on trail segments of particular interest to managers. For example, managers may be particularly interested in monitoring change on segments where pronounced erosion has already occurred or where some new type of trail design is being used. Such situations can be more efficiently studied by locating samples purposively, rather than randomly or systematically. With purposive sampling, it is not possible to assess the condition of the entire trail, however.

The trail conditions that management considers to be a problem will determine what should be measured. Perhaps the most common problem at specific locations is erosion. Soil erosion can be assessed by successively measuring the cross-sectional area between the trail tread and a taut line stretched between two fixed points on each side of the trail. The change in cross-sectional area between successive measurements documents erosion (if area increases) or deposition (if area decreases) of material.

Leonard and Whitney (1977) provide a detailed description of this technique, using nails in trees as fixed points. This means of locating fixed points limits sample locations to forested areas. By using other fixed points such as rods set in the ground or rods temporarily placed in receptacles permanently buried in the ground, sample points can be located in a greater variety of situations.

After locating the two fixed points, stretch a taut line and/or tape measure between the two points. Fixed points should always be far enough apart to allow for future increases in trail width. Take a series of vertical measurements of the distance between line and trail tread at fixed intervals along the tape. The interval should be small enough to permit at least 20 vertical measurements per transect. Measurements will be most precise when (1) the line is elevated above any vegetation or microtopography along the edge of the trail, (2) the line is kept taut, and (3) a plumb bob or level is used to take vertical measurements. The cross-sectional area below the taut line can be computed from the vertical measurements using the formula in Fig. 7.

When trail segments are to be reexamined, the fixed points should be relocated, and the taut line should be repositioned at precisely the same height above the fixed point as in the original sample. Vertical measurements should be taken at the same interval and starting from the same

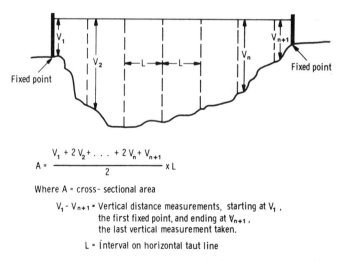

$$A = \frac{V_1 + 2V_2 + \ldots + 2V_n + V_{n+1}}{2} \times L$$

Where A = cross-sectional area

$V_1 - V_{n+1}$ = Vertical distance measurements, starting at V_1, the first fixed point, and ending at V_{n+1}, the last vertical measurement taken.

L = interval on horizontal taut line

Figure 7. Layout of trail transect and formula for calculating cross-sectional area. (*Source:* D. N. Cole 1983b.)

side as in the original measurements. The idea is to remeasure precisely each vertical measurement. Precise relocation becomes increasingly important as the number of vertical measurements per transect decreases. Results show changes over time in the cross-sectional area of the trail (Fig. 8).

Rinehart, Hardy, and Rosenau (1978) developed a technique for measuring cross-sectional area with stereo photographs. As with the quadrapod photographic method of monitoring conditions on campsites, this technique does not really save time, and interpretation of results can be difficult.

The location of the fixed points must be well-documented. One means of doing this is to measure the distance from the trailhead to the trail transect with a measuring wheel (cyclometer). If markers identifying the fixed points are readily visible, this may be all that is necessary. A less obtrusive option is to bury metal stakes that can be relocated with pin locators (a type of metal detector). The cyclometer and photos of the transect identify the approximate location of the transect. Exact locations are referenced to landmarks, and the pin locator leads to the metal stakes.

Detailed measurements of this type are most useful to researchers investigating the relationship between trail condition and factors that influence trail condition. Managers may find it useful for evaluating the effectiveness of alternative trail construction and design techniques. For example, if a new method of trail hardening is being tried, change could be followed both on the hardened segment and a similar unhardened segment. By comparing differences in the amount of change on hardened and unhardened segments, the benefits of hardening could be assessed in relation to its cost before investing in its widespread use.

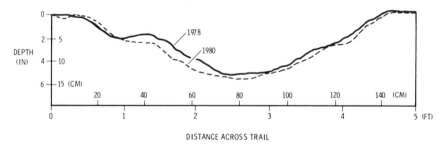

DISTANCE ACROSS TRAIL

Figure 8. Cross-sectional profiles for the same trail transect in 1978 and 1980. Over this 2-year period 17 in^2 of material were eroded away. (*Source:* D. N. Cole 1983b.)

Rapid Survey Samples

As with campsites, a useful alternative to time-consuming sampling of a few places is to make rapid assessments of many trail segments. This approach is particularly useful on trail systems because there are usually many trail miles to assess. Moreover, simply measuring trail width and depth is often as meaningful a means of assessing trail condition as taking cross-sectional measurements, and width and depth measurements can be taken in little time. In rapid surveys much of the time is saved by not relocating sample points. The resulting loss of precision is compensated for by the ability to take a much larger sample in the same amount of time. Monitoring involves comparing two independent samples, each consisting of a large number of observations, instead of reexamining a single, small sample of sites.

To conduct a rapid survey, simply hike a specified distance along the trail, collect data on trail condition, and then hike on to the next sample point. Distances between sample points have varied from 50 to 500 m. Appropriate distances between sample points will depend on the trail mileage to be surveyed and the complexity of situations involved. There should probably be at least 100 observations for each situation of concern. For example, only 100 observations would be needed to assess the condition of a trail. However, if a low use portion were to be compared with a high use portion, 200 observations would be needed. The most common measures taken at each sample point are width of the trail (either the tread or the entire zone of disturbed soil and vegetation), width of bare ground, and maximum depth of the trail. Bayfield and Lloyd (1973) also noted the number of parallel trails and the presence or absence of the following "detracting features": rutting, stepping, surface deterioration, gullying, lateral erosion, bad drainage, esthetic intrusions, vandalism, and litter.

From this data it is possible to calculate mean width and depth of the trail and the proportion of the trail on which there are particular detracting features. Such data provide a useful characterization of trail conditions and problems and permit an assessment of change over time and a comparison of different trails. It is also possible from such data to estimate the percentage of the trail that exceeds certain depth and width standards. If objectives state, for example, that no more than 1 percent of all trails will be more than 1 ft deep, this can be monitored easily using survey techniques.

Census Techniques

Other trail monitoring techniques involve censusing entire trail systems. In Great Smoky Mountains National Park, Bratton, Hickler, and Graves (1979) divided all trails into 0.5 km segments. After walking each segment, they estimated the percent of the segment affected by water erosion, rutting, horse impact and foot impact, or that had mud, bare rock, exposed roots, wild boar rooting, bank erosion, or vehicle tracks. As with rapid survey techniques, these data provide a characterization of trail condition in terms of the mean percent of the trail system that has experienced each of these types of impact. They found, for example, that 8.2 percent of the trail was eroded by water and 8.9 percent was muddy.

Working on horse trails in Rocky Mountain National Park, Summer (1980) divided each trail into segments and then placed each trail segment in one of four erosion classes (Table 1). She used these data to

TABLE 1. Erosion Classes for Horse Trails in the Rocky Mountains

Erosion Class	Evaluation of Present Stability
Negligible	No marked disturbance within trail; some gravel and soil may be moving imperceptibly downslope; on monitored sites, maximum mean incision is less than 2 cm and widening is less than 25 cm.
Low	Some deepening and/or widening of trail; cobbles and soil may begin to accumulate along trail edge; on monitored sites, maximum mean incision is 2 to 6 cm and/or widening is 25 to 50 cm.
Moderate	Noticeable deepening and widening; hoof prints less than 5 cm deep; boulders and cobbles may or may not show evidence of movement; soil and vegetation disrupted; on monitored sites, maximum mean incision is 6 to 8 cm and/or widening is 50 to 100 cm.
High	Very noticeable deepening and widening; hoof prints greater than 5 cm deep; boulders and cobbles obviously moved downslope or beyond trail edge; soil and vegetation disrupted and moved downslope; on monitored sites, maximum mean incision is greater than 8 cm and/or widening is greater than 100 cm.

Source: Summer, 1980. Appeared in *Journal of Soil and Water Conservation,* Copyright © 1980 by Soil Conservation Society of America.

relate the extent and severity of trail erosion to the geomorphic surface on which the trail was located. Summer found, for example, that most trail segments on alluvial terraces fell into either the negligible or low erosion classes; segments on alluvial-colluvial fans where boglike conditions prevail usually were in the high erosion class. She used this information to make suggestions about where trails should or should not be located. Although this was not done, it would be possible and useful to develop objectives limiting the percent of the trail system in high erosion classes, and then monitor the percent of the trail system in each erosion class. Where conditions were deteriorating, particularly where the percent of the trail in high erosion classes exceeded objectives, management actions would be called for.

Another useful approach is to census all trail "problems." The first step here is to define in precise terms exactly what will be considered a problem. The number and length of problems can be recorded while walking the trail; then the location of each trail problem can be mapped. This information can be useful in budgeting for trail maintenance and in allocating manpower to various trail segments. By noting the segment, site, design, and use characteristics of each problem, it should be possible to identify consistent patterns of problem occurrence. Knowledge of occurrence patterns can be used to develop guidelines for trail location, design, and maintenance.

On a trail system in the Selway-Bitteroot Wilderness, for example, Cole (1983b) censused all trail segments that were either incised more than 10 in. or muddy for at least part of the use season and that were at least 3 ft long. At each problem segment, maximum depth and width of the segment, habitat type (vegetation, soils, and topography), and slope of the trail were noted. Over two-thirds of the muddy segments were in one vegetation type. If future trails avoid this type, most of the muddiness problems should be eliminated. Incision problems were strongly correlated with trail slope; almost 90 percent of the problems were on segments with slopes greater than 4.7 degrees. The solution here is to make better use of water-bars on stretches where steep pitches cannot be avoided. Development of such guidelines could greatly increase the cost-effectiveness of trail building and maintenance programs. It basically amounts to learning from past mistakes.

Censuses can also be used to relate trail conditions to objectives. How this is done depends on how objectives are written. One option is for objectives to state that no segments will be more than, say, 1 ft deep. In this case, trails will need to be censused to see if any segments are deeper than 1 ft. An option that is usually more realistic and efficient is to write probabilistic objectives (e.g., no more than 1 percent of the trail will be more than 1 ft deep). In this case, trails could either be censused or rapid survey techniques could be used.

WATER BODIES

Monitoring of water is a critical concern in a variety of situations. Health aspects of water quality are important where drinking water is provided and in bodies of water where swimming occurs. Physical and chemical aspects of water quality are important in areas with objectives that stress maintenance of substantially natural conditions and in areas that maintain populations of sensitive fish species. Some of the situations where monitoring of water quality may be necessary include natural and artificial lakes where heavy boating use may be affecting water quality, roaded areas where recreational use of roads may cause deterioration of water quality, and wilderness areas where the strong emphasis on natural conditions is reflected in stringent water quality standards.

Many techniques for monitoring water quality require sophisticated equipment, laboratory analyses, and highly trained technicians. However, recent advances in development of "user-friendly" techniques and equipment are changing this situation. For example, probes have been developed that allow evaluators to read off chemical concentrations when the probe is inserted in the water (Fig. 9).

It is important to consider where sampling will occur, the frequency and duration of sampling, and the types of measurements that should be made. All of these considerations depend on the objectives for the area. When monitoring lakes, sampling is often done at the outlet. This provides a good indication of the condition of the lake as a whole. However, where localized pollution is expected, adjacent to a boat ramp or a campsite for example, sampling should be conducted in this area. Along streams it may be necessary to establish several sampling locations if the objective is to characterize an entire stream system.

It is usually desirable to monitor water quality in undisturbed places as well, to establish a control for comparison with disturbed conditions. For a lake this commonly involves sampling the inlet stream or part of the lake away from heavily used parts. With streams it is sometimes

Figure 9. Because of health hazards, water quality is monitored in heavily used wildland recreation areas. (*Photo:* National Park Service.)

necessary, but undesirable, to establish control sampling locations on an entirely different stream.

The frequency and duration of sampling can only be decided on after some idea of data variability has been obtained. Bacteriological contamination can vary greatly in relation to the timing of recreational use (Varness, Pacha, and Lapen 1978) and precipitation events. Sampling frequency and duration must be adequate to reveal such patterns.

The final consideration is what parameters to measure. Monitoring procedures and standards of quality for drinking water and water to swim in are well-developed and generally agreed upon. The primary measurement technique involves counting coliform bacteria in a sample of water. Coliform bacteria, while not pathogenic themselves, are often found in the company of organisms that represent health hazards to humans. They are counted because they are convenient to work with, and they have been shown to be good indicators of bacteriological contamination. The standard membrane filter technique involves filtering and incubating water samples and then counting the number of indicator organisms in each sample. Refer to American Public Health Association (1975) for more detail. The number of organisms found can then be compared with various health standards that have been advanced. For drinking water, acceptable coliform counts are usually on the order of one or two per 100 ml of water (depending on whether federal or state standards are used). Acceptable levels for full-body contact, such as swimming, are more variable between states but are usually on the order of hundreds of coliform bacteria per 100 ml of water. Some experts believe it is better to base health standards on the number of fecal coliforms rather than on total coliform counts. Managers should determine what federal, state, or local requirements apply—in this case objectives already exist—and take whatever measures are appropriate.

Although monitoring water is not as simple as campsite and trail monitoring, it is now possible to buy the equipment to conduct membrane filter monitoring for only $1200 to $1500. Additional disposable materials cost about $1 per sample. Training only takes about a day.

Recently, increasing numbers of water bodies, even in remote areas, have been contaminated with the protozoan *Giardia lamblia*. This organism is currently a more significant health threat in wildland recreation areas than bacteria. Moreover, it is difficult to monitor. *Giardia* samples must be large (on the order of hundreds of gallons), and the presence of *Giardia* cysts must be identified by experts using microscopes. However, improved procedures for monitoring *Giardia* contamination are being developed.

A wide variety of physical and chemical water quality parameters can be examined. It can also be useful to sample plankton, algae, and other aquatic biota. In a study designed to determine baseline conditions and possible effects of visitor use on some subalpine lakes in Kings Canyon National Park, Silverman and Erman (1979) measured orthophosphate and nitrate concentration, pH, conductivity, temperature, dissolved oxygen, plankton, and periphyton. In Guadalupe Mountains National Park, Dasher, Urban, Dvoracek and Fish (1981) measured many of these same parameters as well as sulfate, chloride, total hardness, calcium hardness, total alkalinity, and total suspended solids. In most cases techniques used are either standard methods recommended by the American Public Health Association (1975) or techniques described in special field analysis test kits.

While it is helpful to collect information on as many parameters as possible, this may be wasteful, particularly if the increased costs associated with this lead to an undesirable reduction in sampling frequency or the number of sample points. If this is the case, one must reexamine objectives and evaluate which parameters are most likely to indicate adverse effects on water quality. Where use of roads in erodible material is common, increased sedimentation can adversely affect fish populations; in such places monitoring of suspended solids is particularly worthwhile. Recreational trampling, even in remote backcountry areas, can lead to increases in the concentration of certain elements. Sometimes growth of aquatic plants can be stimulated by increases in the concentration of elements that formerly limited plant growth. In Kings Canyon National Park, for example, recreation-related increases in iron stimulated aquatic insects, worms, and small clams, and a depletion of nitrate (Taylor and Erman 1980). In Gatineau Park, Quebec, trampling increased phosphorus levels in a small lake. This stimulated growth of phytoplankton and reduced the transparency of the water (Dickman and Dorais 1977). Thus, in one case, it is most important to monitor iron and biota on the bottom of the lake; in the other case, it is most important to monitor phosphorus and suspended plankton.

These case studies illustrate the complexity of monitoring water quality. A relatively high level of expertise is needed to do more than simply monitor bacteria levels. It is probably best to start out monitoring many parameters at various times and places. This should give some idea of temporal and spatial variability to help decide on sampling frequencies and locations that are both effective and efficient. It will also become clear which parameters are the best indicators of adverse impact. Although something of a "shotgun approach" is required at first, the program should become increasingly efficient over time.

AERIAL PHOTOGRAPHY

There are a number of situations in which aerial photography can be a useful and cost-effective means of monitoring impact. Wherever tree cover is lacking, air photos are a good way to monitor change in the number and area of devegetated places. Price (1983) has shown how air photos can be used to monitor visitor impact on meadows around Sunshine Ski Area in Banff National Park, Alberta. Repeat photos show where new trails are developing and where existing trails are widening or becoming braided.

In Grand Canyon National Park, backcountry campsites are often clustered closely together in accessible places where water is available. These locations develop mazes of informal trails and tent pads. It is difficult to monitor changes in these trail and campsite complexes using only the field measurements and rapid estimation techniques discussed previously. With air photos, however, the number and area of both trails and tent pads can be traced onto maps. Overlays drawn from repeat photos, taken at later dates, can be used to identify changes over time.

A final situation in which air photos are useful is in monitoring impacts resulting from use of off-road vehicles in areas without a dense canopy cover. Such use leads to the development of tracks and large devegetated areas in places of concentrated use. This situation is analogous to the Grand Canyon trail and campsite complexes just described. Overlay maps can again be used to monitor change in the number and size of tracks and devegetated areas.

REFERENCES

American Public Health Association. 1975. Standard Methods for the Examination of Water and Wastewater. 14th ed. American Public Health Association, Washington, DC. 1193 pp.

Bayfield, N. G., and R. J. Lloyd. 1973. An Approach to Assessing the Impact of Use on a Long Distance Footpath—The Pennine Way. *Recreation News Supplement* 8:11–17.

Bratton, S. P., M. G. Hickler, and J. H. Graves. 1978. Visitor Impact on Backcountry Campsites in the Great Smoky Mountains. *Environmental Management* 2:431–442.

Bratton, S. P., M. G. Hickler, and J. H. Graves. 1979. Trail Erosion Patterns in Great Smoky Mountains National Park. *Environmental Management* 3:431–445.

Brewer, L., and D. Berrier. 1984. Photographic Techniques for Monitoring Resource Change at Backcountry Sites. USDA Forest Service General Technical Report NE-86. 13 pp.

Cole, D. N. 1982. Wilderness Campsite Impacts: Effect of Amount of Use. USDA Forest Service Research Paper INT-284. 34 pp.

Cole, D. N. 1983a. Monitoring the Condition of Wilderness Campsites. USDA Forest Service Research Paper INT-302. 10 pp.

Cole, D. N. 1983b. Asssessing and Monitoring Backcountry Trail Conditions. USDA Forest Service Research Paper INT-303. 10 pp.

Cole, D. N., and E. G. S. Schreiner. 1981. Impacts of Backcountry Recreation:

Site Management and Rehabilitation—An Annotated Bibliography. USDA Forest Service General Technical Report INT-121. 58 pp.

Dasher, D. H., L. V. Urban, M. J. Dvoracek, and E. B. Fish. 1981. Effects of Recreation on Water Quality in Guadalupe Mountains National Park. *Transactions of the American Society of Agricultural Engineers Conference* 24:1181–1187.

Dickman, M., and M. Dorais. 1977. The Impact of Human Trampling on Phosphorus Loading to a Small Lake in Gatineau Park, Quebec, Canada. *Journal of Environmental Management* 5:335–344.

Frissell, S. S. 1978. Judging Recreation Impacts on Wilderness Campsites. *Journal of Forestry* 76:481–483.

Hendee, J. C., R. N. Clark, M. L. Hogans, D. Wood, and R. W. Koch. 1976. Code-A-Site: A System for Inventory of Dispersed Recreational Sites in Roaded Areas, Backcountry, and Wilderness. USDA Forest Service Research Paper PNW-209. 33 pp.

Leonard, R. E., and A. M. Whitney. 1977. Trail Transect: A Method for Documenting Trail Changes. USDA Forest Service Research Paper NE-389. 8 pp.

Parsons, D. J., and S. A. MacLeod. 1980. Measuring Impacts of Wilderness Use. *Parks* 5(3):8–12.

Price, M. F. 1983. Management Planning in the Sunshine Area of Canada's Banff National Park. *Parks* 7(4):6–10.

Rinehart, R. P., C. C. Hardy, and H. G. Rosenau. 1978. Measuring Trail Conditions with Stereo Photography. *Journal of Forestry* 76:501–503.

Silverman, G., and D. C. Erman. 1979. Alpine Lakes in Kings Canyon National Park, California: Baseline Conditions and Possible Effects of Visitor Use. *Journal of Environmental Management* 8:73–87.

Summer, R. M. 1980. Impact of Horse Traffic on Trails in Rocky Mountain National Park. *Journal of Soil and Water Conservation* 35:85–87.

Taylor, T. P., and D. C. Erman. 1980. The Littoral Bottom Fauna of High Elevation Lakes in Kings Canyon National Park. *California Fish and Game* 66(2):112–119.

Varness, K. J., R. E. Pacha, and R. F. Lapen. 1978. Effects of Dispersed Recreational Activities on the Microbiological Quality of Forest Surface Water. *Applied Environmental Microbiology* 36:95–104.

11 Visitor Management

It is useful to distinguish between visitor management techniques and site management techniques. However, the distinction between the two is not perfect. Site manipulation can be a potent means of managing the amount and distribution of visitor use, and manipulation of where visitors go can be an effective means of managing site condition. For our purposes we will restrict visitor management to regulation, information, and education designed to influence the number, type, and behavior of visitors. Site management involves management of where use occurs, as well as physical manipulation of the resource.

Although images of trail building and facilities may first spring to mind when we think of impact management, visitor management is generally the first line of defense. Regulations—the "do's and don'ts" on park signs—and the information that comes in brochures and from contacts with rangers do the bulk of the job in controlling visitor impact. This is particularly true in legally designated wilderness. In wilderness, extensive engineering and environmental modification and strict control of where use occurs are clearly inappropriate. As we move away from the primitive end of the opportunity spectrum, the appropriateness of facilities, engineering, and extensive environmental modification increases. In developed campgrounds, for example, site management may rival visitor management in importance. Even here, however, visitor management techniques such as restrictions on the number of people or prohibition of dogs or horses are critical to managing impact.

243

VISITOR MANAGEMENT TECHNIQUES

Although management of the amount, type, and behavior of users is often critical to effective management of recreational impacts, managers must never forget the interests and desires of their recreational clientele. After all, much of the manager's job should be directed toward maximizing visitor satisfaction. It is important to temper a concern for resource protection with a concern for promoting recreational opportunities. The relative importance of these two concerns will vary from area to area, along with management goals and objectives.

A wider variety of visitor management techniques is potentially useful in large recreation areas toward the primitive end of the recreation opportunity spectrum. Therefore, many of the techniques described in this chapter are most applicable to backcountry areas. In fact, most of the examples are taken from wilderness, where research on how visitor management can be used to reduce impacts has been particularly active. The opposite is the case with site management. Many of the techniques described in Chapter 12 will be of limited utility in wilderness, where intensive and extensive site modification is inappropriate.

Limitations on Amount of Use

Although limiting use will be the first technique discussed, it should not be the first line of defense against impact. Reducing use can be a convenient way to limit impact without either having to understand the real cause of problems or getting involved in more direct and active management of problems. However, use limitations conflict with one of the primary objectives of recreation management—providing opportunities for recreational use and enjoyment. It is justified in places where demand is so great that there is little alternative to use reductions or where the only other option is a program of numerous restrictions that preclude many preferred uses. However, other options should be explored first. Use should be limited only after a thorough analysis shows that it is the only way to avoid both unacceptable levels of impact and a program of restrictions that would eliminate much of the joy of visiting the area.

Because the relationship between amount of use and amount of impact is not linear, reducing use will not necessarily reduce impact substantially. A little use causes considerable impact while further increases in use have less and less additional effect on the resource. On already impacted sites all use may have to be curtailed before recovery can occur. In fact, in some situations such as on incised trails where erosion is occurring, even elimination of all use may be ineffective. Active site rehabilitation may be necessary before any recovery occurs.

In popular places, where use levels are high—the most common situation where use reductions have been applied—changes in amount of use will usually have more of an effect on the *number* of impacted sites than on the *severity* of impact on individual sites. Consider the example of a popular wilderness lake basin with 10 campsites. Limiting use to a maximum of five parties per night would probably not reduce use of any of these sites to the point where recovery could occur. However, there would no longer be need for more than five campsites in the basin. Therefore, if managers closed five of these sites, the number of impacted sites would eventually be reduced by the cutback in use. Not only is the severity of impact on individual sites not reduced, but without the supporting action of closing certain campsites, even the number of sites would not have been affected. Use reductions in high use areas are a justifiable means of avoiding crowding but are less useful in avoiding ecological impacts. Where implemented, they must be complemented with a use concentration program to have any ecological benefit at all. In developed recreation areas, use limitation is also a means of seeing that the physical capacity of the area (the number of available campsites, for example) is not exceeded.

In lightly used areas the situation is quite different. Remember that at low use levels, differences in amount of use can have significant effects on amount of impact. If use levels can be kept very low, the severity of impact will also be very low. In such a situation, use limitations can contribute substantially to maintaining low levels of impact. The trick is to keep use low on all sites and to make sure that visitors avoid fragile sites and do not engage in highly destructive behaviors. Even one party of vandals can inflict serious damage. Therefore, a program of use limitation in low use areas—to keep impact levels very low—will only be effective if supported by programs that teach visitors to choose lightly used, resistant recreation sites and to practice low impact techniques. We will discuss these actions, use dispersal and visitor education, in more detail later. Such a program is probably justified only in wilderness-type areas where only very low levels of impact are acceptable.

There are many different ways to limit use. Most involve requiring visitors to obtain use permits. There are also numerous ways to allocate a limited number of permits. Permits can be requested in advance through some sort of reservation system. For example, permits to camp in Yosemite National Park can be reserved through Ticketron, a commercial booking and reservation service that also books concerts and other commercial events. An alternative is to issue permits to visitors on a first-come, first served basis when they arrive at the area. When capacity is reached, additional visitors must be turned away. When demand for permits is many times greater than the number available, lotteries are sometimes used to determine who gets a permit. This is a common means of allocating permits for river trips. People desiring permits submit an application, noting their preferred dates for departure. Then, applications are picked randomly, up to the maximum allowable number, and those parties selected are issued permits. By attaching a fee to a permit or requiring some minimum level of skill or knowledge before qualifying for a permit, demand can be reduced. These can also be a means of rationing (limiting) use.

Each of these methods has certain advantages and disadvantages. Some benefit certain users and are costly to others. Costs to administer are variable, as is the acceptability of the method to visitors. Stankey and Baden (1977) evaluated the pros and cons of each of these means of limiting use. Although they were specifically concerned with rationing wilderness use, their conclusions also apply to other wildland recreation areas. Table 1 summarizes their conclusions. Stankey and Baden (1977) advance five general guidelines to consider when limiting use:

1. Start with an accurate base of knowledge about use, users, and impacts.

2. Reduce use levels only after less restrictive measures have failed to solve the problem.

3. Combine rationing techniques (e.g., issue half of the permits through advance reservation and half first-come, first-served on arrival) to minimize and equalize costs to users and administrators.

4. Establish a system that tends to allocate permits to those people who place the highest value on the permit.

5. Monitor the use limitation program to make sure it is solving problems and is fair.

Both the type of use being limited and where the limitations are applied can vary. In many places overnight use is limited but day use is not. This is justifiable, from an ecological standpoint, where campsite impacts present problems, but trail impacts do not. Campsite impacts are caused almost entirely by overnight users, while trail impacts are caused by both overnight and day users. It is also common to limit permits to float rivers but allow unlimited backpacking in the same area. This is a result of high demand for limited space along the river corridor and low demand elsewhere.

In large nonroaded areas there is an important difference between (1) programs that limit entry to an area but permit free travel once entry has been obtained, and (2) programs that issue a limited number of permits for specific campsites or zones within the area. In this latter case free and spontaneous movement within the area is curtailed because visitors are required to stick to itineraries they agree to before entering the area.

Entry quotas are not as efficient as fixed itineraries in controlling use levels at popular interior locations. Use levels in the interior are affected both by how many people enter the area and by the routes they travel and the places where they choose to camp within the area. Within limits, however, use distribution patterns are consistent and predictable. Therefore, it is possible to devise trailhead quotas that keep use levels at interior locations close to desired levels (Parsons, Stohlgren, and Fodor 1981). Although less efficient, this means of rationing has the advantage of allowing visitors free choice to move about as they please and change their routes and activities in response to circumstances they encounter (such as blisters, bad weather, or new destinations that they see on a map or from some viewpoint).

These freedoms are taken away where visitors are required to stick to fixed itineraries (where limited permits are issued either for specific campsites or zones). Currently, this is a common practice in the back-country of some of the popular national parks, such as Glacier, Yellowstone, Rocky Mountain, Great Smoky Mountains, and Mt. Rainier. Visitors to these parks must state where they are going to camp every night they are in the backcountry. Assuming there are openings available, they are issued a permit to camp in the specific places they have reserved. There is no opportunity, legally, to change their mind even if they overestimated their abilities or if bad weather sets in. With such a program, administrative costs climb because rangers must patrol more

TABLE 1. Evaluation of Impacts and Consequences of Alternative Systems for Rationing Use

Rationing System	Clientele Group Benefited by System	Clientele Group Adversely Affected by System	Experience to Date with Use of System in Wilderness	Acceptability of System to Wilderness Users
		Evaluation Criteria		
Request (Reservation)	Those able and/or willing to plan ahead; i.e., persons with structured life styles.	Those unable or unwilling to plan ahead; e.g., persons with occupations that do not permit long-range planning, such as many professionals.	Main type of rationing system used in both National Forest and National Park wilderness.	Generally high. Good acceptance in areas where used. Seen as best way to ration by users in areas not currently rationed.
Lottery (Chance)	No one identifiable group benefited. Those who examine probabilities of success at different areas have better chance.	No one identifiable group discriminated against. Can discriminate against the unsuccessful applicant to whom wilderness is very important	None. However, is a common method for allocating big-game hunting permits.	Low.

248

Queuing (First-come first-served)	Those with low opportunity cost for their time (e.g., unemployed). Also favors users who live nearby.	Those persons with high opportunity cost of time. Also those persons who live some distance from areas. The cost of time is not recovered by anyone.	Used in conjunction with reservation system in San Jacinto Wilderness. Also used in some National Park Wildernesses.	Low to moderate.
Pricing (Fee)	Those able or willing to pay entry costs.	Those unwilling or unable to pay entry costs.	None.	Low to moderate.
Merit (Skill and knowledge)	Those able or willing to invest time and effort to meet requirements.	Those unable or unwilling to invest time and effort to meet requirements.	None. Merit is used to allocate use for some related activities such as river running.	Not clearly known. Could vary considerably depending on level of training required to attain necessary proficiency and knowledge level.

Table 1. (*Continued*)

		Evaluation Criteria		
	Difficulty for Administrators	Efficiency—Extent to which System Can Minimize Problems of Suboptimization	Principal Way in which Use Impact is Controlled	How System Affects User Behavior
Request (Reservation)	Moderately difficult. Requires extra staffing, expanded hours. Record keeping can be substantial.	Low to moderate. Under utilization can occur because of "no shows," thus denying entry to others. Allocation of permits to applicants has little relationship to value of the experience as judged by the applicant.	Reducing visitor numbers. Controlling distribution of use in space and time by varying number of permits available at different trailheads or at different times.	Affects both spatial and temporal behavior.
Lottery (Chance)	Difficult to moderately difficult. Allocating permits over an entire use season could be very cumbersome.	Low. Because permits are assigned randomly, persons who place little value on wilderness stand equal chance of gaining entry as those who place high value on opportunity.	Reducing visitor numbers. Controlling distribution of use in space and time by number of permits available at different places or times, thus varying probability of success.	Affects both spatial and temporal behavior.

Queuing (First-come first-served)	Low difficulty to moderate. Could require development of facilities to support visitors waiting in line.	Moderate. Because system rations primarily through a cost of time, it requires some measure of worth by participants.	Reducing visitor numbers. Controlling distribution of use in space and time by number of persons permitted to enter at different places or times.	Affects both spatial and temporal behavior. User must consider cost of time of waiting in line.
Pricing (Fee)	Moderate difficulty. Possibly some legal questions about imposing a fee for wilderness entry.	Moderate to high. Imposing a fee requires user to judge worth of experience against costs. Uncertain as to how well use could be "fine tuned" with price.	Reducing visitor numbers. Controlling distribution of use in space and time by using differential prices.	Affects both temporal and spatial behavior. User must consider cost in dollars.
Merit (Skill and knowledge)	Difficult to moderately difficult. Initial investments to establish licensing program could be substantial.	Moderate to high. Requires users to make expenditures of time and effort (maybe dollars) to gain entry.	Some reduction in numbers as well as shifts in time and space. Major reduction in per capita impact.	Affects style of user's behavior.

Source: Stankey and Baden, 1977.

widely to make certain that visitors are keeping to their itineraries. Some limited data from Grand Canyon National Park suggest that over one-third of all parties deviate from their itineraries and, therefore, are subject to citation.

Both increased administrative costs and loss of visitor freedom are accepted for an increase in efficiency. Because use distribution is more tightly controlled at the interior locations of concern, there is less chance that desired use levels will be exceeded. In most situations, however, carrying capacities are sufficiently arbitrary to make this difference in level of efficiency of little importance. A little more impact may be an acceptable trade-off for avoiding the loss of freedom and spontaneity associated with fixed itineraries.

Several studies have asked visitors for their opinions about the acceptability of various use limitation techniques, particularly in wilderness and on whitewater rivers. Most visitors accept use limits if they are necessary to prevent overuse. In San Jacinto and San Gorgonio Wildernesses in California, even parties that did not receive permits and were denied access to the area generally thought the use limits were appropriate (Stankey 1979). Visitors generally prefer rationing techniques with which they are familiar. Lottery is looked at unfavorably in most wildernesses (Stankey and Baden 1977), but it is acceptable on rivers such as the Middle Fork of the Salmon where it has been used successfully for the last decade (McCool and Utter 1981). Fixed itineraries, however, are one of the most disliked of all management alternatives in wilderness (Lucas 1980).

Permits can be used for purposes other than to limit use. They can provide valuable information on users. For example, permits used in Forest Service Wilderness collect data on size of the group, where the party leader lives, main method of travel, date of entry and exit, and location of entry and exit. It is also possible to obtain a rough idea of the party's travel route, although there is no obligation to stick to this itinerary.

Such information can be useful in developing management programs suited to a particular clientele. Permits also provide a means of establishing contact with the user in order to either pass along information or clearly state regulations in force in the area. They can also be used for safety purposes. If a party gets lost, a permit can alert managers to their predicament and help locate them. However, this potential use of permits or a registration system is often not used to advantage because managers do not check for returned permits. This should probably be made clear to visitors who may think they will be rescued if they do not come out by a certain date.

Visitors are generally receptive to nonrationed permits if they are convenient to obtain. For example, in nine wilderness and roadless areas in Montana and California, no more than 15 percent of users found mandatory registration to be undesirable (Lucas 1980). However, compliance with permit systems is highly variable. Compliance is greatest when permits are mandatory and easy to obtain. Self-issued permits at trailheads are a convenient alternative to requiring visitors to come to agency offices during specific hours (Fig. 1). Hendee, Stankey, and Lucas (1978) report compliance rates of 91 to 95 percent with self-issued permits in seven national forest wildernesses in Oregon.

Dispersal of Use

The high level of use concentration in popular parts of dispersed use areas is often blamed for ecological impact problems. For example, in a

Figure 1. Visitors can obtain a free but mandatory permit at this trailhead station. Information on low-impact use techniques, visitor safety concerns, rules, and regulations can be communicated to the visitor at the same time. (*Photo:* R. C. Lucas.)

recent survey Washburne and Cole (1983) asked wilderness managers what their most significant problem was. The most frequent response was "local resource degradation and lack of solitude as a result of concentrated use." The most frequently mentioned "most effective" management technique for dealing with significant problems was personal contact with visitors, leading to increased use dispersal. Dispersal, however, can mean different things to different people. Think about camping, for example. Dispersal could involve (1) spreading people out on the same number of campsites but with greater distance between parties, (2) spreading people out on more sites with or without increasing the distance between parties, or (3) spreading people out in time (increasing off-season use) with or without changing spatial distribution. Each of these types of dispersal has different implications for management of ecological impacts. The appropriateness of each as a means of reducing crowding problems may also be very different from their appropriateness as a means of reducing impact.

Spreading parties out so that they are generally farther apart, but using the same number of recreation sites, will have little positive or negative effect on soils, vegetation, or water (Fig. 2). As long as the

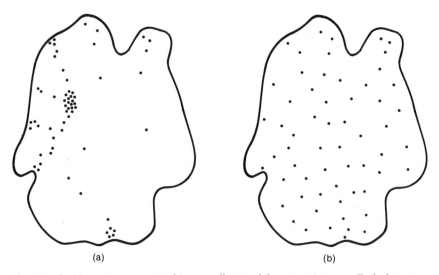

(a)   (b)

Figure 2. In (a) use is concentrated in a small part of the recreation area. Each dot represents a camped party. In (b) use disperal has increased the distance between sites without changing the number of sites. (*Source:* D. N. Cole.)

number of places being impacted remains constant, the distance between impacted sites is irrelevant. The major negative ecological impact associated with this type of dispersal is a likely increase in wildlife disturbance. Certain animals (e.g., grizzly bear, elk, bighorn sheep) retreat to parts of a recreation area where contact with people is infrequent. As more of these safe retreats become frequently used, these wildlife species will have less "safe" habitat, and their populations are likely to suffer. The major advantage to this type of use dispersal is to decrease social crowding at places where parties tend to cluster together. Even on the social side, dispersal can have the negative effect of increased crowding in infrequently used places currently sought out by parties wanting to experience high levels of solitude.

This type of dispersal can be practiced at many scales. Managers can attempt to spread use out over all parts of a recreation area. This is where the problems with wildlife disturbance and loss of high levels of solitude are likely to occur. These two problems are not likely to be severe if use is dispersed on a local level rather than throughout large areas. For example, rather than have numerous sites clustered at one end of a lake, managers might disperse sites around the entire lake. This would reduce crowding and as long as there was no attempt to disperse use to other lakes or other parts of the area not receiving increased use, this would not negatively impact wildlife or high levels of solitude. In general, then, increasing the distance between parties is a positive action, particularly in large wilderness-type areas, if done on a localized scale. On an area-wide scale it has some potentially negative consequences.

When spreading use out entails an increase in the number of sites (and this is probably the most common form of use dispersal), the pros and cons become more complex and difficult to evaluate (Fig. 3). The appropriateness of this type of dispersal depends on amount of use, type of use, user behavior, and resistance of the environment. Spreading use out over more sites is likely to reduce impact in resistant environments, where use levels are low and the type and behavior of most use have little potential for inflicting damage. It is likely to be a disaster in popular areas frequented by large parties, horse parties, or parties that know little about low-impact camping, particularly if the area is fragile (Cole 1981). Let's explore why this is so.

As is so often the case, these management implications reflect the nature of the relationship between amount of use and amount of impact.

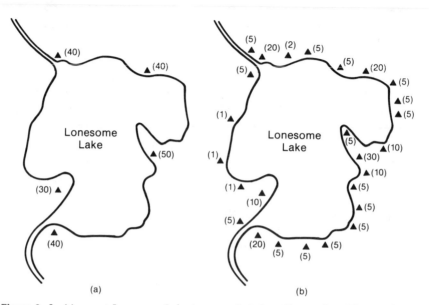

Figure 3. In (*a*) use at Lonesome Lake is concentrated on 5 campsites. The number in parentheses is the nights per year that the site is used. In (*b*) the same amount of use has been dispersed over 26 campsites. (*Source:* D. N. Cole.)

The idea behind this type of use dispersal is to reduce use to levels low enough to keep impact levels low. From the use-impact relationship we know that use levels must be very low before a reduction in amount of use is likely to substantially reduce impact. We also know that to reduce use on one site, use must be increased on other sites. Moreover, increased use of lightly used or unused sites leads to rapid increases in impact.

Let's use a study of lakeside campsites in subalpine forests in the Eagle Cap Wilderness as a case study (Cole 1982a). This is a relatively fragile environment; growing seasons are short, and the vegetation is easily destroyed by trampling. The study examined the condition of campsites receiving three levels of use. An impact rating based on camp area and impact to trees, ground cover vegetation, and soil was calculated for each site. Unused sites had a rating of 1.0, while the most heavily impacted sites had a rating of 3.0. This can be compared with the mean ratings of 1.6 for low use sites, used a few times per year; 2.0 for moderate use sites, used 10 to 20 times per year; and 2.1 for high use sites, used 25 to 50 times per year.

In order to evaluate the desirability of dispersing use in this area, let's assume we need to accommodate 4000 parties around these lakes over the 2 to 3 month summer season. The available options would be to have fewer than 100 high use sites, over 250 moderate use sites, or about 2000 low use sites. Given the great difference in number of sites and relatively small difference in impact rating—even low use sites are over one-half as impacted as high use sites—it seems most reasonable to concentrate use on the 100 high use sites.

The consequence of attempting to spread use out over a large number of campsites in an area with heavy use was documented in the Eagle Cap Wilderness. Over 220 campsites were found in a 325-acre area around two popular lakes (Cole 1982b). Over one-half of these sites had lost more than 25 percent of their vegetation cover, and most were in sight of the trail. While this still represents disturbance of only 1.3 percent of this popular area, one has the perception that impact is everywhere. Moreover, there is no need for so many sites. The average number of parties using the area is about 10 per night, with use perhaps several times as high on peak use nights. Management policy at the time of the study was to ask people not to camp on highly impacted sites, that is, to spread out over more sites. By doing the opposite, concentrating use on a few selected sites, disturbance could be confined to perhaps one-fifth of these sites, effectively reducing impact by about 80 percent. Most parties prefer using the more highly impacted sites anyway.

How well would this type of dispersal work in a lightly used area? What if we only had to accommodate 30 parties per year? One option would be to concentrate all that use on one high-use, high-impact site. However, another option would be to spread this use out over 30 or more sites. If enough potential campsites were available, no site would have to be used even once per year. We do not have data from the Eagle Cap study to predict the impact associated with just one night of use per year. There are many resistant sites, however, where such low use levels would cause essentially no impact. This is particularly true if the party's potential for inflicting damage is low (e.g., if the party is small, travels on foot, and is knowledgeable about low-impact camping). Therefore, spreading use over more sites makes good sense under conditions of low use, resistant environments, and low-impact users.

The implications of this type of management apply primarily to vegetation and soil impact on trails and campsites, particularly in large areas. Water and wildlife probably are less affected by how frequently individual sites are used. Some animals are only highly disturbed on high use sites. In Yosemite National Park, for example, problems with black bears are much more pronounced in high use areas (Keay and van Wagtendonk 1983). Bear problems are aggravated by concentrating use on a few sites. However, smaller animals are likely to be more adversely affected by the creation of many moderately impacted sites than a few highly impacted sites. On the social side this type of dispersal will have no effect on that aspect of crowding related to how frequently recreationists meet other people. It will mean that recreationists see more impacted sites.

Generally, then, dispersal of use among many sites by promoting use of unused or lightly used trails, campsites, or places is likely to substantially increase impact in these places, with little compensatory improvement in the condition of the more popular places, which were the original problems. The exception to this is in low use areas, where dispersal of use, combined with management of where people camp (on very lightly used, resistant sites) and user behavior, can help maintain low levels of impact.

The third type of dispersal, spreading use out over a longer use season, can certainly be beneficial in terms of reducing crowding. However, the ecological effects are, again, complex. Moving use from summer to spring or fall often constitutes moving use to a season when the environment is more fragile. Higher precipitation and snowmelt saturate the soil with water, making it more prone to compaction and erosion. Plants may be more vulnerable in spring when they are initiating growth or in fall when woody plant parts are brittle and easily broken. Wildlife may be vulnerable in spring when they are regaining strength after the winter or in fall when they are getting ready for the winter. Such effects differ greatly from area to area, but they ought to be considered before off-season use is promoted.

In sum, use dispersal is an action that has diverse aspects and implications. It is seldom the panacea that it has sometimes been considered. Even with regard to reducing crowding, it has certain drawbacks. The ecological disadvantages are usually more pronounced. However, there are situations where it can be useful. The key is to use it at the scale and in the places where it will be beneficial. It is most beneficial when applied to localized areas or in places where use levels are low. Usually it will have to be supported with programs designed to manage where and how people engage in recreational activities. The effects of the program should also be monitored because the potential for merely spreading problems around is high.

Where dispersal is desired, it can be accomplished in either a regulatory or a manipulative manner. Regulatory means are comparable to those employed to limit amount of use. Quotas can be established for popular trails, campsites, or zones; when these places are full, additional users must go elsewhere. This technique can be used to increase the distance between parties and/or to avoid concentrated use at certain locations. Of these methods, the highest level of control can be achieved by requiring use of designated dispersed campsites, as is done in the backcountry of Yellowstone National Park. In such a system, visitors must keep to a fixed itinerary, camping at designated campsites, each of which is located a considerable distance from all other sites. In many of the national parks, visitors are required to camp in designated sites. Quotas are set for campsites, but the campsites are clustered in a group. This means that use is locally concentrated but dispersed throughout the park. For reasons previously discussed, this is the worst of both worlds; campsite solitude is lacking, and all parts of the park receive impact. This is often done to make it easier to provide facilities such as toilets.

Spreading use over more sites can be accomplished by establishing use quotas for individual campsites (closing sites to camping after they have been used a certain number of nights) or by requiring that visitors camp on sites that are not highly impacted. One of the only examples is provided by the wilderness management program of Shenandoah National Park, Virginia. Parties are required to camp out of sight of any trail or of signs set up in "no camping" areas. When a campsite shows impact, it is posted as a "no camping" area and allowed to recover. This spreads use out over a large number of sites.

Quotas can also be used to spread visitation out over time. If no permits are available during popular use seasons, there is little alternative but to go during the off-season. Many private parties float the Colorado River through Grand Canyon during the winter months when permits are much easier to obtain than they are during the summer months.

Dispersal can also be accomplished through information and persuasion. This management style is particularly common in Forest Service wilderness areas where freedom and spontaneity are valued highly. Of these, information is preferable to persuasion because it is more subtle and the visitor does not feel pressured to conform, perhaps against his will, to the desires of the manager. Information can be presented in brochures, on signs, or through personal contact (Fig. 4). Use redistribution will be most effective if information is provided during the planning

Figure 4. Personal contact by rangers is a particularly effective means of providing visitors with information. (*Photo:* R. C. Lucas.)

stages of a trip (Lucas 1981). By the time visitors reach the area, it is usually too late to change their minds about where they want to go. This means that written material will usually be the primary informational medium, except in cases where people call and request information.

Visitors also appear to want more information than simply the amount of use that different places receive. In several studies, provision of information on amount of use in different places was ineffective in redistributing use (Lucas 1981). Krumpe and Brown (1982) developed an innovative tool that was successful in redistributing use in Yellowstone National Park. They developed a decision tree (Fig. 5) that permitted visitors to match their preferences for different types of trips with the conditions they were likely to encounter on various trails. This technique redistributed 23 percent of all use from more popular areas to these selected trails.

Advertising the attractiveness of winter in the parks has been effective in increasing off-season use of many national parks. An appeal based entirely on the low use in winter would probably have been less effective. While providing such information is promising, managers must avoid providing too much information and taking away the sense of discovery and exploration that is important to many recreationists.

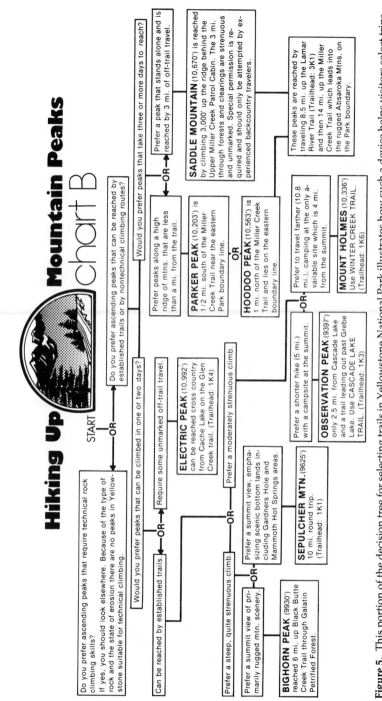

Hiking Up Mountain Peaks
chart B

START

—OR—

Do you prefer ascending peaks that require technical rock climbing skills?
If yes, you should look elsewhere. Because of the type of rock and the state of erosion there are no peaks in Yellowstone suitable for technical climbing.

Do you prefer ascending peaks that can be reached by established trails or by nontechnical climbing routes?

—OR—

Would you prefer peaks that can be climbed in one or two days?

Would you prefer peaks that take three or more days to reach?

—OR—

Can be reached by established trails.

Require some unmarked off-trail travel.

ELECTRIC PEAK (10,992') can be reached cross country from Cache Lake on the Glen Creek trail. (Trailhead: 1K4)

Prefer a moderately strenuous climb.

Prefer a steep, quite strenuous climb.

—OR—

Prefer a summit view, emphasizing scenic bottom lands including Gardners Hole and Mammoth Hot Springs areas.

BIGHORN PEAK (9930') reached 6 mi. up Black Butte Creek Trail through Galatin Petrified Forest.

Prefer a summit view of primarily rugged mtn. scenery.

—OR—

SEPULCHER MTN. (9625) 10 mi. round trip. (Trailhead: 1K1)

Prefer a shorter hike (5 mi.) with a campsite at the summit.

OBSERVATION PEAK (9397') only 2.5 mi. from Cascade Lake and a trail leading out past Grebe Lake. Use CASCADE LAKE TRAIL. (Trailhead: 1K3)

Prefer peaks along a high ridge of mtns. that are less than a mi. from the trail.

PARKER PEAK (10,203') is 1/2 mi. south of the Miller Creek Trail near the eastern Park boundary line.

OR

HOODOO PEAK (10,563') is 1 mi. north of the Miller Creek Trail and lies on the eastern boundary line.

Prefer to travel farther (10.8 mi.), camping at the only available site which is 4 mi. from the summit.

MOUNT HOLMES (10,336') Use WINTER CREEK TRAIL. (Trailhead: 1K6)

Prefer a peak that stands alone and is reached by 3 mi. of off-trail travel.

—OR—

SADDLE MOUNTAIN (10,670') is reached by climbing 3,000' up the ridge behind the Upper Miller Creek Patrol Cabin. The 3 mi. through forests and clearings are strenuous and unmarked. Special permission is required and should only be attempted by experienced backcountry travelers.

These peaks are reached by traveling 8.5 mi. up the Lamar River Trail (Trailhead: 3K1) and then 14 mi. up the Miller Creek Trail which leads into the rugged Absaroka Mtns. on the Park boundary.

Figure 5. This portion of the decision tree for selecting trails in Yellowstone National Park illustrates how such a device helps visitors select trips more likely to match their preferences. (*Source:* Krumpe and Brown 1982. Reprinted with permission.)

261

They must also be cautious about providing only selected information and, of course, should never provide false information.

Signs and personal contact, means of providing information once the visitor enters the area, are most likely to affect local dispersal of use. Utilizing information, for example, Roggenbuck and Berrier (1981) were able to reduce the number of parties that clustered on popular campsites in Shining Rock Gap in Shining Rock Wilderness, North Carolina. The information provided told of the crowded and impacted conditions at the Gap, as well as trail and campsite conditions in some nearby (within 1 mi) alternative camping areas. The number of parties camping at the Gap dropped from 62 per weekend (when no information was provided) to 44 (when information was on a brochure) to 33 (when both a brochure and personal contact with a ranger were used). For experienced hikers the brochure was adequate to redistribute use; for novices personal contact was more effective. Similar techniques could be used to increase the distance between parties or to spread use over more sites.

Concentration of Use

Concentrating use is the opposite of use dispersal. As with dispersal, it can operate in a variety of ways. Distances between parties can be reduced without changing the number of sites; use can be concentrated on fewer sites; or use can be more concentrated in time. The first and third of these options may serve to reduce impact on wildlife in certain situations. Generally, however, they entail high costs to visitors, particularly in increased crowding, and are unlikely to substantially reduce impacts. The most common action taken is to concentrate use on as few campsites and as small a proportion of each campsite as possible.

Spatial concentration of use is one of the premier principles of managing developed recreation areas. Spatial concentration can be applied at several scales. For example, campers are usually required to camp on developed campsites rather than in some undisturbed area of their choice. Within the designated campsite, tent-pads are commonly provided and campers are encouraged to set up their tents on these pads. Both of these actions are variations on the use concentration strategy. Site management techniques intended to confine use to a small proportion of each campsite will be described in Chapter 12.

As was discussed under dispersal of use, use concentration can be appropriate even in large wilderness areas, particularly in places that are heavily used, where it is likely to be the only means of keeping impact from proliferating widely. Use dispersal can be used to maintain very lightly impacted areas, but in popular places there is little alternative to use concentration. Trail construction is a good example of use concentration that serves to avoid the creation of numerous user-created trails criss-crossing the landscape. To provide diversity, large portions of wilderness should remain trailless. Where use is consistent, however, trails need to be built, to provide easier access certainly, but also to avoid development of multiple user-created trail systems. Keeping people on trails and from cutting switchbacks or walking on adjacent braided trails are other examples of concentrating trail use to avoid resource damage.

Concentration of use is particularly important to campsite management (Cole 1981; McEwen and Tocher 1976). Concentration can be accomplished either through regulation or persuasion. The regulatory option is to allow only camping on designated sites. The persuasive option is to ask visitors to use only existing sites. Regulation is seldom necessary because most visitors prefer camping on sites that are already well-used anyway (Cole 1982b). If education does not work, a regulation can be imposed. If illegal sites continue to develop, the only option may be to reduce use levels.

Once a use concentration strategy is implemented successfully, it may be possible to reduce the number of sites. Certain sites can be closed—preferably those that are poorly located or highly damaged. Once use of these sites is eliminated, they may have to be actively rehabilitated. This will shorten the period that they will need to be identified with "no camping" signs or whatever other technique is used to keep people off. More detail on such site management techniques is provided in the next chapter.

Use concentration becomes increasingly important as the potential for users to inflict damage increases. Therefore, it is a particularly important strategy for managing recreational stock and off-road vehicles. In many places these uses are prohibited on certain trails or in certain areas. In Sequoia and Kings Canyon National Parks, for example, a new management plan is proposing to prohibit stock in places that have never received regular stock use. Alternatively, these uses can only be allowed in certain areas established specifically for their use. This is a common strategy for use of off-road vehicles (Fig. 6). In Yellowstone National Park, snowmobiles are only allowed on roads. In the Land Between the Lakes area administered by the Tennessee Valley Authority, off-road

Figure 6. Concentrated motorcycle use in California has denuded this area of vegetation and eroded the bedrock. (*Photo:* D. N. Cole.)

vehicle use is prohibited except in the specially-designated 2350-acre Turkey Bay Off-Road Vehicle Area, where relatively unrestricted vehicle use is allowed.

Limitations on Length of Stay

Use levels can also be reduced by limiting the amount of time visitors can spend in the area. Length of stay limits have been placed on time spent both in the entire recreation area and at specific sites within the area. Area-wide limits are unlikely to have any effect on site impacts. Limits for specific sites will also have little effect if those specific sites are popular. It makes little difference if one party uses a site for seven days or if seven parties use it for one day. The main effect of such a limit is to keep anyone from "homesteading" a particular site. If demand exceeds the supply of campsites or permitted users, a length of stay limit will also allow more parties to use the area. These reasons, to prohibit homesteading and to allow access to more parties, are probably the most common ones for length of stay limits, particularly in more highly developed recreation areas.

In terms of managing ecological impacts, the most important place to impose length of stay limits is in lightly used places, particularly wilderness areas. In places where dispersal is the policy—to avoid substantial impact on all sites—a long stay in one place can cause unacceptable impact. Where dispersal is practiced, length of stay limits should be no more than a night or two at individual sites. No area-wide limits are needed, however, and there should be no need to impose a regulation. Dispersal will only be effective if visitors are highly conscientious about minimizing impact. Keeping their stays at individual sites short should be one of the techniques that all conscientious campers use to keep their impact to a minimum.

Seasonal Limitations on Use

As we discussed in Chapter 7, many environments are particularly fragile during certain seasons of the year. The most common examples are seasons when wildlife are particularly vulnerable and when soils are water-saturated and prone to disturbance. Thus, it is common for recreational use to be limited during these periods. To prevent wildlife disturbance, critical areas may be closed to all use, overnight use, and use by recreational stock or motor vehicles. Soil disturbance problems are most pronounced when use is by stock or motorized vehicles. Thus, it is common to close roads and prohibit travel with stock before some opening date in the summer when soils have had a chance to dry out. Seasonal stock prohibitions reduce damage to trails and to meadows used for grazing.

In Sequoia and Kings Canyon National Parks, for example, there has been a long history of use of meadows by packstock. In an attempt to reduce soil damage, managers have set an objective to keep hoofprints less than 1 in. deep. Managers feel that achieving this objective would avoid damage to the sod cover of meadows—damage that in the past has led to accelerated erosion. To accomplish this objective, opening dates have been set for each forage area in the parks. These opening dates, set in order to keep stock out when soils are water-saturated, vary depending on whether the preceding winter rainy season has been a wet, dry, or normal season. Potential users request opening date information for the places they wish to visit. Opening dates are selected early enough so that visitors have enough advance time to plan their trips.

Zoning

Another management option is to separate different types of users or to prohibit particularly destructive users from using parts of the area. Zoning is a common means of accounting for differences in the impact caused by different modes of travel. The most likely actions to be taken are to create zones in which all use, overnight use, or use by parties with stock or motorized vehicles is prohibited (Fig. 7). National forests, being divided into wilderness and nonwilderness areas, are already zoned in relation to motor vehicles; all motorized traffic (with a few exceptions) is prohibited in wilderness. Even outside of wilderness, motorized vehicles are excluded from some areas for either social or ecological reasons. Prohibitions on motorized use are a common means of reducing wildlife

Figure 7. Closing areas to certain types of users and uses is a common management action. In the Rattlesnake National Recreation Area, Montana, hiking, horse riding, and bicycling are allowed; motorcycling is prohibited, as are shooting and camping within three miles of the trailhead. (*Photo:* D. N. Cole.)

disturbance and deterioration of water quality. Protection of wildlife and of water quality are also the most common justification for excluding either all use or overnight use. Examples include areas that are municipal watersheds and places where encounters with grizzly bears have been a problem.

Excluding stock from certain zones can produce numerous benefits. Hikers who dislike encountering stock are provided with the opportunity of avoiding them if they visit places where stock are prohibited. Selected areas are spared the added impact of stock use, and trail construction and maintenance costs are reduced. In Sequoia and Kings Canyon National Parks, a new management plan proposes to prohibit stock use in a series of meadows that provide representative examples of pristine meadow ecosystems (DeBenedetti and Parsons 1983).

The important concern with zoning is that opportunities are not unfairly denied to legitimate users. All areas cannot provide opportunities for all users. Managers should cater to those users most appropriate in their area, basing appropriateness to some extent on regional opportunities for specific uses. For example, a local prohibition on motor vehicles is easier to justify if motorized recreation opportunities are generally available in the region.

Party Size Limits

Party size limits can be used effectively to avoid certain social conflicts. Large parties can dominate recreational facilities and in wilderness areas, at least, they contribute inordinately to crowding problems (Stankey 1973). It is more difficult to evaluate their effect on environmental conditions. Without question, large groups are likely to create larger disturbed areas simply because they must spread out over a larger area (Fig. 8). A large group can also disturb an area more rapidly than a small party. However, the severity of impact to central concentrated-use parts of any site is unlikely to be affected by party size. It should make little difference if the central part of a site is used by 10 parties of 30 or 100 parties of three; the same number of feet are trampling the area. Certain impacts—use of firewood, for example (Davilla 1979)—may even be reduced when use is by large parties. Wildlife are also likely to be less disturbed by occasional large parties than by frequent small parties.

Party size limits, imposed in order to keep disturbed areas small,

Figure 8. By spreading out over a large area, this large party has created an unusually large area of impact. (*Photo:* U.S. Forest Service.)

seem particularly appropriate in wilderness areas. As with so many visitor management actions, restrictions are most important in lightly used places where a dispersal policy is intended to keep impact levels very low. A small party will find it much easier to leave little trace of their visit than a large party that inadvertently can disturb an area rapidly. In such places limits must be quite low, much lower than the most common current limit of 25 persons per party in wilderness (Washburne and Cole 1983). Along with length of stay limits and other recommended low impact behavior, party size limits in low use places are likely to be most effective as part of an overall educational program for appropriate use of places "off the beaten track."

In more popular places party size limits may also be needed to keep disturbed areas from enlarging and coalescing into huge impacted areas with few buffer strips. This can be unsightly and reduce privacy, reducing the desirability of the area for recreation. In such places limits need to be supported by site management techniques designed to confine use and maintain relatively undisturbed intersite zones (McEwen and Tocher 1976). In many developed recreation areas, specific sites are designated for use by large groups. In Grand Canyon National Park, special large party sites have also been designated in more popular parts of the backcountry.

Low Impact Education

Throughout this discussion we have frequently referred to the need to support certain actions with a strong educational program. Low impact education is one of the real keys to reducing impact in all recreation areas, from the most primitive to the most developed. It is not a panacea; it will not solve all problems. However, without educated and caring users, impact management will remain primarily reactionary in nature. Managers will seldom be able to get beyond treating symptoms to dealing with the cause of problems. Education is the basic foundation on which to build a complete management program.

In our typology of visitor actions in Chapter 9, we distinguished between illegal, careless, unskilled, and uninformed actions and unavoidable impacts. Education can alleviate impact problems caused by the first four types of action; other steps are needed to control unavoidable impacts. On campsites it should be possible, through education, to virtually eliminate damage to trees and pollution of the site with campfire ashes, food remains, soap, and other waste products. On raft trips through the Grand Canyon, collection of firewood is not permitted (except during the off season when driftwood can be collected), all fires must be contained in fire pans that protect the ground, and all ashes, garbage, and human waste must be carried out of the Canyon. Even dishwater is poured through screens into the river and what does not go through the screen is hauled out. As a result, even beaches that are used almost every night by large parties are not polluted and have little tree damage.

In contrast to some of the avoidable impacts, trampling of vegetation and soil is largely unavoidable. On Grand Canyon beaches, vegetation and soil deterioration is not too serious because most use occurs on barren sand. Trampling does contribute to beach erosion, however (Valentine and Dolan 1979). In less resistant places trampling, even by low-impact users, can severely alter soil and vegetation conditions. In such places the amount and distribution of use must also be managed.

A frequently forgotten but obvious point to remember is that educational messages must be tailored to individual places. Behavior that is appropriate in one place may be disastrous in another place. For example, in many frequently used places, site impacts can be most effectively minimized if use is concentrated on a few places (Cole 1981). In such places educational programs should stress using existing sites and keeping them pleasant so that repeat use is encouraged. In lightly used areas, where dispersal is considered to be more appropriate, education should stress the opposite—avoiding already-impacted sites and hiding all evidence of use. Generalized educational programs can teach an ethic of caring for the land, but many of the specific behavioral recommendations must be site-specific, varying even within the same recreation area.

The following points should be considered when developing a low-impact educational program. Other worthwhile sources of information are Bradley (1979), Fazio (1979), and Fazio and Gilbert (1981).

1. *Focus the Message.* It is better to deal with a few critical problems and desired behaviors than to overwhelm the visitor with huge quantities of material. It is important to clearly state the problem, the type of behavior that aggravates the problem, and how a change in behavior will improve the situation. If concepts and the rationale behind suggested behavior are clearly laid out, visitors will be better able to vary their behavior appropriately in different situations. It is important that the suggested behavior be reasonable and adequately communicated to visitors. While personal contact often facilitates initial receptiveness to suggestions, written material may help with retention.

2. *Identify the Audience.* By learning about which visitor groups use the area, messages can be tailored to these specific groups. It is particularly worthwhile to identify "problem users," those that contribute most to critical problems. Programs are likely to be most effective if different messages are developed for each user group rather than hitting everyone with the same message. For example, there is no reason to burden backpackers with all of the details of low-impact stock use.

3. *Select Communication Methods.* Various media can potentially be used to educate visitors. Some media have been tried, many have not, and few have been evaluated. Personal contact is often considered to be the most effective means of communication, although brochures can also be effective (Roggenbuck and Berrier 1981). Where they exist, visitor centers can be effective places to deliver educational messages. Mass media such as television, radio, and newspapers are other options, but

they frequently fail to reach the right audience (Fazio 1979). Demonstrations and field programs have been used in town, at universities, club meetings, and at the recreation area. Except in the latter case, these have the advantages of being tailored to a specific group and of providing the information during the planning stages of a trip. This is also true of the low-impact information that is increasingly being added to guidebooks and how-to manuals. Managers should seek to contribute to and review material for books written about their area. The most effective programs will use a variety of media, each tailored for a particular user group and message (Bradley 1979).

4. *Decide Where to Contact the Audience.*   Again, this depends on the targeted user group and the communication media selected. Some visitors can be contacted at home if they request information or are required to obtain reserved permits. This has worked very well on whitewater rivers such as the Colorado River through Grand Canyon. Advance information is critical where required behavior demands special equipment. Local residents—the most frequent users of most recreation areas—can be reached through special programs in the community, on radio and television, or through the newspaper. College students can be reached on campus; horse clubs, Boy Scouts, and other organized groups can be contacted directly.

We want to stress again that the appropriate *content* of an educational program will vary from place to place, with environmental conditions, management objectives, and amount and type of use. Off-road vehicle users, parties with stock, and hikers each require different skills to practice low-impact use. Appropriate behavior in a low use, undeveloped wilderness setting is very different from that in a high use, developed, roaded area. Finally, different areas with different regulations will require unique programs. The point here is that one must choose from among the following and other suggestions and develop a program tailored to specific situations.

Perhaps most emphasis is given to education of wilderness users. Certainly education is particularly important there, where management seeks to avoid regulation and where minimal impact is an overriding management objective. Most low-impact suggestions pertain to campsite use. These are some of the more generally useful and noncontroversial techniques.

1. *Take Along Proper Equipment.*   Lightweight, self-contained tents

Figure 9. An illustration of various states of campsite deterioration and recommended user responses. (*Drawings:* W. Sydoriak.)

eliminate the need to cut down trees for tent poles or lean-to's. Air mattresses or foam pads eliminate the need for bough beds. Waterproof floors eliminate the need to ditch tents. Stoves mean either no or less firewood gathering and campfire impact.

2. *Keep Party Size Small.* As mentioned before, this is particularly important to avoid disturbing sites in low use areas.

3. *Select Resistant and Appropriate Campsites.* This is a particularly important skill. Large parties, parties with packstock, and parties

Table: Campsite Condition and Recommended User Responses

CONDITION CLASS	VISIBLE INDICATORS	RECOMMENDED USER RESPONSES
1. PRISTINE	The site appears never to have been used before.	USE WITH CAUTION IN CERTAIN SITUATIONS The keys to proper use of these sites are minimum impact, selection of resistant sites away from attractions, and *no* repeat use. These are ideal sites in lightly used areas *if* you are careful to minimize impacts. In high use areas, it is preferable to select a moderately impacted site unless your party is small, has no packstock, uses a stove, is highly experienced in low impact camping, and chooses a resistant site away from more popular locations.
2. SEMI-PRISTINE	Sites are barely recognizable as campsites. Vegetation has been flattened, but bare areas have not been created.	DO NOT USE These sites will rapidly deteriorate if used repeatedly. In low use areas select a pristine site; in high use areas, select a moderately impacted site.
3. LIGHTLY IMPACTED	Ground vegetation worn away around the fireplace or center of activity.	USE ONLY IF NECESSARY Unless these sites are particularly resistant (e.g., sandy beaches, rocky outcrops, dry meadows, or grasslands), they will deteriorate rapidly if use increases. Moderately impacted sites are always preferable and in low use areas, pristine sites are preferable.
4. MODERATELY IMPACTED	Ground vegetation worn away on most of the site, but humus, litter decomposing leaves and needles are usually present on much of the site.	USE WHERE POSSIBLE These sites are not highly susceptible to further damage. They retain most of their desirable attributes and site impact is not irreversible. If possible, choose screened, forested sites, out of sight and sound of other parties. Do not damage overstory trees. For campfires, collect only dead and down wood that you can break by hand. Avoid trampling seedlings.
5. HIGHLY IMPACTED	Ground vegetation, humus and litter has been worn away on most of the site exposing gritty, dusty, or muddy bare mineral soil. Tree roots may be exposed if stock have been tied to trees but soil erosion is not obvious. Firewood is usually scarce in the vicinity of the campsite. Some overlapping of campsites may occur.	USE ONLY IF NECESSARY Where possible, these sites should be avoided to encourage site recovery. In low use areas these sites should never be used. Managers should be encouraged to close and rehabilitate them. In high use areas, this level of deterioration may have to be accepted as the norm. However, select moderately impacted sites if they exist. When using these sites, avoid spreading out or any other practice that might contribute to site enlargement. Minimize the use of wood fires.
6. SEVERELY IMPACTED	Soil erosion is obvious. Exposure of tree roots and rocks is pronounced and widespread. Trees may be reduced in vigor or dead. Individual campsites may coalesce to create large disturbed areas with multiple fire rings. Firewood is scarce for a considerable distance around the campsite.	DO NOT USE Unless managing agencies require the use of such sites, they should never be used. Damage is already almost irreversible. Managers should be encouraged to permanently close these sites to use.

knowing little about low-impact camping should choose existing, well-used campsites that are unlikely to deteriorate further. This is particularly important in heavily used areas. In low use areas it is better to select pristine sites *if* a party knows how to minimize impact. It is particularly important in such places to allow sufficient time and energy at the end of the day to find an impact-resistant site. As an educational tool, Cole and Benedict (1983) provide a table and set of drawings of campsites in various states of deterioration (Fig. 9). They list the conditions under which these sites should or should not be used. The idea, as previously discussed, is to direct use either to pristine sites or sites that are unlikely to deteriorate further. Lightly impacted sites are to be avoided because they are likely to deteriorate with further use while, if left unused, they should recover quickly. The most severely impacted sites are also to be avoided because they are either poorly located or have suffered excessively as a result of poor camping practices in the past.

4. *Be Careful with Use of Fire.*   This is extremely important in both high and low use areas. In high use areas the goal is to keep sites attractive so that others will be encouraged to also use the same sites rather than damage new areas. In low use areas the goal is to eliminate all traces of your visit so others will *not* be attracted to the site.

5. *Avoid Site Engineering.* Do not level or ditch tent pads or build rock walls as windbreaks.

6. *Minimize Site Pollution.* Pack out all garbage and use only biodegradable soaps in small quantities and away from water sources.

7. *Properly Dispose of Human Waste.*   Use toilets if they are provided. Use a latrine if traveling with a large group in a heavily used area. This minimizes the number of disposal sites that inadvertently might be uncovered. Otherwise, use the "cat-hole" method in which individuals bury their waste in a shallow hole (about 6 to 8 in. deep) well away from water bodies and campsites.

8. *Keep Lengths of Stay to a Night or Two on Sites in Low Use Areas.* Concern for the exact location of tent and fire sites and where you walk (particularly avoiding tree seedlings) can also reduce impact.

9. *Cleanup Is Very Important.*   High use sites should be left clean and

pleasant; low use sites should show no evidence of your visit. Judicious spreading of duff and litter can effectively camouflage trampling damage to low use sites.

For hikers the most important aspects of low-impact trail use are to stay on the bare tread and, particularly, to avoid cutting switchbacks or walking on lightly used segments of braided trails. Closed trails and impromptu trails just beginning to develop should never be used. Where parties are traveling cross-country, it is best to spread out and not trample the same path. With small parties this may not be necessary unless the vegetation is particularly fragile. The point is to avoid creating a new trail.

Parties with stock could reduce their impact greatly by avoiding certain destructive behaviors. First of all, stock should never be allowed on campsites. Keeping stock off the site will limit soil disturbance and avoid fouling the ground with manure. Proper containment of stock is extremely important. Tying horses directly to trees causes root exposure and damage and can girdle and kill small trees. Picketing a horse in one place for a long time results in spotty overgrazing unless picket pins are rotated frequently. Less destructive approaches are to use hobbles when horses are grazing and to tie horses to a rope strung between trees when they are not grazing or when they are eating supplemental feed. Lightweight electric fencing is available for use in creating temporary corrals. Again, it is important not to overuse selected spots. Stock parties would do well to avoid use of trails or meadows when they are wet and prone to damage. Finally, grazing impacts could be sharply reduced if parties carried at least some of their own feed. It is important, particularly in wilderness, that the feed not contain nonnative weeds.

A range of styles can be used to teach people low-impact behaviors. Low-impact techniques can be required; this involves establishing and enforcing regulations. Visitors can also be persuaded to behave in a certain manner through contacts either on-site or at the trailhead. The least obtrusive method is to conduct off-site programs and to concentrate on teaching concepts—about impacts, their causes, and how they can be avoided. This approach allows visitors to develop their own means of minimizing impact. If concepts are communicated well, visitors should be capable of developing adequate means of avoiding impact, and their level of commitment to these techniques should be high.

In more developed situations the most important aspects of user behavior relate to keeping the area attractive and staying on paths and other disturbed areas so that intersite buffer zones are maintained in a relatively undisturbed state. Concern for disturbing or infringing on other users is also very important. Much of the educational message unique to water-based recreation also relates to not disturbing others. Obvious examples are convincing motor boaters to give swimmers a wide berth and to slow down when passing nonmotorized craft. Concern for polluting waters with petroleum products is also important.

Education can also be a potent means of reducing the impact of off-road vehicles. Snowmobilers should learn about problems related to the harassment of wildlife in winter, and they should learn to avoid approaching animals. Although potential impacts are greatest with snowmobilers, skiers and even summer users also need to be aware of and avoid harassment of animals. With other types of off-road vehicles, much of the problem is with erosion. Erosion's effects on water quality and site productivity need to be understood. Riding techniques and locations can be selected to minimize erosion. These concerns, as usual, are more important in dispersed use situations than in areas set aside and managed intensively for off-road vehicle recreation.

CAMPFIRE MANAGEMENT ALTERNATIVES

To illustrate how a wide variety of techniques is usually available for dealing with any specific problem, let us take a look at some alternative campfire management programs. Table 2 presents some alternatives to the last resort of a policy in which all campfires are banned (Hammitt 1982). While there may be situations in which there is no alternative other than the complete prohibition of backcountry campfires, such a policy should be implemented only after considering less restrictive alternatives. The proposed alternatives vary from those that are most *indirect* in controlling user opportunities to experience campfires to those that are most *direct*.

Information Programs

The most indirect of the management alternatives is the provision of information to park users about impacts of the campfire and its proper

TABLE 2. Alternatives for Managing the Use of Campfires in Backcountry Recreation Areas

Type of Management	Alternative	Specific Examples
Indirect (Emphasizes modifying user behavior; preserving campfire opportunities)	Information programs	Promote desired campfire policies. Educate users of campfire impacts. Redistribute users to underused areas or more tolerant sites.
	Alternative fuels	Encourage use of lightweight stoves, lanterns, and alternative fuels.
Direct (Emphasizes regulation of user; removal of opportunities)	Elevational zoning	Restrict fires above treeline and in adjacent high elevation plant communities.
	Forest type and site zoning	Restrict fires from forest types that lack fuelwood (e.g., spruce-fir forest). Restrict fires from non-forested areas (e.g., grassy balds, beech gaps). Restrict fires by specific sites that lack fuelwood or present a fire danger.
	Temporal zoning	Restrict fires to hours of darkness only. (Require stoves for cooking.)
	Seasonal zoning	Restrict fires to winter and cool weather seasons.
	Communal fires	Require several parties to share a common fire.
	Rationing	Ration campfires to ½ and ⅓ of the nights camped by a party.
	Total ban	Eliminate fires on a park wide basis.

use. Many parks are already using this alternative through interpretive programs and low-impact use brochures. The objective is not to restrict user behavior but to modify it. Information on campfire impacts, low-impact camping, park policies governing the use of campfires and resource preservation, and underused areas where campfire impacts are less of a concern may modify user behavior such that campfire impacts are greatly reduced.

Alternative Fuels

An action that is closely related to providing general information on campfire impact and use is encouraging the use of alternative fuels. By informing campers of the advantages of lightweight stoves for cooking, campers may choose to use fewer open fires. The use of lightweight lanterns as a substitute for the social campfire might also be encouraged.

Elevational Zoning

As a more direct alternative to campfire management, the manager may want to restrict the use of campfires above certain elevations. The small quantities of fuelwood above treeline and in adjacent subalpine plant communities may make it necessary to eliminate the use of campfires in these areas. Because of the short growing season and slow rate of wood production at these elevations, fuelwood production is insufficient to support campfires.

Forest Type and Site Zoning

As an extension of the elevational zoning alternative, certain forest types and nonforested areas of a wildland area may need to be zoned as no-fire camping areas. Zones where campfires are prohibited may be those where fuelwood production is insufficient to meet the supply needs of campers. This alternative can also apply to specific sites or locations where use is heavy and fuelwood has been greatly depleted or where forest fire danger is high during the fire season.

Temporal Zoning

The philosophy behind temporal zoning is to limit campfires to an aesthetic function that occurs only after dark. Many backcountry users are already using lightweight stoves for their cooking. Stoves are more dependable and efficient than campfires for cooking. However, the presence of a stove does not eliminate the desire to have a campfire. Most campers still consider the fire to be an important esthetic and social component of the camping experience. By requiring campers to use stoves for their cooking and to build campfires only after dark, far less fuelwood would be used. Instead of three campfires per day (breakfast, lunch, dinner) or, as sometimes occurs, the all day cooking fire, the campfire would be limited to a few hours of darkness during the typical summer evening. This action might reduce the demand for fuelwood to the point where the forest could produce enough fuel to meet the needs of campers.

Seasonal Zoning

A further restriction on campfire use would be to restrict its use to winter and cool season camping. Fuel is needed for heat and comfort during these seasons, but demand is light because of low use at this time of year. This would have the added advantage of encouraging off-season use, in places where a shift toward increased off-season use is desirable.

Communal Fires

Another means of reducing the number of backcountry campfires and the consumption of fuelwood is to have several parties share the same fire. On South Manitou Island at Great Sleeping Bear National Lakeshore, Michigan, a communal campfire pit is supplied for every 6 to 10 camping sites. Fires are prohibited except in designated pits. The technique appears to be quite successful, with essentially no evidence of tree chopping or removal of horizontal screening vegetation within and between individual campsites. Although this alternative would not serve the needs of all types of campers (i.e., those oriented to solitude), it does provide an opportunity within the spectrum of campfire alternatives for many campers to experience campfires.

The communal fire concept deserves further adaptation to various backcountry areas. Alpine lakes and other destination areas where campers tend to concentrate would be likely areas where the communal fire alternative might be tried.

Rationing

Rather than eliminate fires entirely from the camping experience, managers may want to limit fires to only one-third or one-half of each party's camping nights. The rationing of campfires could occur at the time hiking permits are issued, by having campers select the nights they want to have fires. Although difficult to enforce, a potential added benefit of this alternative might be an increase in the quality of campfire experiences. Because it would make sitting around a campfire a less common experience, rationing may cause the camper to place a higher value on the campfire experience when it is permitted.

Total Ban

Little explanation is needed for this alternative (Fig. 10). However, much deliberation is needed before resorting to it. Recreation resource management should provide a spectrum of recreational opportunities so that the needs of a diversity of users are met. The campfire is an important

Figure 10. Extensive campfire impacts, as illustrated in this scene, have led to the banning of campfires in some backcountry recreation areas. (*Photo:* W. E. Hammitt.)

component of the camping experience, and we need to provide for its enjoyment when and where possible.

VISITOR INFORMATION NEEDED TO MANAGE RECREATION IMPACTS

To effectively manage visitors, certain types of information are needed. The most obvious is how many people are using the area. It may also be important to know how people are distributed, both in space and over time. User characteristics such as their mode of travel, party size, and length of stay may influence management decisions. Knowing where people come from will help in contacting users for an educational program. Finally, knowing visitors' attitudes about conditions in the area and their management preferences can also help in development of a management program that is sensitive to the visitor's desires and needs.

As was mentioned before, much of this information can be obtained from permits. Information commonly collected on permits provides data on amount of use, its spatial and temporal distribution, mode of travel, party size, length of stay, and the residence of the person with the permit. Registration is basically the same thing as a permit, except that it is often not mandatory and, therefore, compliance rates are often low (Lucas 1983). Registration rates can be adjusted to compensate for non-registrants, but this requires separate studies of registration behavior. Numbers of people entering an area can be counted with automatic counters. These are sometimes linked to cameras that take low-resolution photographs. This makes it possible to determine method of travel and party size. This is costly, however, and the question of invading privacy can be a concern. Number of people can be observed directly at a sample of times and places, but this is costly too, and the use estimates obtained are not likely to be very accurate. Air photos have been used to count people, particularly those engaged in water-based recreation or at an off-road vehicle area. Of all these options, however, permits are the least costly, most precise, and most informative.

Specialized information on visitor opinions and preferences is more difficult to obtain. The most common method is to use a survey or questionnaire. These need to be carefully constructed and administered in a systematic manner, following established sampling theory. Otherwise, results will be biased and will not provide the information managers are seeking. Surveys conducted or sponsored by federal agencies must be approved by the Office of Management and Budget, a difficult procedure. Other options are direct observation of behavior or use of some sort of diary or self-reporting form in which visitors keep track of certain items of interest to the manager. Observation has been used to determine such things as how much time people actually spend fishing at lakes. Diaries have been used to record information that might be difficult to recall later such as the high point of a day or the number of fish caught in specific places.

All information is costly to obtain; consequently, it is important to have specific reasons for each bit of information collected. It is almost always better to systematically collect a few types of information than to haphazardly collect many types. Finally, it is important to be sensitive to the visitor. All efforts should be made to avoid unnecessarily inconveniencing or intruding on the visitor. In many cases the visitor is only too happy to provide information, and there are other cases where the information is important enough to demand compliance. Concern for efficiently and sensitively collecting only useful information will avoid most problems and will add considerably to development of a management program.

REFERENCES

Bradley, J. 1979. A Human Approach to Reducing Wildland Impacts. In Ittner, R., D. R. Potter, J. K. Agee and S. Anschell, eds., *Recreational Impact on Wildlands Conference Proceedings*. USDA Forest Service, Pacific Northwest Region, Portland, OR. pp. 222–226.

Cole, D. N. 1981. Managing Ecological Impacts at Wilderness Campsites: An Evaluation of Techniques. *Journal of Forestry* 79:86–89.

Cole, D. N. 1982a. Wilderness Campsite Impacts: Effect of Amount of Use. USDA Forest Service Research Paper INT-284. 34 pp.

Cole, D. N. 1982b. Controlling the Spread of Campsites at Popular Wilderness Destinations. *Journal of Soil and Water Conservation* 37:291–295.

Cole, D. N., and J. Benedict. 1983. Wilderness Campsite Selection—What Should Users Be Told? *Park Science* 3(4):5–7.

Davilla, B. 1979. Firewood Production, Use, and Availability in the High Sierra. In Stanley, Jr., J. T., H. T. Harvey, and R. J. Hartesveldt, eds., *A Report on the Wilderness Impact Study: The Effects of Human Recreational Activities on Wilderness Ecosystems with Special Emphasis on Sierra Club Wilderness Outings in the Sierra Nevada*. Outing Committee, Sierra Club, San Francisco, CA. pp. 94–128.

DeBenedetti, S. H., and D. J. Parsons. 1983. Protecting Mountain Meadows: A Grazing Management Plan. *Parks* 8(3):11–13.

Fazio, J. R. 1979. Communicating with the Wilderness User. Bulletin 28, College of Forestry, Wildlife and Range Sciences, University of Idaho, Moscow. 65 pp.

Fazio, J. R., and D. L. Gilbert. 1981. Public Relations and Communications for Natural Resource Managers. Dubuque, IA: Kendall/Hunt. 400 pp.

Hammitt, W. E. 1982. Alternatives to Banning Campfires. *Parks* 7(3):8–9.

Hendee, J. C., G. H. Stankey, and R. C. Lucas. 1978. Wilderness Management. USDA Forest Service Miscellaneous Publication 1365. 381 pp.

Keay, J. A., and J. W. van Wagtendonk. 1983. Effect of Yosemite Backcountry Use Levels on Incidents with Black Bears. In Meslow, E. C., ed., *Bears—Their Biology and Management*. International Conference for Bear Research and Management 5:307–311.

Krumpe, E. E., and P. J. Brown. 1982. Redistributing Backcountry Use Through Information Related to Recreation Experiences. *Journal of Forestry* 80:360–364.

Lucas, R. C. 1980. Use Patterns and Visitor Characteristics, Attitudes and Preferences in Nine Wilderness and Other Roadless Areas. USDA Forest Service Research Paper INT-253. 89 pp.

Lucas, R. C. 1981. Redistributing Wilderness Use Through Information Supplied to Visitors. USDA Forest Service Research Paper INT-277. 15 pp.

Lucas, R. C. 1983. Low and Variable Visitor Compliance Rates at Voluntary Trail Registers. USDA Forest Service Research Note INT-326. 5 pp.

McCool, S. F., and J. Utter. 1981. Preferences for Allocating River Recreation Use. *Water Resources Bulletin* 17:431–437.

McEwen, D., and S. R. Tocher. 1976. Zone Management: Key to Controlling Recreational Impact in Developed Campsites. *Journal of Forestry* 74:90–93.

Parsons, D. J., T. J. Stohlgren, and P. A. Fodor. 1981. Establishing Backcountry Use Quotas: An Example from Mineral King, California. *Environmental Management* 5:335–340.

Roggenbuck, J. W., and D. L. Berrier. 1981. Communications to Disperse Wilderness Campers. *Journal of Forestry* 79:295–297.

Stankey, G. H. 1973. Visitor Perception of Wilderness Recreation Carrying Capacity. USDA Forest Service Research Paper INT-142. 61 pp.

Stankey, G. H. 1979. Use Rationing in Two Southern California Wildernesses. *Journal of Forestry* 77:347–349.

Stankey, G. H., and J. H. Baden. 1977. Rationing Wilderness Use: Methods, Problems and Guidelines. USDA Forest Service Research Paper INT-192. 20 pp.

Valentine, S., and R. Dolan. 1979. Footstep-induced Sediment Displacement in the Grand Canyon. *Environmental Management* 3:531–533.

Washburne, R. F., and D. N. Cole. 1983. Problems and Practices in Wilderness Management: A Survey of Managers. USDA Forest Service Research Paper INT-304. 56 pp.

12 Site Management

Managers can also strive to control impact through management of where use occurs and through manipulation of the site itself. Impacts will be reduced if use occurs on relatively durable sites. Design and treatment of sites can also do much to keep impacts within acceptable limits. Site management can affect the amount, type, and distribution of visitors, as well as the durability of the resource and can be used to restore places that have been excessively damaged. Generally, site management is likely to increase in intensiveness and importance toward the more developed end of the recreation opportunity spectrum. Everywhere, effective management will require a mix of both visitor and site management.

When developing site management plans, it is important to strive to maintain a natural appearance, particularly in wildland recreation areas. Even in wilderness, however, managers should not be paralyzed by a concern with avoidance of engineering if it is the only means of avoiding equally "unnatural" resource damage. Curiously, many managers in wilderness have little problem with highly engineered trails, but they resist similar engineering levels for campsites and stock-use areas. The obtrusiveness of site manipulation must be carefully weighed against the obtrusiveness of site impacts and other means of solving problems.

Another concern in site management is cost, both to the visitor and to management. Closure of all sites at a lake to permit recovery and closure of a road to move a trailhead back 10 miles are costly actions for visitors. They may be justified, but evaluation of the severity of the problem at hand, the likely effectiveness of alternative actions, and costs to the visitor must all be considered. Many site management actions entail significant costs for management. These range from the high costs of installing irrigation systems to improve plant growth on campsites to lesser costs for building a corral or a hitchrail. Some actions are only costly in the construction phase; others entail significant ongoing maintenance costs. It is particularly wasteful to make an initial investment in a program that proves ineffective because of insufficient maintenance funds.

LOCATING USE ON RESISTANT SITES

One effective means of reducing impact is to see that most use occurs on durable sites. For example, in a number of experimental trampling studies, the vegetation loss associated with walking along an experimental path 100 times ranged from less than 5 percent in a mountain grassland in Montana to almost 90 percent in a lodgepole pine forest in Alberta (Cole 1985). This suggests that the grassland might be able to receive over 10 times as much use as the forest, with no more impact. It is difficult to generalize about what makes a site durable because a good location for a trail may not be a good location for a campsite. Even with campsites, a durable low use site may not be a durable high use site. Moreover, generalizations about durability are extremely site-specific; they vary from region to region. Given the importance of this action, however, some generalizations for specific situations will be offered. Additional information is provided in Chapter 7.

On high use campsites the most important durability considerations are probably overstory trees and the soil's erodibility, drainage, and depth. Other aesthetic considerations should also be evaluated. Because tree regeneration is sharply curtailed on campsites, it is wise to locate campsites in stands of relatively young, long-lived trees that are not susceptible to disease. This will prolong the time that campsites will be forested. In the West, aspen groves should be avoided because they are highly susceptible to canker diseases when mechanically injured (e.g., through initial carving) by campers (Hinds 1976). Forested campsite life spans in aspen are on the order of 20 years. Ripley (1962) provides an index of the susceptibility of 27 Southern Appalachian trees and shrubs to disease infection, insect infection, and decline (Table 1). This provides

TABLE 1. Rankings of Trees from Most to Least Able to Withstand the Impacts of Recreation Use

Hardwoods		Conifers
1. Hickories	12. Red maple	1. Shortleaf pine
2. Persimmon	13. American holly	2. Hemlocks
3. Sycamore	14. Sourwood	3. White pine
4. White ash	15. Black birch	4. Pitch pine
5. Beech	16. White oaks	5. Virginia pine
6. Sassafras	17. Black walnut	
7. Buckeye	18. Red oaks	
8. Yellow-poplar	19. Black locust	
9. Dogwood	20. Magnolia	
10. Blackgum	21. Black cherry	
11. Yellow birch	22. Blue beech	

Source: Ripley 1962.

a useful guide for deciding on campsite locations. The durability of ground cover vegetation is much less important because, with heavy use, even resistant ground cover is unlikely to survive.

It is important for erosion potential to be minimal, because heavy use campsites must be used for a long time. It is best to locate sites on relatively deep soils with a wide mix of particle sizes (e.g., loams) and at least a moderate amount of organic matter as such soils have good drainage. Soils with drainage do not have serious problems with flooding and excessive runoff. Primarily organic soils should be avoided. However, thick organic horizons minimize the exposure of mineral soil that results from campsite use. Deep soils with moderately rapid drainage are also required for many human waste disposal systems that depend upon on-site decomposition. Leonard, Spencer, and Plumley (1981) provide a useful table of limitations posed by certain physical site characteristics for overnight facilities (Table 2). Some of these guidelines only apply to the northern Appalachians, for which the table was developed; others are more general in applicability.

On lightly used campsites such as those in a portion of wilderness where use dispersal is being practiced, the most important durability consideration is the resistance of the ground cover vegetation. If properly managed, soil damage in such places should be minimal, and tree damage should not occur. The main problem is avoiding devegetation

TABLE 2. Physical Site Characteristics and Limitations for Overnight Facility Locations

	Limitations		
	None to slight	Moderate	Severe
Topography			
Slope	2 to 15 percent	15 to 30 percent	Greater than 30 percent
Landform	Valleys, footslopes, low-elevation ridges, terraces or benches on side slopes	Midslopes of mountains	Steep mountain side slopes, depressions, ravine floors, pond shorelines, bog lands
Aspect	East, south	West, north	Northwest, southeast (or aspects receiving most frequent storm winds)
Soil			
Depth to impervious layer or seasonal high-water table	Greater than 5 feet	2½ to 5 feet	Less than 2½ feet
Drainage	Rapid to moderately well drained	Moderately well to imperfectly drained or excessively rapid	Poorly or imperfectly drained
Flooding	None		One to 2 times per year during use season.

Soil texture	Moderately coarse to medium texture (sandy loam to silt loams)	Moderately fine or slightly coarse texture (clay loams, silt-clay loams, or sandy soils of 65 percent sand)	Fine texture (clays), loose sand, or organic soils
Rockiness/stoniness	Cobbles/gravel—20 percent Surface rocks—25 feet apart	Cobbles—20 to 50 percent Surface rocks—5 to 25 feet apart	Cobbles—50 percent Surface rocks—5 feet apart
Vegetation types	Beech, maple, oak, hickory, pine stands	Spruce, fir, hemlocks, birch, alders, willows	Alpine, subalpine, bog, krummholz
Water supply For huts	Available potable water source provides quantity sufficient for daily consumption throughout season, e.g., 12 gal./person/day	Water source has decreasing flow during season to ¾ the quantity needed and water must be stored	Inconsistent flow from the water source and quantity is less than 12 gal./person/day
For shelter or tentsites	Water flows from a spring, and the flow and quality are reliable all season. Spring outlet is within 250 yards of site	Water flows from a spring but flow is decreased to a trickle at the end of season. Spring outlet is ¼ mile away	Reliable spring water is over ½ mile away

Source: Leonard et al. 1981. Copyright © 1981 by Appalachian Mountain Club, used with permission of publisher.

which, once it occurs, tends to attract further use to the site. It is always best to select sites without any vegetation at all. Examples include sheets of bare rock, sand beaches, gravel bars, and some dense forests. Where vegetation is present, considerable information or experience may be needed to evaluate durability. Many of the resistant plant characteristics mentioned in Chapter 3 can be used to evaluate the resistance of different vegetation types. The most useful general guideline is that grasslands and meadows are more resistant than the undergrowth in forests (Fig. 1). Dry vegetation types are usually more resistant than moist types.

Selecting a durable route is often the most important tool in managing impacts on trails. It is certainly the least costly tool and should be the first line of defense, particularly in wilderness where the other major management option—engineering—is to be avoided as much as possible. The most important environmental factors affecting trail durability are usually topography, soil moisture, and soil erodibility. The slope of the trail and the extent to which the trail intercepts runoff from upslope

Figure 1. Vegetation loss at this outfitter site in the Bob Marshall Wilderness, Montana, is low because it is located in a resistant dry grassland. (*Photo:* D. N. Cole.)

are particularly important. Trails with steep slopes are likely to deteriorate rapidly unless steps are taken to control erosion. The same is true of
trails that run straight up slopes and are depressed well below the
ground surface. Such trails intercept overland flow and are quickly
eroded by running water. On the other hand, trails with no slope at all
often have trouble draining. The best trail locations are on slight grades,
usually between 1 and 7 percent, on side hills where water will not be
diverted onto the trail. Where such a location cannot be sustained, engineering techniques will need to be used to mitigate the potential problems of a less than ideal location.

In many mountainous areas the most comon cause of trail damage
from the users's point of view is excessive soil moisture, which leads to
development of muddy trails (Fig. 2). Muddy stretches are difficult to
walk through. Moreover, in an attempt to avoid the mud, hikers and
horses frequently skirt the stretch and, in doing so, widen the quagmire.
In the Bob Marshall Wilderness "trail bogs" knee-deep in mud may be
100 yds long and almost as wide.

Areas of late snowmelt, high water tables, and places where water

Figure 2. This trail traverses an area of high soil moisture. It is widening, developing
parallel trails and is difficult for hikers to negotiate. (*Photo:* D. N. Cole.)

drains onto the trail are common situations in which problems with muddy trails occur. Locating trails on south-facing slopes is a general means of avoiding problems with late snowmelt. Before locating a trail, it is often useful to observe where snow lasts longest, either in the field or with the aid of aerial photography. High water tables can often be identified by using vegetational indicators. On a trail system in the Selway-Bitterroot Wilderness, for example, over two-thirds of the muddiness problems were in one vegetation type, which, along with the vigorous growth of four individual species, indicates quite accurately where muddiness problems are likely to occur (Cole 1983). Soil color can also be used as an indicator of potential muddiness problems. Blue-gray and dark organic colors often indicate poor drainage, while yellows and reds often indicate good aeration and, therefore, good drainage. Soils that are primarily organic (e.g., peat or muck soils) and fine-textured soils are also likely to be muddy because drainage is poor. Again, engineering can compensate for a poor location, if necessary.

Certain soils are also less suceptible to erosion than others. Erosiveness is lowest in soils with good drainage and the ability to resist the detachment of soil particles. These properties are optimized in loams with a substantial organic matter content. Sandy soils have good drainage, but they are easily displaced; they are of intermediate desirability as trail locations. Clay soils resist detachment, but drainage is poor; they are even less desirable than sands. The most erosive soils are those with homogeneous textures of a moderate particle size (i.e., fine sands and silts) (Bryan 1977). The prominent trail erosion problems in many mountain meadows result from the erosiveness of the homogeneous, fine-textured soils that have developed on the glacial outwash or lacustrine deposits characteristic of these meadows.

Rather than focusing use on resistant sites, managers can also prohibit use of certain sites or ecosystem types. One of the most common prohibitions is against camping within a specified distance of water bodies, particularly lakes. In wilderness, setbacks range from 20 ft to as much as one-half mile; the most common distance is 100 ft (Washburne and Cole 1983). Both social and ecological justifications have been provided for this action. Social reasons include: (1) preserving the aesthetic qualities of the lake that attracted people to the area in the first place, (2) reducing the visibility of campers—they are highly visible along the lakeshore, and (3) preserving the lakeshore as common space for all to use. Ecological reasons include: (1) avoiding use of particularly fragile lakeshores, (2) reducing the potential for water pollution, and (3) avoiding the braided trails that often form when campsites are located close to the shore.

There is no doubt that the social justifications are significant. However, the ecological reasons are suspect. Lakeshores are not more fragile than places set back from water. In the Eagle Cap Wilderness there was little difference in impact on lakeshore sites and sites more than 200 ft from lakes (Cole 1982a). Water quality is seldom a problem except where use is very heavy. Therefore, in most backcountry situations this is not a valid justification. There are certainly places where avoiding use of sites close to waterbodies is important; there are also many places where this is unnecessary. Since such a prohibition keeps parties from camping where they most want to, the action should only be taken where it is necessary. Many of the same things could be accomplished through educating people about not damaging shorelines or polluting waters. Since social reasons for setbacks are the most telling, setbacks are more appropriate in heavy use areas than in low use areas.

INFLUENCING VISITOR USE

Site manipulation can be used both to influence the spatial distribution of visitor use and to increase the durability of the sites on which use occurs. Trails provide an excellent example of how site manipulation influences use patterns. People seldom venture off trails, so managers can control where most people go simply through careful consideration of where they build trails. Three primary means of affecting visitor use are manipulation of ease of access, development of facilities in some places and not in others, and design of concentrated-use sites, such that traffic flow is contained.

Ease of access is primarily related to the number, distribution, and condition of roads and trails. Roads can be closed to make roaded areas only accessible to nonmotorized users or to increase the difficulty of reaching some internal destination. This is likely to reduce total use of the area and to shift the balance of types of use. This can be beneficial to wildlife and water quality, which will be less disturbed because of the shift away from motorized use. Internal destinations are likely to be less crowded and impacted because of reductions in use. The principal costs are borne by motorized users and those with less time to get to internal destinations, as well as by neighboring areas where use and impact may increase. These costs can be minimized by providing alternative, attractive areas for displaced users—areas where increased use can be planned for and accommodated.

A somewhat less effective and drastic means of accomplishing the same thing is to not maintain or to reduce the quality of access roads. This may exclude legitimate users that lack vehicles capable of driving the roads, while permitting access to inappropriate users that visit the area primarily for the challenge of driving the rough roads. Such a program may also lead to resource damage problems, particularly erosion of the road surface and a reduction in water quality. Another alternative is to build new roads or to improve the quality of existing roads in areas into which management wants to divert use.

Trail systems can be manipulated toward the same ends. Building new trails and improving the quality of existing trails are likely to increase use, while closing or not maintaining trails is likely to decrease use. Type of use can be altered as well. Low levels of maintenance are likely to exclude use by stock or motorized vehicles. Pristine areas are more likely to remain that way if they are left trailless. Usually the effectiveness of such attempts to manipulate use distribution will be increased if combined with information about the distribution and condition of roads and trails.

Nonmaintenance of trails, which serves as a "psychological barrier" to use for certain visitors, is a common practice in some backcountry areas. Removal or nonreplacement of trail signs and log bridges across streams are also means of reducing use. When these practices are used by management, visitors should be made aware of them so they can plan their trips accordingly.

Trailhead facilities also affect ease of access and, therefore, visitor use. Developed boat ramps will attract motor boats while removal of a ramp will decrease motorized use. Similarly, a ramp for unloading horses from stock trucks and trailers will increase horse use (Fig. 3). Providing a campground and overnight horse-holding facilities at a trailhead will increase use of that trail. Even the size of the parking lot provided will influence amount of use.

Development of facilities within a recreation area will also change use patterns. For example, building a horse camp at a lake is likely to attract more horse use to that area, particularly by novice users that are highly dependent on such facilities. Hikers that dislike contact with horse par-

Figure 3. Provision of trailhead facilities for loading and unloading horses is likely to increase use by parties with horses. (*Photo:* R. C. Lucas.)

ties and that know of the facility are likely to avoid the area. In many cases—because some users are likely to be attracted, while others are repelled—development of facilities may have more effect on the type of use than on the total amount of use. The most common internal facilities for attracting use in backcountry areas are trails, huts and shelters, horse-holding facilities, and improved potable water supplies. In roaded areas interpretive facilities, developed swimming beaches, and improved picnic areas and campsites are common attractants. Stocking a lake with fish and improving fish or wildlife habitat are also effective means of increasing particular types of use. Dismantling facilities or not stocking lakes can have the opposite effect. To effect a change it is important that the public be informed of the change. Word of mouth can be effective, but it may be desirable to advertise attractions, facilities, or management improvements.

Facilities can reduce resource damage in several other ways. They usually concentrate use, which, as we discussed in the last chapter, is desirable in many situations. Use concentration is most desirable where use levels are high, the usual case in situations where facilities are provided. The best examples are in camp and picnic areas. Tables and fireplaces concentrate the impact associated with preparing and eating food. Toilets concentrate human waste, and garbage cans, if provided, concentrate litter. Horse-holding facilities concentrate the impact of horses (Fig. 4). Facilities can also shield the resource from impact; we will discuss this in more detail later.

It is also important to design traffic flow on and between sites in such a way that as little area as possible is frequently trampled. This is particularly relevant to the design of developed multisite campgrounds. Impact occurs wherever people walk between sleeping areas, eating areas, water sources, toilets, garbage cans, and attractions. Total impact is closely related to the proportion of the area that is frequently walked on (Orr 1971). This proportion can be minimized through the use of barriers, signs, and the attractiveness and location of trails and other facilities provided. People tend to take the shortest path between facilities, although this is influenced by visibility, signing, ease of travel, and attractiveness. Routes between facilities will tend to be used if they meet these criteria; impact will be minimized if the location of facilities and attrac-

Figure 4. Hitchrails confine packstock trampling to a small area and avoid damage resulting from tying stock to trees. (*Photo:* D. N. Cole.)

tions channels use along as few routes as possible. For this reason, Leonard et al. (1981) advocate a linear arrangement of facilities in densely forested backcountry areas in the Northeast (Fig. 5).

If shortcuts develop between facilities, it is often best to try to incorporate these into the existing trail system (McEwen and Tocher 1976).

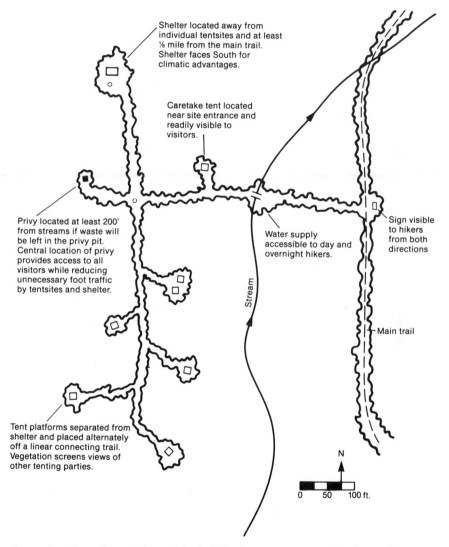

Figure 5. A linear layout of overnight facilities that concentrates traffic flow and impact but separates and disperses visitor groups. (*Source:* Leonard et al. 1981.)

Sometimes this is unacceptable, and the manager must turn to barriers or signs, more obtrusive means of management. Barriers range from the undesirable extreme of barbed wire fencing through earthen barriers to unobtrusive plantings of shrubs and trees. Signs such as "Please stay on the path" are another less than desirable option. This is another place where effectiveness and obtrusiveness must be balanced.

Trail impact can also be reduced by confining use distribution. The most common problems are shortcutting switchbacks and trail widening, leading to development of either a continuous wide bare area or to a system of multiple trails. The key to avoiding such problems is to make staying on the trail the easiest alternative for the hiker. Switchback cutting can be minimized by keeping them few in number and out of sight of each other, utilizing wide turns where possible, and building barriers between the upper and lower legs of the switchback. These considerations need to be balanced with a concern for proper trail drainage, as discussed below.

Wide trails occur where the trail tread is relatively rough or wet relative to the adjacent land. These conditions cause the hiker to walk off the trail, widening it. Widening is also a problem with horse use on sidehills. Horses tend to walk on the downhill side of the trail, which breaks down this outer edge and widens the trail. Trail roughness can be reduced by removing rocks or surfacing the trail. Alternatively, the roughness of adjacent land can be increased by piling rocks along the trail. Piling rocks on the outside of wide trails caused by heavy horse use is a common use of this technique. Trail wetness problems require some sort of bridging and drainage control.

SITE HARDENING AND SHIELDING

Engineering—after proper location—is the major defense managers have against deterioration of trails. While excessive engineering is to be avoided, particularly in more primitive recreation areas, engineering solutions are often necessary and appropriate. After all, trails are a largely artificial, visually obvious addition to the landscape—a flat, barren, compacted strip through the environment. Most visitors do not mind the artificiality; they accept it as the price for increased accessibility.

The problems that most commonly require engineering solutions are trail erosion and damage to areas that are wet or poorly drained. The two simplest, least costly, and lowest maintenance techniques for erosion control are outsloping of the trail tread and incorporation of drainage dips. Outsloping involves building the trail such that the outer edge is lower than the inner edge. This causes water to drain off the trail. Drainage dips are short sections of trail built with a grade opposite to the prevailing grade of the trail. If a trail is climbing uphill, for example, short sections of downgrade provide periodic interruptions of what would be a continuous down-trail channel. Coarse material at the low point of dips helps prevent erosion there.

Two other tools for controlling erosion are water bars and steps (Proudman 1977). Both should be part of the original trail construction design; they will be much less effective once substantial amounts of erosion have occurred. Water bars, made of wood or stone, are oriented at an angle to the slope and trail and divert water off the tread (Fig. 6). Steps are oriented perpendicular to the slope; they slow water down and hold soil. Both are placed closer together and become more important with increases in slope, the amount of water on the tread, and soil instability.

Water bars are particularly important at the top of slopes where water can be diverted before picking up momentum. It is important that they be oriented at the proper angle to the trail—usually 30 to 40 degrees. A steeper angle encourages erosion; a shallower angle leads to excessive sedimentation behind the bar. It is important to be concerned with what happens to the water after it is diverted off the tread. Sometimes a ditch is needed to handle the diverted water. Where drop-offs adjacent to the trail are steep, rocks may help dissipate the energy of the falling, diverted water. This will help avoid gully erosion and undercutting of the trail. Frequent maintenance is required to keep water bars from filling in with sediment and becoming highly-erosive little waterfalls. Periodically disturbed bars (horses, particularly, have a habit of dislodging them) and rotted wooden bars need to be replaced.

Not allowing water to flow onto the trail is as important as diverting water off the trail. Water is particularly likely to flow onto the trail where it crosses small drainageways. In such places water should be kept off the trail with culverts under the trail or, if the drainage is very small, with rock-lined ditches across the trail. Even with culverts it is critical to use a system large enough to handle floods. Where water seeps onto the trail in many places and the trail cannot be outsloped, it may be neces-

Figure 6. Rock water bars divert water off this trail in Yosemite National Park. The rock steps in the foreground also reduce the potential for erosion. (*Photo:* D. N. Cole.)

sary to construct parallel ditches along the trail. If there is much gradient to the ditches, erosion may occur unless ditches are rock-lined and have check dams or periodic side-ditches to drain them.

Where erosion is particularly severe, primarily at off-road vehicle concentrated-use areas, it is important to control where eroded material is deposited. Otherwise, it will be carried into streams, where it reduces water quality and adversely affects fish populations. At off-road vehicle areas in California, debris basins have been built to trap sediment. Initially under-engineered, many early sedimentation basins were washed out in floods. Proper engineering is critical if these basins are to remain functional (Smith 1980).

Bridges, in addition to serving a visitor safety purpose, protect against erosion at stream crossings. They should be considered wherever a steep bank of erosive material must be negotiated. Various types of bridging are the only means of avoiding serious resource damage where trails intercept springs or cross wet areas or areas with a high water table. Any trampling of water-saturated soil causes both churning and compaction of the soil. The end result is a quagmire that widens and lengthens over time.

If the wet area is neither too deep nor long, it can be bridged with stepping stones. Three more elaborate options are to build turnpike, puncheon, or corduroy. Turnpiking involves building up the trail bed, using material from parallel ditches. The trail material is held in place with logs or rock (Fig. 7). The base of the trail should be above the water

Figure 7. Turnpiking can be used to elevate sections of trail above surrounding wet areas. The trail surface is sand held in place by log stringers. Culverts allow water to pass beneath the trail. (*Photo:* D. N. Cole.)

level in the ditches, and the trail material should provide reasonably good drainage. It may be necessary to import gravel or some other well-drained material to build up the trail. Where drainage problems are more severe, puncheon can be used to elevate the trail above the wet area without disrupting drainage. Puncheon consists of a decking of logs or timbers set on log or timber stringers along the side. It is important to maintain good drainage under the trail and to extend the stretch of puncheon into areas of good drainage at either end. Corduroy, the most common form of bridging in more primitive areas, is merely a primitive form of puncheon construction. Native logs are laid perpendicular to log stringers. Drainage control is less elaborate. Corduroy deteriorates rapidly and must be replaced periodically.

Surfacing of trails may be necessary where use is very heavy, particularly where use is by horses or motorized vehicles. It is also necessary where trails cross wet areas or rockslides. Gravel should be used on segments that cross wet areas or rockslides. On heavy use trails other options include wood chips, soil cement, and as a last resort, paving (Fig. 8).

The major means of increasing the resource durability of camp and picnic areas are to surface areas that receive concentrated use and to construct facilities that shield the resource, such as tent pads, shelters, fire grates, and toilets. In heavy use areas, it is possible to minimize compaction, improve drainage, and avoid the creation of muddy, wet areas by surfacing tentsites, eating areas, and trails between facilities with gravel or wood chips. This will also serve to concentrate use and avoid damage to intersite zones. While such surfacing is generally inappropriate in wilderness areas, it is debatable whether surfaced areas are any less "natural" than barren, dusty or muddy, devegetated areas.

More elaborate means of shielding the ground, used particularly in the eastern United States, are construction of tent platforms and shelters. Tent platforms are flat wooden structures that elevate and separate tents from the ground surface. They can either be portable or not and can be built to accommodate one or several tents (Leonard et al. 1981). Shelters can be created by placing a roof and sides on the platform. Shelters attract visitation; this results in more concentrated use and impact (Fig. 9). In Great Smoky Mountains National Park, shelters receive 35 percent of backcountry use; however, they account for only 7 percent of the area of bare soil and 11 percent of the intensive damage (the combined area of bare soil, leaf litter, and trampled vegetation) on over-

Figure 8. This motorcycle trail has been hardened in an inconspicuous manner with soil cement. (*Photo:* R. F. Washburne.)

night sites (Bratton, Hickler, and Graves 1978). Overnight sites with developed facilities tend to be large and highly impacted, but properly designed facilities keep impacts to acceptable levels and the amount of impact per person is low because use and impact are concentrated on shielded sites.

At water-based recreation areas, it is important to surface boat ramps. This reduces erosion and also increases accessibility and public safety. The boat ramp in Fig. 10 allows rafters on Idaho's Middle Fork of the Salmon River to get their rafts down to the river without damaging the riverbank excessively.

Figure 9. Backcountry shelters concentrate use and impacts, but if properly designed, lead to low amounts of impact per visitor night of use. (*Photo:* W. E. Hammitt.)

Provision of fire grates is another means of concentrating impact and/ or shielding the site. A fire pit on the ground concentrates impact at one point. This keeps campfire impact from spreading and disturbing a large area. Grates that are elevated also shield the ground from the impact of the fire.

A final facility that concentrates impact and shields the resource is the toilet. Toilets are standard in developed areas and have become increasingly common in heavily used parts of wilderness. Over one-quarter of wildernesses used toilets in at least some places in 1980 (Washburne and Cole 1983). Some toilet systems merely concentrate waste in pits. When the pit is full, it is covered over and a new pit is built elsewhere. In other systems waste is either removed from the site or treated and then redeposited in the vicinity. Waste can be either chemically treated or composted. Leonard et al. (1981) provide a table that displays alternative waste disposal methods, their appropriateness at various sites and use levels, aesthetic considerations, and associated costs (Table 3).

Outside of wilderness and other areas where preservation of natural conditions is paramount, durability of vegetation can be increased either

Figure 10. A boat ramp on Idaho's Middle Fork of the Salmon River reduces damage to the riverbank. (*Photo:* D. N. Cole.)

by altering the vegetation composition in favor of more resistant species or by applying cultural treatments that make existing plants more resistant. Both are common practices in developed recreation areas and have a place in many wildland settings where use is at least moderately high.

An example of species replacement is planting turf grasses in a picnic ground to take the place of natives that have been eliminated by trampling. Generally, the only resistant plants available are (1) grasses, usually commercially available mixes of exotic species, or (2) shrubs and trees large enough to avoid being trampled. Thorny shrubs can be par-

TABLE 3. Methods for Disposing of Human Waste in Wildland Recreation Areas

Method	Decomposition Process	Site Requirements	Visitor Levels	Aesthetic Considerations	Costs
Soil leaching Cathole (no facilities)	Waste is partially decomposed aerobically within surface organic soil layers before it is leached through soil beneath	At least 1′ of well-drained soil and some surface organic matter	No more than 2 persons/night, since visitors do not disperse widely around an overnight site	No odors, no contact with others' waste	None
Pit privy or chum	Waste remains buried and undergoes slow anaerobic decomposition while being leached	Well-drained soils; 3 to 5′ deep beneath pit bottom and above seasonal high water-table; site must have space for a new pit every 2 to 3 years; privies must be well away from streams and pond or lake shores (200′ recommended)	Pit 3 × 3′ will accommodate 20 persons/night for 2 years	Usually malodorous; user is exposed to others' waste	Initial costs may be $300 to $500 per unit; little maintenance needed during season; at high-use sites, relocation may be costly
Mechanical-chemical Waste removal (flyout system)	All waste removed from site	Any terrain, if helicopter landing site is available	No limit; a 55-gallon barrel accommodates 200 to 250 overnight visitors and weighs about 500 pounds	Collection barrel often malodorous; heliport may lessen wildland experience for some visitors	Installation costs $750 to $1000 per unit, including airlift of materials to site; annual operating expense

Type	Waste treatment	Off-site disposal	Capacity	Advantages	Cost and limitations
Chemical toilet	Waste is transformed into pathogen-free chemical sludge that can be either removed or deposited on the site	Sludge should be deposited on site with at least 6' of good leaching soil	475 overnight visitors before sludge must be pumped from unit	No odor, no contact with others' waste	is high—about $400 for a site with 1000 visitors (data Appalachian Mountain Club, White Mountains, New Hampshire) $850 to $1000 for noncontained unit plus $500 for housing; sludge disposal costs are additional, and some units require electricity; malfunctions require skill to correct; backcountry use has been too limited to provide operating costs
Composting Composting toilet (Clivus multrum, Toathrone)	Waste aerobically decomposed in container beneath privy and can be spread on forest floor after 2 or 3 years	None	1500 overnight visitors per season	No odor when working correctly; units are large and may not be visually compatible with wildland site	$2000 to $4000 for purchasing, airlifting, and housing one unit; little routine maintenance, but compost environment often needs modification; malfunction requires skill to correct

307

TABLE 3. (*Continued*)

Method	Decomposition Process	Site Requirements	Visitor Levels	Aesthetic Considerations	Costs
Bin composter	Waste is aerobically decomposed in bin separate from privy, and can be spread on forest floor in 2 to 3 weeks	None	One bin suffices for 2000 overnight visitors per season;	Little odor if well maintained; bin is inconspicuous	Requires 1000 pounds per season of bark or other material, transfer of waste to bin, and mixing of compost pile; costs per unit at a site with 1000 visitors, $120 (data from Green Mountain Club, Vermont)

Source: Leonard, Spencer and Plumley. 1981. Copyright © 1981 by Appalchian Mountain Club, used with permission of publisher.

ticularly useful. In the Grand Canyon, for example, expansion of back-country campsites is being controlled by planting prickly pear cactus. The cactus establishes well from transplants and effectively discourages use of areas that are being rehabilitated. In deciding on which species to use, it is important to match species to local environmental conditions, particularly to amount of shade, soil fertility, and moisture. Trees should be long-lived, resistant to insects, diseases, and windthrow, and relatively small in size (Ripley 1965). It is also important to decide whether or not to encourage growth of exotic species. Exotics are often attractive, durable, and easy to establish; however, they often require more maintenance and are "unnatural."

The durability of vegetation can also be increased through use of various cultural treatments. Perhaps the simplest treatment is to thin the overstory. Numerous studies have documented a negative relationship between overstory canopy cover and ground cover vegetation impact. Generally, as shade decreases, vegetation cover increases, and the amount of vegetation loss caused by recreational use decreases (Marion and Merriam 1985). Shade discourages the growth of grasses, which are almost always more resistant to impact than other plant types. Even within the same species, plants growing in a shady environment tend to be particularly flimsy as they spread out to capture sunlight. On camp-grounds in the southern Appalachians, reducing canopy cover from 90 to 60 percent doubled grass cover; a further reduction to 30 percent cover tripled grass cover (Cordell, James, and Tyre 1974). Thinning trees, then, can increase both the quantity and hardiness of the ground cover. Thinning can also increase the vigor of the remaining overstory trees, improve wildlife habitat, and enhance aesthetics and recreational opportunities. It is important, however, to maintain adequate screening between sites and to not increase susceptibility to windthrow.

Other treatments include irrigation and fertilization. These two treatments are likely to be particularly important when trying to maintain a sod of exotic grasses in a dry climate. In an area with a wet climate watering may not be necessary.

The importance of fertilization varies with soil conditions. Where trace elements are limiting, their inclusion in soil amendments can lead to spectacular increases in growth. It is always worth investing in soil testing to identify any nutritional deficiencies. Even in soils without known deficiencies, exotic grasses usually respond well to additions of complete nitrogen-phosphorus-potassium fertilizers. Wagar (1965) recommends a ratio of twice as much nitrogen as phosphorus and potassium. He also recommends using a slow-release type of fertilizer such as urea formaldehyde. This reduces the danger of burning the vegetation, and fertilization is not required as frequently. Surface application is best for ground cover vegetation while putting fertilizer in holes drilled in the ground will get more fertilizer to the tree roots.

The pH of soil is also important. Native plants in coniferous forests grow best in moderately acidic soils (pH about 5.0), while exotic grasses prefer a neutral pH. Coniferous soils are likely to need liming to reduce acidity if conversion to grasses is desired. Where naturally acidic coniferous soils are neutralized by recreation use—remember that campfires tend to increase pH—an amendment like peat moss will promote growth of acid-loving native species.

Either flood or aerial irrigation can be used to water plants (Jubenville 1978). With flood irrigation, water is diverted by ditch systems to the recreation area, where it is spread out across the ground. The developed campgrounds in the bottom of the Grand Canyon utilize flood irrigation to maintain cottonwood trees and some brushy screening between sites. Aerial irrigation can be used more flexibly. Either portable above-ground sprinklers or a buried underground system can be used. Either system is costly. A buried irrigation system used at a developed campground in Idaho cost almost $100 per unit per year in the late 1960s (Beardsley, Herrington, and Wagar 1974); this would be over $300 per unit per year in the 1980s—a cost approaching $1.00 per visitor-day of use. Another problem with irrigation is related to the susceptibility of soil to compaction when it is wet. Watering should occur after, not before, periods of heavy use. If feasible, it may be best to close the campground or portions of the campground (loops) one day per week for watering.

Despite these problems, the value of irrigation and fertilization was illustrated in an experimental renovation and maintenance program conducted on the previously mentioned campground in Idaho (Beardsley et al. 1974). Largely devegetated campsites were all seeded yearly with a mixture of exotic grasses. On some sites this seeding was the only treatment applied. Other sites were also either fertilized once per year, watered once a week—at a rate three times the normal summer rainfall—or both. Vegetation cover was monitored over a four year period. As you can see from Fig. 11, seeding, by itself, resulted in little improvement in vegetation cover. This is not surprising because exotic grasses are poorly adapted to a coniferous forest environment. Both

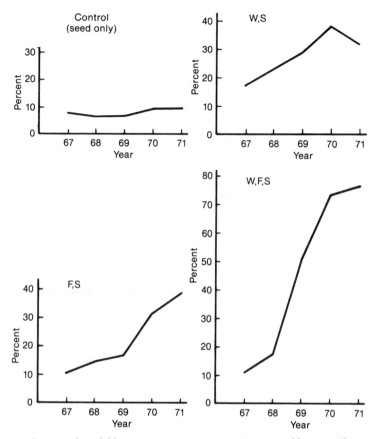

Figure 11. Percent of available growing space on campsites covered by ground vegetation after various combinations of watering (W), fertilizing (F), and seeding (S). Treatments were initiated in 1967 and continued for 4 years. Data are from Point Campground in Idaho. (*Source:* Beardsley et al. 1974.)

watering and fertilization, by themselves, caused pronounced increases in cover, but the combination of the two was twice as effective as either one by itself.

Similar results were found in a campground in an aspen grove in Utah (Beardsley and Wagar 1971). Watering and fertilization, together, caused the greatest increase in ground cover. Fertilization, by itself, was less effective than watering, and fertilization without seeding or watering was no more effective than doing nothing at all. An interesting result of this study was that while these treatments did increase ground cover under aspen, similar treatments under a dense coniferous overstory had little effect. Without thinning and, perhaps, some removal of organic horizons, it is unlikely that any treatments can establish much vegetation under a dense coniferous overstory.

A final conclusion derived from these evaluations of cultural treatments is that they will only be effective when combined with careful site design and surfacing of concentrated-use areas. As discussed earlier in this chapter, good design channels traffic along paths and roads and minimizes the area that is frequently trampled. Areas used so heavily that vegetation and organic horizons are entirely eliminated should be surfaced to promote drainage, reduce compaction, and minimize problems with dust and mud.

In some situations site durability can also be increased by improving soil conditions, particularly by relieving soil compaction and increasing the organic matter content of soils. At a campground in Texas, Legg, Farnham, and Miller (1980) experimented with various means of relieving soil compaction without closing the entire campground. They experimented with various lengths and seasons of closure, with rototilling, and with incorporating wood chips and grass seed into the soil. Rototilling proved to be detrimental if it was done without closure or incorporation of wood chips into the soil. Rototilling destroyed soil structure, and this apparently prevented the overwinter recovery that usually occurs in these soils. Merely closing campsites during winter to promote overwinter recovery allowed compaction levels to return to near-normal. Incorporation of wood chips into the soil greatly reduced bulk density, and the seeding of grasses resulted in less erosion during winter. The authors conclude that, at least in this area, rest-rotation of campsites is feasible, particularly if organic matter is incorporated into the soil. Where organic matter is added to soil, the populations of soil microorganisms that decompose this material can increase. These organisms may tie up much of the available nitrogen in the soil and deprive plants of nitrogen. It may be necessary to compensate for this by adding high-nitrogen fertilizer, along with organic amendments.

Surface application of wood chips—mulching—was effective in encouraging plant growth on closed day-use picnic areas in four Maryland state parks (Little and Mohr 1979). Surface application promotes moisture retention and inhibits surface runoff. The authors felt that scarification, breaking up the soil with rototillers or hand tools, can cause problems in forested areas because it can disturb tree roots. Moreover, in their study, scarification did not increase vegetation growth. Their primary suggestions for rehabilitation were to confine use to hardened parts of the site and to mulch little-used parts of the area.

TEMPORARY SITE CLOSURES

In some areas, highly impacted sites have been temporarily closed to allow them to recover. Once they have recovered, these sites can be reopened for use. Other sites must be available for recreational use until the closed sites can be reopened. This action has been called "rest-rotation" because there is a rotation of open and closed sites. It bears some similarity to the type of dispersal in which use is spread among a larger number of sites. The major difference is that management formally controls which sites are open and which are closed. With rest-rotation, sites are also likely to be either open or closed for longer periods of time than sites in an area where managers are attempting to disperse use. Consequently, they become more highly impacted after periods of use. A rest-rotation strategy could be applied in a number of recreational situations but is most important in campsite management. Temporary campsite closures have been used in both developed and backcountry campsite situations.

The critical factor in assessing the appropriateness of rest-rotation is the relationship between the length of recovery periods and the period of time it takes for impact to occur. If recovery takes much longer than deterioration, a rest-rotation system will require either that there be many closed sites for each open site or that the capacity of the area to serve normal visitor loads be reduced.

As described earlier, deterioration of campsites often occurs within the first few years after a site is opened to use. This has been demonstrated both on wilderness campsites in the Boundary Waters Canoe Area (Merriam et al. 1973) and on car-camping sites in Pennsylvania (LaPage 1967). In both cases impact increased dramatically for about two years and then tended to level off.

Although a two-year deterioration period may be relatively standard on sites that receive at least a moderate level of use, recovery periods are much more variable. Recovery rates vary greatly in response to such factors as length of the growing season and moisture regime. Around a backcountry lake in Kings Canyon National Park, Parsons and DeBenedetti (1979) found that soil compaction had returned to pre-use levels within 15 years after closure; however, quantities of organic matter were still low, and ground cover vegetation was still disturbed. In an oak stand in Minnesota, soil recovered from compaction in just under a decade (Thorud and Frissell 1976). While there are undoubtedly more resilient environments than these, it is doubtful that any place can recover as rapidly as it deteriorates.

Difficulties with rest-rotation are most serious in wilderness areas where active revegetation is difficult and, many feel, not appropriate on a major scale. Moreover, recovery periods are often particularly long because of harsh growing conditions. The effectiveness of temporary closures was evaluated at Big Creek Lake in the Selway-Bitterroot Wilderness, Montana, where seven of 15 campsites were temporarily closed to allow recovery. Eight years after closure, vegetation cover on closed sites was still only one-third of normal, and bare soil was exposed on 25 percent of the site compared with just 0.1 percent on controls (Cole and Ranz 1983). The most dramatic change over the eight-year period was the development and deterioration of seven new campsites near the closed sites. Within eight years after their creation, vegetation loss and bare soil were as pronounced on these sites as on long-established sites in the area. The major effect of the temporary closure, then, was to increase the number of impacted sites. Recognizing this, area managers eventually reopened the closed sites and abandoned the idea of rotating sites.

In resilient environments, where active rehabilitation is feasible, rest-rotation may work. Legg et al. (1980) demonstrated how over winter closure of developed campsites in Texas, when aided by rototilling organic matter into the soil, allowed soil compaction levels to quickly return to normal. Even on resilient developed sites, it would be prudent to be cautious when attempting rotation. By experimentally closing and revegetating one site, recovery periods can be estimated. If recovery is sufficiently rapid, funding and manpower are available to do the revegetation, and the number of sites is sufficient to accommodate both open and closed sites, then rest-rotation might be worth implementing on a large scale.

REHABILITATION OF CLOSED SITES

In some situations there is no option but to permanently close and rehabilitate recreation sites. Common reasons for such an action include excessive site damage that cannot be controlled with continued use, a decision to relocate the facility on a more durable or desirable site, and rehabilitation of previous damage that is unlikely to occur in the future because of a change in either type of use or management. Many of the cultural treatments we have been discussing—watering, fertilizing, seeding, mulching, and so on—also can be used to rehabilitate closed sites. Some are not appropriate; replacing native vegetation with exotic, trampling-resistant species or thinning the overstory to encourage grasses makes little sense if use of the site is to be curtailed. Other techniques, particularly eliminating all use on the site, become even more important.

Rehabilitation of camp or picnic sites and trails is most common. Other recreation sites that may require rehabilitation work are overgrazed meadows and off-road vehicle areas. Although a considerable amount of rehabilitation work has been done, little of it has been documented. Most experience in site rehabilitation comes from revegetation of mines and rangelands. Cole and Schreiner (1981) provide an annotated bibliography of references that provide useful information for rehabilitating recreation sites.

Regardless of the facility being rehabilitated, five basic steps are required:

1. *Eliminate Use.* Some effective means must be devised for keeping visitors off closed sites. Particularly in fragile areas, very little use can destroy the fruits of years of work. Providing attractive alternative use areas is of critical importance. Channeling use away from the area, using either attractants or barriers, may also be helpful. A sign to a viewpoint, away from the closed area, may be effective. Brushing in a trail may keep people from using it. "Planting" rocks or logs on a site will discourage overnight use but may not curtail day use. Signs or other information about the closure, reasons for the closure, and the location of replacement facilities may be necessary (Fig. 12). In primitive areas, especially, these should be a last resort. Where closed areas are intermixed with open areas, it may be necessary to delineate closed areas with some sort of fencing to keep use off. The fencing material can vary from string to stouter materials, such as lumber.

Keeping users off closed sites can be a particularly serious problem in wilderness areas, where management strives to be as inobtrusive as possible. Because even people walking across a site to go fishing can destroy rehabilitation work, there may be no alternative to obtrusive

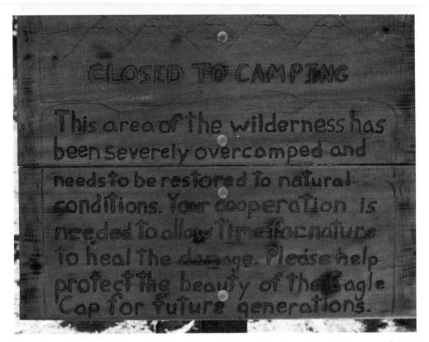

Figure 12. Sign used to keep visitors off a campsite in the Eagle Cap Wilderness, Oregon, while the site was being rehabilitated. (*Photo:* D. N. Cole.)

fencing until substantial recovery occurs. Information about the location of and reasons for rehabilitation programs will increase compliance because visitors know what to expect and why and how to comply.

2. *Control Drainage and Erosion on the Site.* On camp and picnic areas it is important to keep drainageways from flooding the site; some sort of mulch may also be needed to control sheet erosion on the site. Control of gully erosion on trails is more difficult. The techniques for minimizing erosion of used trails, described in the preceding section, are all appropriate. On closed trails check dams, built across the trail, can be used to reduce erosion and encourage sedimentation behind the dams. Mulching can also be useful.

3. *Prepare the Soil.* The nature of soil preparation is highly variable; it ranges from doing almost nothing on lightly disturbed backcountry sites to extensive grading in severely eroded off-road vehicle areas. The principal objectives of this step are to reduce soil compaction and to improve the organic matter content, fertility, and moisture content of the soil.

Exactly what treatments are needed will depend on characteristics of both the undisturbed and damaged soil, as well as the nature of the vegetation to be reestablished. Soil scarification, which ranges from light raking to rototilling, can reduce compaction. The value of scarification can be more than offset by destruction of roots and plant parts that are capable of vegetatively reproducing. Also, as Legg et al. (1980) found, scarification may be of little value unless organic matter is either incorporated into or spread on top of the soil.

The value of adding organic matter to the soil and the best type to add depends on soil pH and the optimum pH for the vegetation to be reestablished. Peat moss and coniferous duff promote acidity, while steer manure is good for basic soils (Schreiner and Moorhead 1981). Liming can also reduce the acidity of soils. Rotting logs can be planted to provide ongoing sources of organic matter and shelter for plantings. It is important to replenish large woody debris on sites where it has been entirely removed because such debris plays a critical role in the functioning of many ecosystems (see Chapter 2). Where substantial quantities of organic matter are added, it may also be necessary to add nitrogen to the soil. Soil nitrogen is likely to be depleted by the increased number of microoganisms that are involved in breaking down the supplemental organic matter.

Fertilization is important where exotic plants are being established. As this is less common on permanently closed sites, fertilization may be less important than in places where recreational use continues. Fertilization appears to be more critical to the establishment of vegetation from seeds than from transplants. Fertilization is often of little value if not accompanied by watering (Beardsley and Wagar 1971). Generally, fertilizers should be used cautiously, particularly in wilderness, where their use tends to favor exotic species and can contribute to eutrophication of nearby waters. Information on desirable soil preparations can often be obtained from university extension services provided by land grant colleges, the federal Soil Conservation Service, state soil testing labs or departments of conservation, and local planning offices.

4. *Plant the Site.* Under certain favorable circumstances, natural revegetation may occur rapidly without much assistance. This is most likely at low elevations, where growing seasons are long, on productive soils, and in places that receive abundant but not excessive light and moisture. Elsewhere, rehabilitation will have to be assisted either by transplanting nursery-grown plants or plants from neighboring areas or by

seeding. This step involves deciding which species to use, preparing propagules for planting, and then doing the actual planting.

In deciding which species to use, the most important consideration is whether or not the species is adapted to the site. As noted before, it is difficult to grow grass in heavy shade or on acidic soils. Similarly, it is difficult to grow forest-floor species in a meadow. With native species it is best to use plants from local and similar environments. Sometimes even the same species from a distant location or elevational zone is poorly adapted, genetically, to the site. Species that successfully colonize neighboring naturally disturbed areas are particularly good choices for revegetating disturbed areas. Resistant species, including exotics, may be desirable in places where it may be difficult to avoid consistent ongoing use.

If seeding is to be done, a seed source must be found. For natives this often means collecting seed yourself. It is important to be aware of the plant's germination requirements. Seeds of many species must receive specific types of dormancy treatments before they will germinate. Some seeds will not germinate unless they are cracked or scratched; others will only germinate after being exposed to low temperatures. References that may help in collecting and treating seeds can be found in Cole and Schreiner (1981). Local expertise in garden clubs, native plant societies, and local nurseries can also be tapped. Seed is either scattered over the soil and covered with 1/2 in. of soil or dropped into holes 1/2 in. deep. Then the soil is tamped down, mulched, and watered. The mulching keeps the seed from washing away, provides insulation, and improves moisture retention. Wood chips, straw, and jute netting are commonly used mulches. The best time to plant seeds varies from place to place and can be critical to success. In the mountainous national parks of the Pacific Northwest, for example, it is best to sow seeds in the late fall, just before the start of the rainy season.

With transplants the first step is to find a source of plants. Transplants can be collected in the field or, if large quantities are needed, grown in nurseries. In the Pacific Northwest, transplanting has been much more successful than seeding. In areas with more summer moisture, seeding may be more successful. When plants are collected in the field, they should be taken from scattered locations to disperse the impact. It is helpful to select short, healthy-looking plants and to water plants a day before transplanting. When digging up the plant, care should be taken not to damage roots. It is preferable to excavate a section of turf rather than individual plants. Where individual plants are excavated, the whole root ball—roots and soil—should be included. Keeping the plant in some of its familiar soil will lessen the shock of the transplant. Plants should be replanted as soon as possible and, while in transit, should be kept cool, moist, and out of direct sunlight. Plants should be placed in a hole slightly larger than the root ball, taking care not to double-up the roots. Any excess space must be filled in with soil and organic matter, leaving a slight depression around the plant. This facilitates watering and reduces the risk of frost heaving, a process in which freezing and thawing of the soil lift small plants out of the soil. Finally the site should be watered and mulched, and any damage to the holes from which the transplants came should be repaired.

Plants for transplanting can also be propagated in greenhouses, either from seeds or cuttings. Miller and Miller (1976) have used a greenhouse in their pioneering work on rehabilitation of subalpine trails and campsites in North Cascades National Park, Washington. Cuttings were collected in the field and transported to the greenhouse. Once rooted and growing, plants either were taken into the backcountry for planting, or were divided further. Plants of certain species were also grown from seed collected in the field. Plants suitable for transplanting, particularly trees, may also be commercially available.

5. *Maintain the Plantings.* Ongoing maintenance activities will vary from place to place. In some situations yearly fertilization and mulching and weekly watering are necessary; in other situations little maintenance is required. "Please water me" signs can be a good means of getting help from visitors. All areas will profit from careful documentation of the rehabilitation techniques that were used, as well as monitoring of how successful the effort was. Photographs and counts of plants can help in evaluating success. Before launching into a full-scale program, experimentation with different species, types of soil preparations, and planting techniques will save much time and money in the long run.

Even with all this effort, revegetation can be an exceedingly slow process. In many cases transplant survival has been high, but growth and spread have been slow. Transplants on roadcuts in the alpine zone of Rocky Mountain National Park were surviving after 40 years, but they had not spread significantly (Stevens 1979). Similar slow growth and spread are common wherever the climate is severe and growing seasons are short (Fig. 13).

Somewhat different techniques may be needed to rehabilitate trails,

Figure 13. These transplants on a campsite in the Eagle Cap Wilderness, Oregon, have survived for five years, but they have not spread. (*Photo:* D. N. Cole.)

primarily because erosion is more of a problem on trails. Palmer (1979) experimented with various means of rehabilitating multiple trails in Tuolumne Meadows, Yosemite National Park, California. The most successful technique involved cutting off the sod ridges between multiple trails at the level of the trail tread and stacking the sod in the shade. The soil beneath both the trails and the ridges was spaded up to eliminate compaction, and sand was added to bring the whole area up to the level of the surrounding meadow. Finally, the vegetation from the sod ridges was divided into transplant plugs and planted in the soil. Utilizing this technique, trail scarring was less obvious, and transplants were spreading within several years.

A final example of restoration is the rehabilitation of meadows in Sequoia and Kings Canyon National Parks, California. These meadows had been severely disturbed by a history of overgrazing by both recreational and domestic livestock. This use led to loss of vegetation cover and shifts in species composition that favored unpalatable and weedy species. The most serious problem was accelerated erosion. Destruction of sod and trampling of streambanks increased erosion. Increased downcutting by streams lowered water tables, drying out meadows. This allowed lodgepole pine seedlings to germinate and become established in meadows. Many meadows were shrinking dramatically as this invasion of trees progressed. Meadow rehabilitation involved both visitor and site management. The amount, distribution, and timing of stock use was controlled. In addition, erosion was controlled by building check dams, grading stream banks, and planting banks with willow cuttings (DeBenedetti and Parsons 1979).

REFERENCES

Beardsley, W. G., R. B. Herrington, and J. A. Wagar. 1974. Recreation Site Management: How to Rehabilitate a Heavily Used Campground Without Stopping Visitor Use. *Journal of Forestry* 72:279–281.

Beardsley, W. G., and J. A. Wagar. 1971. Vegetation Management on a Forested Recreation Site. *Journal of Forestry* 69:728–731.

Bratton, S. P., M. G. Hickler, and J. H. Graves. 1978. Visitor Impact on Backcountry Campsites in the Great Smoky Mountains. *Environmental Management* 2:431–442.

Bryan, R. B. 1977. The Influence of Soil Properties on Degradation of Mountain Hiking Trails at Grovelsjon. *Geografiska Annaler* 59A(1-2):49–65.

Cole, D. N. 1981. Managing Ecological Impacts at Wilderness Campsites: An Evaluation of Techniques. *Journal of Forestry* 79:86–89.

Cole, D. N. 1982a. Wilderness Campsite Impacts: Effect of Amount of Use. USDA Forest Service Research Paper INT-284. 34 pp.

Cole, D. N. 1982b. Controlling the Spread of Campsites at Popular Wilderness Destinations. *Journal of Soil and Water Conservation* 37:291–295.

Cole, D. N. 1983. Assessing and Monitoring Backcountry Trail Conditions. USDA Forest Service Research Paper INT-303. 10 pp.

Cole, D. N. 1985. Recreational Trampling Effects on Six Habitat Types in Western Montana. USDA Forest Service Research Paper INT-350. 43 pp.

Cole, D. N., and B. Ranz. 1983. Temporary Campsite Closures in the Selway-Bitterroot Wilderness. *Journal of Forestry* 81:729–732.

Cole, D. N., and E. G. S. Schreiner. 1981. Impacts of Backcountry Recreation: Site Management and Rehabilitation—An Annotated Bibliography. USDA Forest Service General Technical Report INT-121. 58 pp.

Cordell, H. K., G. A. James, and G. L. Tyre. 1974. Grass Establishment on Developed Recreation Sites. *Journal of Soil and Water Conservation* 29:268–271.

DeBenedetti, S. H., and D. J. Parsons. 1979. Mountain Meadow Management and Research in Sequoia and Kings Canyon National Parks: A Review and

Update. In Linn, R. M., ed. *Proceedings of the Conference on Scientific Research in the National Parks.* USDI National Park Service, Transactions and Proceedings Series 5, U. S. Government Printing Office, Washington, DC. pp. 1305–1311.

Hinds, T. E. 1976. Aspen Mortality in Rocky Mountain Campgrounds. USDA Forest Service Research Paper RM-164. 20 pp.

Jubenville, A. 1978. *Outdoor Recreation Management.* Philadelphia: Saunders. 290 pp.

LaPage, W. F. 1967. Some Observations on Campground Trampling and Ground Cover Response. USDA Forest Service Research Paper NE-68. 11 pp.

Leeson, B. F. 1979. Research on Wildland Recreation Impact in the Canadian Rockies. In Ittner, R., D. R. Potter, J. K. Agee and S. Anschell, eds. *Recreational Impact on Wildlands Conference Proceedings.* USDA Forest Service, Pacific Northwest Region, R-6-001-1979, Portland, OR. pp. 64–65.

Legg, M., K. Farnham, and E. Miller. 1980. Soil Restoration on Deteriorated Campsites in Texas. *Southern Journal of Applied Forestry* 4(4):189–193.

Leonard, R. E., E. L. Spencer, and H. J. Plumley. 1981. *Backcountry Facilities: Design and Maintenance.* Boston: Appalachian Mountain Club. 214 pp.

Little, S., and J. J. Mohr. 1979. Reestablishing Understory Plants in Overused Wooded Areas of Maryland State Parks. USDA Forest Service Research Paper NE-431. 9 pp.

Marion, J. L., and L. C. Merriam. 1985. Recreational Impacts on Well-established Campsites in the Boundary Waters Canoe Area. University of Minnesota Agricultural Experiment Station Bulletin AD-SB-2502, St. Paul, MN. 16 pp.

McEwen, D., and S. R. Tocher. 1976. Zone Management: Key to Controlling Recreational Impact in Developed Campsites. *Journal of Forestry* 74:90–93.

Merriam, Jr., L. C., C. K. Smith, D. E. Miller, C. Huang, J. C. Tappeiner, II, K. Goeckermann, J. A. Blomendal and T. M. Costello. 1973. Newly Developed Campsites in the Boundary Waters Canoe Area—A Study of Five Years' Use. University of Minnesota Agricultural Experiment Station, St. Paul, Bulletin 511. 27 pp.

Miller, J. W., and M. M. Miller. 1976. Revegetation in the Subalpine Zone. *University of Washington Arboretum Bulletin* 39(4):12–16.

Orr, H. R. 1971. Design and Layout of Recreation Facilities. In *Recreation Symposium Proceedings.* USDA Forest Service, Northeast Forest Experiment Station, Broomall, PA. pp. 23–27.

Palmer, R. 1979. Progress Report on Trail Revegetation Studies. In Stanley, Jr., J. T., H. T. Harvey, and R. J. Hartesveldt, eds. *A Report on the Wilderness Study: The Effects of Human Recreational Activities on Wilderness Ecosystems with Special Emphasis on Sierra Club Wilderness Outings in the Sierra Nevada,* Outing Committee, Sierra Club, San Francisco, CA. pp. 193–196.

Parsons, D. J., and S. H. DeBenedetti. 1979. Wilderness Protection in the High Sierra: Effects of a 15-Year Closure. In Linn, R. M., ed. *Proceedings of the*

Conference on Scientific Research in the National Parks, National Park Service, Transactions and Proceedings Series 5, U. S. Government Printing Office, Washington, DC. pp. 1313–1318.

Proudman, R. D. 1977. *AMC Field Guide to Trail Building and Maintenance.* Boston: Appalachian Mountain Club. 103 pp.

Ripley, T. H. 1962. Tree and Shrub Response to Recreation Use. USDA Forest Service Research Note SE-171. 2 pp.

Ripley, T. H. 1965. Rehabilitation of Forest Recreation Sites. *Proceedings, Society of American Foresters* 61:35–36.

Schreiner, E., and B. B. Moorhead. 1981. Human Impact Inventory and Back-country Rehabilitation in Olympic National Park: Research and Its Application. *Park Science* 1(2):1–4.

Smith, T. C. 1980. ORV's and the California Department of Parks and Recreation Resource Management Efforts: A Summary. In Andrews, R. N. L. and P. F. Nowak, eds. *Off-road Vehicle Use: A Management Challenge.* USDA Office of Environmental Quality. pp. 169–172.

Stevens, D. R. 1979. Problems of Revegetation of Alpine Tundra. In Linn, R. M., ed. *Proceedings of the Conference on Scientific Research in the National Parks.* National Park Service, Transactions and Proceedings Series 5, U.S. Government Printing Office, Washington, DC. pp. 241–245.

Thorud, D. B., and S. S. Frissell. 1976. Time Changes in Soil Density Following Compaction Under an Oak Forest. Minnesota Forest Research Note 257. 4 pp.

Wagar, J. A. 1965. Cultural Treatment of Vegetation on Recreation Sites. *Proceedings, Society of American Foresters* 61:37–39.

Washburne, R. F., and D. N. Cole. 1983. Problems and Practices in Wilderness Management: A Survey of Managers. USDA Forest Service Research Paper INT-304. 56 pp.

V CONCLUSION

13 A Lasting Impact

In the preceding 12 chapters we have characterized wildland recreation use and resource impacts as long-term phenomena worthy of resource management. We began by pointing out the importance of wildland recreation and resource impacts. Next, we stressed the need to understand the ecological parameters and impacts associated with the four basic resource components of wildland areas—soil, vegetation, wildlife, and water. Having provided the basic ecological knowledge required to understand resource impacts, we discussed the role of environmental durability and visitor use as factors that influence resource impacts. Building on an ecological understanding of impacts, and the relationship of environment and visitors to impacts, we then presented the tools available to manage environmental impacts and recreational use in wildlands. In this last chapter we want to summarize the major points presented concerning recreational use and impacts in wildland recreation areas.

WILDLAND RECREATION AND RESOURCE IMPACTS: NECESSITIES

Wildland recreation, because it occurs in natural environments, inevitably causes some degradation of natural conditions. Wildland recreation, even under light to moderate levels of use, will lead to changes in resource conditions of most wildland environments. These changes are

usually negative in an ecological sense, and when resulting from recreational use, are termed recreation resource *impacts.*

Because wildland recreation is increasing in popularity and because
resource impacts naturally accompany use of wildland areas, both recreation and impact management are necessities in wildland ecosytems.
The option of eliminating recreational use in wildland areas is not available or desired in most wildland recreation environments. Public policy
has made these areas available for recreational use, and resource managers must aim to satisfy public use benefits as well as protect the resource base that provides these benefits.

The job of the recreation resource manager is not easy. The resource
impacts caused by recreation are complex, interrelated, and are often
either synergistic or compensatory. They are not evenly distributed in
space or time. They vary by type of environment and type of use. Also,
they are seldom related to amount of recreational use in a direct and
linear fashion. For recreation resource managers to do their job, it is
essential that they have an understanding of resource impacts and their
spatial and temporal patterns in relationship to visitor use. Once these
are understood, limits of acceptable change in resource conditions can
be developed and conditions can be manipulated in such a way that
impacts are minimized while recreational opportunities are preserved.

UNDERSTANDING THE RESOURCE

Before one can manage the resources that are impacted by recreational
use in wildland areas, an ecological knowledge and understanding of
how resource conditions respond to human use is necessary. Managing
of resource conditions within the "limits of acceptable change" framework presupposes a working knowledge of resource ecology, ecological
impacts, and the ability to monitor change in resource conditions.

Vegetational changes are among the first to occur as a result of
wildland recreation and are the most readily evident to visitors. Herbaceous, ground cover plants are quickly broken and bruised by the trampling of recreationists. This leads to significant reductions in vegetation
cover and changes in species composition. Closely associated with the
effects of trampling on ground cover vegetation are the pulverization of
leaf litter and the compaction of surface soils. Most impact to the surface
vegetation and soils occurs during the first few years of recreational use.
However, other impacts like tree damage increase gradually over much

longer periods of time. Compaction of soils to the point where tree regeneration is impossible, in concert with long term damage to trees on campsites, means that tree cover on campsites may disappear after the current generation dies. This type of impact will have a long lasting effect on site conditions.

The effects of wildland recreation on wildlife resources are little known and deserve more research. Comparative studies of wildlife before and after recreational use in an area are particularly needed. Two general responses of wildlife to recreation are (1) alteration of typical behavior and (2) displacement from original habitat. Both of these responses lead to changes in species composition and structure among wildlife populations. A major source of wildlife impact is the recreationist who innocently produces stressful situations, primarily through unintentional harassment of wild animals. Stress, whether the result of unintentional or intentional actions of users, is particularly harmful to wildlife during certain times of the year when they are already under physiological stress (e.g., winter or mating season). Management can best avoid serious wildlife impacts by managing use during critical times of the year and at key locations.

Water related impacts, because they are more directly related to human health than soil, vegetation, and wildlife impacts, are a major concern in wildland recreation. The concern about water quality and human health is compounded by the fact that water is a major attractant for recreational users. While water is often treated in front country and developed recreation areas, this is seldom the case in backcountry. However, while water quality is a major concern, it is not a prevalent recreation-caused impact in wildland areas. Research to date has shown that recreation does not present a health problem, at least at a large scale. Moreover, the dominant source of pathogens in contaminated water is usually wildlife. Thus, boiling and treatment of water by visitors, as precautionary measures, are more useful than management of recreationists. In the eyes of recreationists, suspended soil solids and turbidity may be a more prevalent water quality problem than bacteria, for clarity of water is directly related to the public's desire to use it.

ENVIRONMENT AND VISITOR INFLUENCES

Both the type of environment and the type and amount of visitors can influence the severity of resource impacts. Environments differ in their degree of resistance and resilience. Visitors differ in their behavior and their potential to alter resources. Moreover, the interaction of environmental conditions and visitor behavior creates consistent patterns of resource impact. Impact patterns, environmental durability, and visitor use characteristics must be understood before management practices can be implemented.

Recreational use and impact are often predictable, exhibiting consistent spatial patterns. At the same time, recreation sites and impacts are not static; they change over time. Backcountry campsites are often concentrated near lakes, streams, and scenic attractions. Over time, these campsites commonly enlarge in size, increase in number, and even acquire new types of impact. Perhaps the most distinctive pattern of recreation use is its highly concentrated nature. This concentration of use means that pronounced resource impacts, while locally severe, only occur in certain zones and a small proportion of any wildland recreation area. Campsite impacts usually consist of three zones: (1) the inner core or bare ground area, (2) the intersite zone between campsites, and (3) the surrounding buffer zone. Different types and degrees of impacts are concentrated in these three zones. However, when the total impacted area of campsites is compared to the total acreage of a wildland area, a very small area (usually less than 1 percent) is substantially disturbed.

Impacts are also concentrated in a temporal sense. In many areas, most soil and vegetation impact occurs during the spring and early summer seasons; such places often recover somewhat during the winter off-season, if they have not been too severely impacted. The bulk of soil compaction and vegetation impacts occurs during the first few years of recreational use. Other impacts like campsite enlargement and nutrient influx in aquatic systems occur over longer time periods.

Environmental durability, the tolerance of resource sites to *resist* and to *recover* (resilience) from ecological damage, is a critical component in recreation resource management. Ideally, one would like to direct recreational use to those sites that demonstrate a high degree of both impact resistance and resilience. Selection of durable sites and manipulation of site factors are primary means of controlling recreational impacts. Visitor management, of course, is the other primary management option. While environmental durability is a key component to minimizing recreational impacts, it is a complex subject that we do not entirely understand. Environmental durability involves many factors, including inherent site conditions (e.g., soil type and vegetation form), weather conditions, elevation and slope, habitat type, and even ecosystem characteristics. Certain animal species and types of water are also more tolerant of recreational use than others. Definitive answers are not presently available to guide managers in all site variables that influence environmental durability. However, many impacts can be minimized if managers become acquainted with what is known about environmental tolerance and durability.

Visitor use interacts with environmental durability to influence the degree, type, and distribution of resource impacts in wildland recreation areas. While amount of use is obviously related to amount and pattern of impacts, mode of travel, party size, and the presence/absence of a minimum impact ethic may be just as—if not more—important. For example, one large party of horse users that camps several nights in a sensitive environment and that uses wood fires will probably have much more impact than many small backpacking parties that camp one night per site, on durable sites, and that use portable stoves. This is not to say that horse impacts can not be managed within acceptable limits; rather it reflects the fact that horse and motorized forms of travel have more potential to cause impact than foot travel. Many characteristics of visitor use can be easily influenced by management to minimize impacts. In fact, management of visitor use is the most important and effective means of managing impacts in many wildland areas, particularly in designated wilderness where policy prohibits widespread resource manipulation. Providing visitors with information concerning methods of appropriate and minimum impact behavior is essential to limiting resource degradation everywhere.

SOME MANAGEMENT TOOLS

Now that we understand the ecological basis of resource impacts and major factors that influence impacts, it is time to apply this knowledge to management. Management cannot—and indeed should not—eliminate impact in wildland recreation areas; cleared trails and campsites, for example, are desirable environmental changes in many recreation areas. However, management can control impacts within acceptable limits— their nature, magnitude, and geographic distribution—by manipulating the factors that influence impact patterns. As change is the norm in natural environments, management will generally not seek to halt change; it will seek to halt undesirable change or the acceleration of change caused by man's recreational use of these areas.

The first task of resource management in wildland areas is to determine what is undesirable change and to set some objective limits on the types and amounts of change that are either desirable or acceptable. It is critical to establish specific management objectives—limits of acceptable change—to determine at what level impact becomes a problem demanding management action. Once management states the conditions it will provide (how much impact and where), it is necessary to inventory conditions to see how they compare to desired conditions as stated in objectives. If the inventoried conditions do not meet stated objectives (limits of acceptable change), then management must initiate action to correct the situation. Figure 2 in Chapter 9 summarized this process.

To make sure that inventoried conditions continue to meet stated management objectives, it is necessary to monitor on-going change in recreational environments. Over time, monitoring allows trends in condition to be recognized. This further aids in the identification of the effectiveness of management practices and can suggest where changes in management are needed. Places where problems are particularly pronounced or where the trend in conditions shows rapid deterioration can be identified as areas of concern.

Once limits of acceptable change and impact management objectives have been defined and resources conditions have been inventoried or monitored, management is in the position to manipulate the two factors influencing resource impacts—visitor use and site resources. While management of these two factors naturally overlap, it is visitor management that is generally the first line of defense in impact management. This is particularly so at the primitive end of the wildland recreation opportunity spectrum. When managing visitors, it is important to use, where appropriate, approaches that do not inhibit visitor behavior—indirect approaches. Information on resource impact sensitivity and minimum impact visitor behavior are powerful management tools. Distribution of use to durable sites is a useful tool, as is redistribution of users to either concentrate or disperse visitors (depending on the situation and management objectives). As we pointed out in Chapter 11, if durable sites do not exist for redistributing use, it is far better to concentrate that use on existing impacted sites, and thus, concentrate the zone of impact. Direct approaches that regulate the use of visitors or prohibit certain behaviors are essential at times. However, management should make a concerted effort to explain the reasoning behind regulatory actions, to improve public acceptance of these actions.

At the more developed end of the wildland recreation opportunity spectrum, in particular, management of site resources may rival visitor management in importance. Usually, site management is undertaken to increase the durability of the resource or as a rehabilitation measure. Silvicultural and horticultural treatments can greatly aid in increasing a site's ability to tolerate impact and in enhancing a site's ability to recover from impact. As a design tool, site management can be used to channel use and influence the amount and type of use a site receives. However, many site management problems and techniques entail significant costs, both to management and to visitors. These range from the high costs of installing irrigation systems to improve plant growth on campsites to the social costs of campsite closures for visitors. Whatever the management action proposed, it is important to evaluate: (1) the severity of the problem at hand, (2) the likely effectiveness of alternative actions, and (3) the costs to visitors and management, before implementation.

LASTING INTO THE FUTURE

Recreational resource impacts in wildland areas are a sign of man's past and current use of these areas. Wildland recreation is a popular form of recreation and will certainly continue into the future. As we look to the future of wildland recreation and resource impacts, what are the major issues? Five of these important issues are the following concerns.

1. Wildland recreation is not a fad; it will continue to be popular in the future and its impacts will not go away. Many of these impacts occur rapidly, are persistent or accumulative as long as use occurs, and are easily distributed to new areas. Impacts compromise objectives for preserving natural conditions and can make areas less attractive, desirable, or functional. A major question today and certainly into the future is, "How much resoure impact is acceptable, both at the site and area level?" Limits of acceptable change in site conditions need to be developed. Each area must grapple with the trade-offs involved in either dispersing or concentrating use and resource impacts.

2. Techniques for monitoring most resource impacts exist, but the implementation of monitoring programs or systems is lacking in most wildland recreation areas. A concerted effort needs to be made in the future to develop and implement inventory monitoring programs concerning major resource impacts. Management of impacts under the concept of acceptable change is dependent on these programs.

3. Too little baseline information is available concerning the ecological impacts of recreation on wildlife, and to a lesser extent, water resources in wildland areas. Future research concerning the impacts of wildlife-human interactions is particularly needed. Currently, we have many speculative suggestions on how wildlife responds to recreational use, but unfortunately, few of these suggestions can be substantiated with a scientific data base. Telemetry and stress physiology techniques will need to be further developed before the behavioral-biological complex of wildlife impacts is understood. Promotion of off-season use should proceed cautiously until more is learned about wildlife impacts.

4. Most site engineering and management techniques have been implemented in developed wildland recreation areas. In the future, more creative and appropriate techniques of site manipulation will be required in the more primitive wildland areas. Even in wilderness, managers should not be paralyzed by a concern with avoidance of site manipulation if it is the *only* means of avoiding equally or more severe unnatural resource damage. Many managers in wilderness have little problem with well-engineered trails, but they resist similar engineering levels for campsites, stock-use areas, and wild river entry locations. Wildland recreation areas need to be preserved in as natural a state as possible. In the future site manipulation must play a bigger role in keeping heavily impacted sites natural.

5. Management of recreational use in wilderness is particularly difficult. In other wildland areas, nature preservation objectives are not so stringent, and concentration of use, facility development, and site manipulation provide powerful means of controlling impact. In wilderness, such strategies reduce solitude, lead to unacceptable levels of impact and are often considered inappropriate. Yet, dispersal can lead to proliferation of impacts. Impact manage-

ment in wilderness is extremely complex. Numerous management alternatives are available and a wide variety of techniques will be needed to balance a concern for avoiding excessive resource damage with sensitivity to maintaining wilderness experiences. The use/preservation balancing act is important in all wildland recreation areas, but is most problematic in wilderness.

Index